The Journey of a Closeted Pastor

The Journey of a Closeted Pastor

RAY MILLER

The Journey of a Closeted Pastor
by Ray Miller
Copyright ©2021

All rights reserved. No part of this book may be reproduced or transmitted in any form or by any means, electronic or mechanical, including photocopying, recording or by any information storage and retrieval system, without written permission from the publisher / copyright owner / author, except for the inclusion of brief quotations in critical articles or reviews.

Cover and interior design by Deanna Estes, LotusDesign.biz

ISBN: 978-1-7361464-3-9 (Print)

Dedicated to my three partners on the journey:

June, Saundra and Warren.

Life is a journey
 …and even if it isn't always easy
 it's always worth it.

THE JOURNEY OF A CLOSETED PASTOR

It was Guatemala that led me to the life God intended for me to live. My love affair with Guatemala began as I assume it does with all affairs (on the other hand I do not know personally about such affairs) by just happening, the confluence of several streams. It seems incredible that my journey to my newly beloved took me from a factory town in Pennsylvania, to a tiny college in a valley snuggled in the mountains of West Virginia, to such locations as Melrose Park, Harvey, and Crystal Lake in Illinois, then through the Rocky Mountains of Colorado, finally taking me to a little town in the mountains of Guatemala. Hardly the most direct route, but the way God led me.

> *I was born before the invention of the ballpoint pen, the electric guitar, suntan lotion, photocopying, the personal computer, wi-fi, cell phones, color TV, nuclear power, the helicopter, silly putty, radar, Birdseye frozen food, walkie-talkies, parking meters and the Internet, which is to say, I am an octogenarian.*

My life began in the bedroom of what I would come to know as home during my growing-up years. It was a small brick house located on Ridge Avenue in Arnold, Pennsylvania, a factory town northeast of Pittsburgh. There were two bedrooms on the second floor plus a bathroom with tub, no shower. Baths were taken on Saturdays and occasionally another time during the week if something special was to happen. In winter a small electric heater could be turned on to take off the chill. A kitchen, too small to permit a refrigerator that was placed in the dining room, a living room and the dining room made up the first floor. There was a basement with a fruit cellar for storing canned goods, a coal bin, a washing machine and a coal furnace.

Later when I was too old to be sleeping in a bed with my sister, four years older than me, Dad divided the larger bedroom, giving me room for a single bed and chest of drawers. My sisters slept in a three-quarter bed in the other part.

There was a narrow door in the closet of my bedroom that led to a stairway into the attic. This was not a finished attic but had planks resting on beams on which we stored Christmas decorations, Halloween costumes and various other things. At night

when I was young I would imagine that during the night some creatures would come out of the attic through that door and into my bedroom. There were times when I would become so frightened thinking about what I thought was a possibility, I would call out to my mother to come in my bedroom until I went to sleep.

A front porch was partially enclosed by a brick wall corresponding to the brick of the house. There was a swing and during the summer all of us at times sat on the porch and greeted neighbors who might be walking by.

The back porch also had a swing and a white picket fence that surrounded it. In the summer we could sit on one of the porches and try to alleviate the heat and humidity. I would often have a jar and roamed around the backyard catching fireflies that we called lightning bugs.

The population of Arnold was preponderantly white. There was a small black community outside the boundaries of our town along a creek that was called Lincoln Beach. I never crossed the bridge to see what that community was like, whether they had a grocery store or any other facilities to service the people who lived there. There were no black students in my school, neither in elementary nor in high school.

I was the second of three children brought into the world in the larger bedroom where all our births took place, overseen by Dr. Thomas who still made house calls. It was March 3, 1935. The Great

Depression was in full swing that caused economic hardship for many, including my parents.

My father, John Henry Miller, born in 1900, was the youngest of seven in his family and grew up on a farm outside the city. His forebears came to the United States from Germany in the mid-19th century. Family legend has it that they were from Berlin.

My mother, Catherine Marie Kuhlman, next to the youngest of seven, was born in 1904 and raised in the borough of Arnold. Her ancestors also came from Germany, the first ones, Cooper and Catherine Sheets in 1852. There was a legend that moved among the family that she was part Indian.

It was 1929 when they were united in marriage. They met at a square dance but other than that I know nothing about their courtship, how the proposal took place, nor their honeymoon destination. Was there a 'falling in love' experience? It is so hard to visualize one's parents in a romantic way when there was never any evidence of intimacy that I saw in my home, but that was characteristic of those times.

My parents' wedding day

However their union took place, a marriage occurred in the parsonage of the pastor of the Arnold Methodist Church with only mother's youngest brother, Clyde, and his soon-to-be wife, Violet Evans, as witnesses. After the wedding, Clyde and Violet accompanied Mother and Dad east on Route 30 for a number of miles, following in their car, as the newlyweds headed for their honeymoon. Theirs was a marriage that lasted for thirty-one years until my father's sudden death in 1960.

They bought a house on the hill at 1728 Ridge Avenue in Arnold in June, 1929, high enough to be unaffected by the occasional flooding of the Allegheny River. Italians lived on the flat area near the river, blacks in an area outside town along a small creek, a town given a racially repulsive name by some of the whites.

1929 was not the most auspicious time to take on the economic responsibilities of a family and a mortgage. I was told that my father, who was employed in the extrusion department of the Alcoa factory in our town, would sometimes get just one day of work in a week during the depression.

Dad was quite a remarkable handyman and took on various jobs to supplement his income from the factory such as: hanging wallpaper, doing small construction jobs, resoling shoes and whatever else someone needed. Still, it was only through the generosity of one of his five sisters, Margaret, were my parents able to keep payment on this house where I was born.

Dad grew up on a farm and as a young man worked as a driller in the oil and gas fields of northwestern Pennsylvania, was a small game trapper and finally became employed in the extrusion department of the Alcoa factory in town.

It was dirty work, and Dad would frequently come home filthy with grease and dirt covering his clothes, face and hands. He did shift work, eight hours at a time, 3 p.m. – 11 p.m., 11 p.m. – 7 a.m., or 7 a.m. – 3 p.m. Often Dad would walk down the hill to the factory and walk home again to save gas and money.

MOTHER

Mother was born on October 22, 1904 in Arnold, Pennsylvania. Before marriage Mother had been a teacher, attending two summers training at Slippery Rock Teacher's College in Pennsylvania. With that meager training, she taught school in a rural one-room schoolhouse one year and then at a school in Arnold. Upon marriage, teaching came to an end and life as a 'stay-at-home housewife,' as we say today, began.

I remember those years of growing up, sitting with my mother in the bay window of the dining room where she taught me to read, write and do numbers before I even started school. She made books for me with the lessons in them, books with padded covers in pretty colors. I believe it was this emphasis on reading that gives me the love of books today. I was a Mama's boy, her favorite son, well her *only son*.

We kids, of course, learned nursery rhymes like all kids did then. One that I remember and loved was recited by Mother, squeezing each toe in turn:

> *This little piggy went to market,*
> *This little piggy stayed home,*
> *This little piggy had roast beef*
> *This little piggy had none.*
> *This little piggy cried, "Wee, Wee, Wee"*
> *All the way home.*

There was another that I remember as well:

Fishy fishy in the brook,
Daddy catch it on a hook
Mommy fry it in a pan,
Raymond eat it like a man.

Mother was short, four feet eleven inches tall at best, something she bequeathed to my younger sister. She was the traditional homemaker: doing laundry, cooking, cleaning, some gardening, and caring for her three offspring. Grocery shopping was done with Dad because he was the only one who knew how to drive. Hers was not an easy life, always trying to juggle all of these balls in the air made more complicated because of Dad's shift work at the Alcoa factory.

Mother was the one who encouraged our studies and extracurricular activities.

She was mother of three, two girls and a boy. Mary Jane, the oldest was born on February 23, 1931. She took piano lessons, sang in the church choir and was a member of the Rainbow Girls, a high school girl's organization sponsored by the Masons. After high school she attended secretarial school, but after marriage did not work outside her home.

She married Donald Speer on a hot and humid day in June, 1951. I was asked to be a groomsman and was so nervous, sweating profusely.

They had five children: James, Marilyn, Nancy, David and Jo An. Prior to marriage Don served in the military during World War II and later trained to be a draftsman and was employed at an architectural firm in Pittsburgh.

One time Don and Mary Jane were going to a state park for a picnic and fishing. Don had a red convertible. They asked me if I wanted to go with them, which I did and thoroughly enjoyed riding in a convertible for the first time.

Kathleen, the younger sister, six years younger than me, was also in Rainbow Girls and was the one whose purpose in life was to antagonize her brother, something she did well. When Kathleen graduated from high school, she began nurses training in Allentown, Pennsylvania and became a registered nurse.

She married Jerry Hobaugh in 1960. She was the mother of 3: Lorraine, Michael, and Susan. Jerry had a career in the navy. All of the places of deployment were in the United States except for one year in Spain. We visited them at every place they were stationed except Spain.

Mother was the first teacher of faith. I remember mother listening on the radio to a woman named Kathryn Kuhlman (no relationship even though my mother's maiden name was Catherine Kuhlman), a faith healer, broadcasting out of Cleveland, Ohio. Listeners would call in with issues: physical, emotional or faith-related. Kuhlman would pray in her husky voice and demand healing for the caller. I occasionally listened with my mother. It seemed weird but also mysterious.

Mother prayed every day and taught us to pray by kneeling by our beds every night before going to bed. She baked delicious apple pies and apple dumplings. We had one of her pies in the freezer when she died and kept it there for a long time because we knew that when we ate it that would be the last of her pies we would ever have.

Mother was characterized by shyness, was somewhat introverted, lacking in positive self-esteem, and she bequeathed many of these qualities to me. However, underneath this was a woman who learned how to persevere.

Dad died quite suddenly. I received a call from home on Monday, September 12, 1960 telling me that he had been taken to the hospital. A few hours later I received another call telling me that Dad had died. He was only 60 years old. I booked a flight on Capital Airlines as soon as I could and took a flight for the first time to Pittsburgh. When I arrived home I found my mother bedridden with grief and that lasted for a week.

I know she felt that her life was over. There was fear, wondering how she could manage all the things she relied on Dad to do. Other than Aunt Violet and Uncle Clyde, she had practically no one she socialized with, and now their get-togethers to play cards on Saturday nights would cease. I now realize how very frightening it must have been for her.

The funeral was held on Friday, September 16 the day before my sister Kathleen to be was married. The trauma surrounding both of these events within 24 hours of each other caused a tremendous psychological impact on all of us, especially mother and me. Results of those two events happening in such close proximity caused problems for me later in my life.

My wife June (we wed in 1960) and her mother traveled to Pennsylvania in time for the funeral and the wedding, something I was very thankful for.

Mother's income now was greatly reduced with only Social Security and perhaps a small pension. Still, she managed her living so well that when she died in 1980, she left an inheritance of approximately $90,000 accrued through her purchase of government bonds and the sale of the house.

After Dad's death mother began living with Kathleen, then me, sometimes for months at a time. Then she would spend time in her own home, where it became the responsibility of Mary Jane to take care of her and to chauffeur her around.

I remember one stint when she lived for four months with my wife June and me. Those months were especially difficult. Of course we were accustomed to living our own lives without having to consider someone who wasn't part of our lives normally, and who didn't share some of our interests. By that time I was a busy pastor and June was busy at school.

When Mother visited us in Harvey, Illinois in the 1970's where I was pastor of the Zella Gamble Memorial Methodist Episcopal Church *(that actually was the official name)*, I would come home at noon for my lunch. June was at school as were the children so Mother would sit at the table with me while I ate. I was accustomed to eating alone, reading the newspaper or relaxing. Mother would say, "What did you do this morning? Who did you see?" mostly I didn't want to talk about that. As a busy pastor, it was my 'alone, contemplative time'.

I now understand that Mother was in a community where she only knew a few people from the church and she undoubtedly felt very lonely. She did make a couple of friends who invited her to various activities at the church and she often attended if asked.

If I am sounding ungrateful for all that my Mother struggled to give to the three of us, I want to be clear that I do not mean to do that. It's just that Mother and I had different personalities, different interests, a different understanding of the faith and while I was often in social situations, Mother felt more comfortable just being with family and at home.

In addition, the relationship between my Mother and June was not always as warm as I would have liked it to be. Sometimes I blamed June for that, but in truth my Mother had made it difficult. I think she believed that June was the reason I never went back to Pennsylvania and that was probably true. Mother had hoped for my return to the Keystone State. She would end practically every letter she wrote to me by saying, "I wish you were closer."

I know that Mother was more than she ever realized she was, and I wished that she could have seen herself as I did, as a giving person with great skills with many reasons to have been positive about her life.

With Dad, the situation was different. He had belittled me when I was young and that had a profound impact upon my life and the way I saw myself. However, now that I have been able to put aside some of the things I experienced from Dad, his calling me 'sissy,' chastising my inability to accomplish 'male' things, occasionally giving me beatings, some of which I must admit I probably deserved, I realize that Dad was doing the best he could. There must have been a lot of pressure on him to provide enough income to support his family of five.

I do remember times when he would take me with him when he was hanging wallpaper and let me apply paste to some of the sheets of paper. There are pictures of Dad with me on the beach at Wildwood-By-The-Sea in New Jersey making a sandcastle, although I do not have that in my memory. Then there were my chores: cutting the grass, filling the wheel barrow with the bituminous coal that was dumped in front of our house, pushing it up the steep, grassy bank to the opening into the coal cellar. Tough, dirty work.

I have regrets for the ill feelings I have had toward Dad when I only remembered the difficult experiences. I like to think that Dad was proud of my academic accomplishments, school activities, service in the National Guard, and my marriage. I regret that he died at the age of 60 when I was just 25, six weeks after my marriage to June. *(More about our marriage later!)*

If he had lived longer I believe we could have shared times fishing in Minnesota, attending Pittsburgh Pirate baseball games, and maybe even sharing something of our lives with each other. It's possible the relationship between my parents and June could also have improved.

I would love to know more about my Dad and Mother, their family origins, the influences on their lives, their hopes as well as discouragements, the things that characterize us as human beings. But that possibility is gone. Tracing one's genealogy is helpful, but the human interactions are more important.

CLUES TO MY HIDDEN IDENTITY

Some of the activities I was involved in as a child should have been an indicator of the direction my life would eventually take. For instance, as a pre-five year old I remember sitting on the ground in the backyard where there was a round, once-upon-a-time flower garden and would dig up small worms. We called them 'cut worms.' I would play with them as if they were mamas, papas, and kids.

Paper dolls, reading, and embroidering occupied some of these early years. During the months of rheumatic fever that afflicted me at the age of nine, Mother bought me a little square loom with materials to weave. With it I made dozens of squares which later mother crocheted into an afghan. While boys were playing kick-the-can in the front street, throwing a football or swinging a bat, I contented myself with more sedate, creative and intellectual activities.

Not that I didn't get into trouble. There was a time when my older sister Mary Jane and I were husking corn on the back porch and something happened, no one remembers what. I grabbed my sister's arm and bit it hard. There was a severe price to pay for that one bite of flesh.

One day my best friend Buddy and I were in my parent's bedroom looking in the drawers of my Mother's dresser, a big 'No, No!' There we found what we thought was chocolate candy. We were so excited to make this find and devoured quite a few pieces. Shortly after, mother discovered what we had done and was horrified. What we thought was candy turned out to be Ex-Lax. I remember sitting on a chair in the middle of the kitchen drinking a 'god-awful' concoction that Dr. Thomas said would counteract the usual results of taking excessive amounts of a laxative.

My younger sister, Kathleen, (six years younger) would irritate me at times and on one occasion I took her shoes and threw them out the window of the second story bedroom into the backyard. The reason for this is unclear. But my sister remembers it vividly and has never let me forget.

I remember the night Kathleen, was born. I have been naïve all my life, believing things that could not possibly be true. That night, I must admit, was a complete surprise. I had no idea that mother was pregnant and about to give birth. In fact I probably did not know what pregnancy was. *Don't the storks deliver babies?* Mother was just getting fat.

I was sleeping with my older sister, Mary Jane. Sometime during the night I heard a noise, a squeal. I said to Mary Jane, "Did we get a cat?" No. It was a sister. I'm not sure if I was disappointed or not, but probably not.

Soon Dad divided the larger bedroom, giving me a room a third the size of the one for my sisters. In the closet of my room there was a door that led to stairs to the unfinished attic. There were planks of wood stretched across the rafters on which were stored Christmas decorations, Halloween costumes and all sorts of things.

One year I went to the attic to get a costume. I found this long white robe and the neatest head covering, a pointed hat with material hanging down the front with eyeholes. I thought, what a great costume. I brought it down from the attic and showed it to Mother. With a horrified look on her face she said it had been

Dad's, but he never wore it much. I learned later it was the dress for the Ku Klux Klan. So that is part of my life story too.

Living in our neighborhood was like living with 'family' everywhere. I was Sonny to all the neighbors. Everyone looked out for everyone else's children. We played together and got into trouble together.

One of the neighborhood girls said to me one day, "If you show me yours, I'll show you mine." There was no show-and-tell that day or any other day.

THE NEIGHBHORHOOD SALESMAN (BOY)

I have been a salesperson all my life, whether selling products or the Gospel. This career in sales began early for me. We had a 'Victory Garden' during World War II, growing vegetables for home consumption to make more available for the troops.

When the abundant crops came in, I would go door-to-door on our street offering to sell extra green beans, peas, radishes and other vegetables that grew in abundance in our garden. I also sold bunches of violets that grew in a vacant lot and tried foisting dandelions on neighbors for a couple pennies as well. I never quite grasped why those lovely yellow flowers did not sell well.

Mother induced me to sell dishcloths. They came in a huge box bundled 12 to a pack. I sold hundreds of those dishcloths, most of the proceeds going into my bank account, money for college, a goal Mother had for me.

Among my entrepreneurial ventures were hamsters, hundreds of hamsters. The first pair I ordered from an ad for 'Golden Hamsters' from somewhere in Alabama. As soon as they arrived I named them Prince and Princess. One night Prince got loose never to be found. But as things happened, he left a pregnant royal Princess. That was the beginning.

During the two or three years that I raised the cute little furry creatures, there was a time when there were as many as 125 in cages in our basement. I wrote to laboratories to see if I could sell them for experimental purposes, but no response. I sold some for pets, and secured the right to show them at a hardware store that had a small pet section. One morning I received a call from someone at the store telling me the hamsters had gotten out of their cages, "Come and find them." Of  course, among all the inventory of the hardware store, find the hamsters? They were gone! Thus ended part of my business.

I kept meticulous records, listing the names of each one of them, or later, assigning them numbers, keeping track of their parents and what happened to them. (A sign of my obsession with detail that has continued to characterize my life.) I didn't earn much money but I learned a lot from this effort, most importantly the value of all living things. To this day I have a soft spot in my heart for those little furry creatures that were skilled at biting fingers.

Later on it was a paper route. Half of each week's profits went into my bank account.

BACK TO MOTHER

I was surrounded with love everyday. But Mother had her own issues to deal with. She was an introvert to the extent that when Dad died she would never call someone from church or other friends to ask for a ride somewhere, a place they would also most likely be going. Mother did not have the confidence that allowed her to learn how to drive a car, despite our encouragement. As a result, this meant after Dad's death she had little

mobility and freedom. She depended exclusively on Mary Jane, who remained in the Arnold area her entire life, for all Mother's needs away from home. This was certainly hard on my sister.

Mother was also a worrier. She bequeathed that characteristic to me. If there is anything to worry about, you can be sure that I, like Mother, will worry about it. She relied on Dad to do everything except take care of the house and raise the children.

She became known as 'The Apron Lady,' making thousands of aprons and selling them for about 25 to 50 cents profit per apron. An article appeared in a national magazine highlighting persons with creativity and how they were using that talent. Mother was featured in one issue. I benefitted from her labors because with some of her earnings she bought my first trumpet.

CHRISTMAS AT HOME

Christmas was a special time in our family. A few weeks before Christmas Mother and Dad would hang blankets over the French doors leading from the living room to the dining room. There was a swinging door between the kitchen and dining room that was never opened when we were around. We children were not permitted to go into the dining room because we were told that Santa Claus was working there and if we went in Santa would leave. So we waited in anticipation. Occasionally we would hear noise in the dining room and we believed that it was Santa Claus working on things for Christmas.

Finally, on Christmas morning none of us except Dad could go downstairs until everybody was up. Dad would start coffee, turn on the tree lights, start the Lionel train running around the tree and windup the toys under the tree.

We could then come down and there it was in all its splendor, the illuminated tree, a few houses glowing through their paper windows in the village Mom had created, each one illuminated by one of the light bulbs from a string of tree lights, the Lionel train running on an oval track, and presents, a small stack for each of the three of us. It was wonderful.

I continued that tradition as much as possible when I got married. In fact, the train and village became so large that one year I had two trains, at least 40 illuminated houses with trains climbing up and down a hill, and an elevated trolley running from the 'suburbs to downtown.' The platform on which all of that was positioned measured about 12' x 6' in the living room. June said you could only go into the living room if you walked sideways between the edge of the platform and the sofa.

The only problem was that after all the work I put into that display, some of the tree lights might not work and some sections of the track lost power and the trains would stop on the track. But that was our magical Christmas.

Surprises were always fun at Christmas, especially for me, although the recipient of the surprise was not always as excited as I had anticipated. For instance, one year when my son Randy was around eight, I decided the perfect gift would be a gas station with an elevator that could move cars manually to the second level. It was made of metal with little tabs to be inserted into the designated slot after which they were to be bent to secure them.

So on Christmas Eve after the kids had gone to bed, I was in the attic trying to get it together. After suffering many sore fingers from bending the metal tabs I brought it down and placed it in front of the tree. On Christmas morning I waited for Randy to exclaim excitedly that this was the best gift of all. Instead he moved it aside to center his attention on his other gifts. I played with the cars and elevator a few times before it went off to Goodwill.

Then a couple years later there was a gift meant to be a surprise for June. After she had gone upstairs to bed with my assurance that I would be joining her soon, I brought out the box and started assembling the pieces. The ant farm took more time to put it together than I had anticipated. But it would be worth it. At one point June came downstairs to see what was detaining me. I shouted that she should not come into the kitchen.

I had ordered the ants so they could be living in their new home on Christmas morning. However, the ants had awakened from their induced slumber so when I opened the cartridge they started coming out and climbing over my hand. Biting. By the time it was over, a number had met their Maker, some were in the farm, and my hand looked red and puffy. I was sure I would die from ant bites, but that didn't happen. I remember June saying, "What made you think I would want an ant farm?" Truth is, *I wanted* an ant farm.

STUBBORN

I did not always comply with what my Father told me to do. One requirement in our home was that you cleaned your plate. Food cost money and was not to be wasted. However, there were times when whatever was prepared was not to my liking, for instance spinach. I would not eat spinach.

Dad said, "You will sit at the table until you eat all of it." I refused. The struggle of wills began. Everyone had left the table and the dishes had all been washed, except mine. I sat there alone. Finally, Mother interceded and I was allowed to leave the table without eating the spinach. I won that time, but paid for it later. Dad remembered such things.

Some would say that I have been stubborn about some things all my life. I can't believe that. I refuse to believe that. Not me!

WW II
Age five to ten

War. Those years leave many memories with still a little of the fear that coursed through my mind and body. I cut out pictures of kings and queens, presidents, and generals and made scrapbooks. There was a smaller scrapbook, with bias tape sewn around the edges of the pages to make them less likely to tear. That one was filled with shoulder patch insignias of various military units as well as letters from cousins and friends who were serving overseas.

The fear would come mostly on Saturday nights when my parents, along with Aunt Violet and Uncle Clyde, would gather at our house for cards, Canasta, Bolivia, Five Hundred and such, after which we kids were sent to bed. Only then would their conversation about the war begin.

Instead of bed, I sat at the head of the stairway and listened: the number of dead, men fighting in places I had never heard of, weaponry that would take down dozens, hundreds even. There was talk of men who were drafted. I figured out that that meant they had to become military people and go to these places where terrible things were happening. I was eight and nine years old, but I trembled with the thought that in a few years I would be killing people.

Of course there were all those other restrictions that affected everyone during the first half of the 1940's: purchasing gasoline only if you had a gas stamp, stamps for shoes, saving rubber to be used for the army, skimming the cream off milk delivered to our front door and turning it into butter, and later squeezing the little yellow capsule inside a plastic bag with a white substance, maybe lard,to make oleo margarine yellow, which we would use instead of butter. There were no new cars manufactured so the factories could produce planes, jeeps, tanks etc, crucial to the war effort, and we planted Victory Gardens. All of these restrictions were put in place because we were all sacrificing, thereby helping to win war.

Then came VE Day May 8, 1945. When the end of the war in Europe was announced, people were out on our street banging pots, pans, anything to make noise, to celebrate the end of that part of World War II. I watched from our front porch because I still wasn't allowed to do anything strenuous. Why? I was still in recovery from rheumatic fever.

MORE 1940s

There was a lot of activity in the streets and alleys in the '30s and '40s. Some were unfortunate men (I do not remember there being women). We called them tramps, bums, or vagabonds. Those names were not being used to cast aspersions on them. That was just how they were seen, their unfortunate place in life, at least for the time being. They were men who were homeless and would come to the back door asking politely for food. Mother would make them a sandwich or bowl of soup or whatever she had. They would then sit on our back porch, not on the swing or in a chair, but on the step, and eat the food.

The *rag man* would move through the alleys calling out, "rags and old iron." It was another way of trying to make a living in those difficult years of depression and recovery. The *scissors sharpener* man would make his rounds, sharpening any knife, scissors, or other implements.

Then there was Frank, the weekly seller of the *freshest* fruits and vegetables. His truck would stop in front of our house and we would buy lettuce, beans, apples, or whatever he had that we needed. It was more than that, also a time for conversation.

I was reminded of these people decades later during my time in Guatemala. These people were like people who were part of the landscape in my early years of life. There in Quiché was the weekly truck loaded with, not fruits and vegetables, but with everything from soap to snacks to cereal and almost any other kind of nonperishable item. The shoemaker made his rounds as well, carrying the tools of his trade, replacing worn-out soles on worn-out shoes.

There was the old woman leading one or two sad looking horses with cut wood on their backs, selling that wood for the little wood-burning stoves found in every kitchen, a stove used only for preparing certain foods. The banana lady, the seller of straw hats and the ice cream vendors playing "Home on the Range." All of these are part of everyday life in Guatemala in the mountains of Quiché.

VACATIONS

Life was rather simple for a little boy, mostly activities around the house and vacation trips to the northwestern part of Pennsylvania to the cabin built by my father and several other men where they lived when hunting deer, bear and turkey.

It was fun in the cabin and a little scary. There was no electricity, just kerosene lamps that provided shadowy light at night. I loved those lamps and rued the day electricity was installed in the cabin.

There was an icebox and another cooling place, cold water coming from an underground source that filled a rectangular vat outside into which the water flowed and provided enough refrigeration to keep perishables from rotting. There were inhabitants in the spring I didn't like, including spiders and other crawly things that caused shivers up my back.

In the kitchen was a wood/coal-burning stove, a fireplace in the living room and an inside toilet, non-flushable, with a rattlesnake skin pinned over the door. When I went in the toilet I prayed that that skin would not fall on me. The toilet had a huge metal bucket into which our excretions collected until time to go home when a hole would be dug, far from the cabin, into which the contents would be dumped and buried.

There was a Victrola record player that required turning a handle to prep it for playing. We would play old-time records, including, "Three Little Fishies."

> *Down in the meadow by a little bitty pool,*
> *Swam three little fishies and a mama fishy too.*
> *"Swim," said the mama fishy, "Swim if you can"*
> *and they swam and they swam all over the dam.*
>
> —Kay Kyser

A little wooden bridge carried our car and us across a small creek *(in Pennsylvania it was called Clear Crick instead of Clear Creek)*. When the creek flooded sometimes the bridge would be a casualty. One time we had to carry our clothes, food, everything across a makeshift walkway being careful not to lose balance and fall into the creek where there were copperheads and water moccasins hanging out. Another year a temporary 'bridge' had been constructed across the creek. You needed to keep the tires of the car on the wooden planks placed there. Of course I was nervous and frightened as Dad drove across that bridge and we were safe on the dirt road leading to the cabin.

Evening drives on the dirt road in front of the cabin to watch for deer and any other wildlife that might be spotted were always fun. It was difficult for me to actually see the deer because of colorblindness, *(they just blended in with the surroundings)*. Mostly I just saw the eyes that shone brightly from the light of the powerful flashlight Dad had. In the morning we would get up quietly to see if there were any deer at the salt lick behind the cabin.

On occasion we did see other wildlife inside and outside the cabin, mice inside and a porcupine trying to chew his way through the screen door to get inside. His life was given up with one shot of a .22 rifle by my Dad, making all his effort futile. Although always being warned of rattlesnakes, I only saw one during all the years of going to the cabin.

Sometimes Dad and I would go to the neighbor's farmhouse for a visit. The family owned the land on which the cabin stood. I heard Archie Bush, the farmer, tell rattlesnake stories, how one time when he was stepping out of the house, there was a rattler lying on the doorstep. Fortunately he didn't step on it. Another time, he was walking in the woods when he felt something beating against his boot. He had stepped on a rattler. Luckily he had snake-proof boots that protected him.

All of us tried target shooting with Dad's .22 rifle. I rarely hit the target and would become frustrated with the failed attempt. Dad would become exasperated with me because I just couldn't do *manly* things like he could.

It was a glimpse into the future in which I always wanted to excel in whatever I attempted. Perfectionism is what it is called, and while it causes one to strive to do even better than one might expect to do, it is a curse, putting the bar of success very high, and the experience of satisfaction even higher.

We made friends with the Bush children. They were about the ages of the three of us. We would go to the State Park pool with water from an underground spring that was icy cold. I never learned to swim, neither there nor anywhere. We engaged in all the other imaginary things kids can dream of.

NEW JERSEY

Our other, more ambitious vacation took place when we would visit Aunt Mame and Uncle Joe Sheets, Mother's aunt and uncle, who lived in Cape May Court House in southern New Jersey. Trips to Wildwood-by-the-Sea took us to a boardwalk and a wonderful sandy beach. We never went to Atlantic City because nothing there was nice, according to Dad.

On the way to New Jersey we amused ourselves by counting cows, each taking one side of the road, sometimes arguing over the accuracy of the others count. We sang songs like,

> *Mairzy doats and dozy doats and liddle lamzy divey*
> *A kiddley ivey too, wouldn't you?*

If the words sound queer and funny to you ear a little bit jumbled and jivey, sing "mares eat oats and does eat oats and little lambs eat ivy...."

And

> *"You are my sunshine..."*

Good grief, Mother thought I could sing so well, she took me to a place where recordings could be made and had me sing that song.

The trip to New Jersey was an experience we always looked forward to, even the long trip east, mostly on the Lincoln Highway, U.S. Route 30. When we crossed over the higher Allegheny Mountains, we often saw cars that had overheated sitting by the side of the road with steam coming out of the hood. It was exciting to reach the top of one mountain, to *Bill's Place*, population eight.

We always stopped and had ice cream. There were telescopes that enabled you to see several counties in Pennsylvania and on clear days, West Virginia, at least that's what it said. When I looked, all I saw were trees and more hills, nothing that marked the counties or even West Virginia. It could have been fake news to say we could see all of that as far as I was concerned.

Building castles in the sand on the beach *(mine never amounted to much)*, trying our luck at some game of chance, riding the Merry-Go-Round, and countless other diversions

awaited us in Wildwood. However, I didn't like getting all sandy. Just not my thing. Even in later adulthood when we would go to Mexico, I would not go into the ocean water because I don't want to deal with the salt and sand on my skin.

Uncle Joe died when I was quite young. As a result of his death, Aunt Mame had little financially to support herself, but through a program of the State of New Jersey she was able to give her house to the state and receive a small income and live in the house until she died. The house was old, furnished mostly with castoffs.

Aunt Mame was one in whom I saw reflected the image of Christ as I thought of him. A humble servant of God, she never complained about anything lacking in her life. She was not permitted to receive any additional money, because of the agreement with the state, but we would slip her a few extra dollars when we visited, and Dad and my uncles would do repairs that were needed.

Although she had little, she would make quilts to be sold to provide funds for her church or for the hospital in town. Her chicken pot pie was to die for and probably contributed to early deaths because it was so rich with slabs of dough in heavy, creamy sauce and chicken hidden somewhere in the mix. I loved the dough most of all. When she was cooking, if ants appeared on the kitchen table while she was kneading dough, she would just wipe them off with her hand and continue on. A little ant protein did not hurt any of us.

One time the 'fishing people' brought home some crabs they had caught while on the water. That was to be dinner. I will never forget the moment when Aunt Mame put the live crabs in the boiling hot water and saw them trying to get out of the pot. It seemed so cruel. I doubt that I ate any crab that night. (It's always easier to eat meat or seafood if you don't think about how the animal was killed.

Behind her house we would find snails. These snails did not have any shells and if we put salt on them we could watch them dissolve. It was fun for us kids, but not so much fun for the snails.

Aunt Mame always sent me birthday cards when I was

growing up. One year I opened a card picturing Salman's Head of Christ. Inside was a lovely expression of sympathy. *(They say it is the thought that counts!)*

Usually there were a number of relatives, aunts and uncles, siblings of my mother and their spouses, who would also make the trip from Pennsylvania to New Jersey at the same time so they could fish together and we could enjoy our time there with them as well. I often slept with Uncle Louis, my mother's brother, who suffered terribly from arthritis. Nothing kept him back from fishing however. His crippled hands managed to turn the reel to bring in fish. I was told, since I was asleep, that I, a restless sleeper, would kick Uncle Louie. He would moan, but he never complained or asked for different sleeping arrangements.

Fishing was a major part of going to New Jersey on vacation. My father and the other adults, except my Mother, went fishing every day. They fished in Delaware Bay in a small boat pulled by a larger boat into the bay. I asked how the man who towed them out knew when they wanted to return to the dock. Uncle Clyde, said, "When we want to come in we tell the boy on a bicycle and he tells them on shore." I believed him. Uncle Clyde never let me forget that.

The fish they caught were scaled, cleaned and taken to the icehouse where they were frozen until the time for returning to Pennsylvania. The fish were shared by all when we returned home. I could barely eat the fish because they smelled so fishy and because when I was young I had gotten a fishbone caught in my throat, but that is a story for another time.

On every trip my Mother would only go fishing one day and that was the day I would go too. We would be out all day for hours, many hours. In the morning it was fairly enjoyable because the fish would be biting and the weather comfortable.

In the afternoon the fish went to sleep and the sun beat down on us. First, Mother would not feel well, and then I would not feel well and would long to return to solid ground. It seemed hours, and probably was, before the decision was made to return to land. Obviously my inability to enjoy fishing did not go over well with my Dad.

There was one incident that became part of family lore. I hooked a fish and was reeling it in when a shark surfaced and chomped down on my fish leaving only the head, which I brought into the boat. Uncle Clyde, always the comedian, never let me forget that I had caught half a fish.

Speaking of fish, when I was very young, perhaps four or five years old, we were eating fish for a meal at home and I got a fishbone caught in my throat. Mom could not get it out so a trip to the doctor was needed to remedy the situation.

The experience left a lasting impression, such that I refused to eat fish for fear of bones. Not until the 1970's when I was going to Weight Watchers for one of my many dieting programs did I eat fish. WW required that you eat two or three servings of fish a week. What to do? WW suggested monkfish that they said was something like lobster. Not quite, but I did eat monkfish to satisfy the need to eat fish three times a week.

And of course, whenever we would have something like fish sticks, who would get the stick with bones? Me, of course.

SPEAKING PITTSBURGHESE

We had our own language in the Pittsburgh area. We had words like:
- pop: soda
- jumbo: baloney for sandwiches
- chipped ham: thinly sliced used to make barbecue
- youns, yous or yinz: plural of you
- slippy: slippery
- redd (not a book): like redd up your room, clean it up
- crick: creek
- stillers: Steelers
- jagoff: a person who is stupid
- gumbands: rubber bands
- nebby: nosy
- sweeper: vacuum cleaner
- buggy: shopping cart or baby carriage
- supper: evening meal, dinner

We knew what someone was saying even if others may not!

Life in those first nine years was wonderful. Games forged from imagination, tents created with blankets draped over chairs in the dining room, fairy wings cut out of crepe paper, kicking a can in the front street became standard kinds of recreation. There was no fear, only a chance to express oneself. In retrospect it was a magical time in my life.

LEARNING TO DRIVE

When I got my driver's license, I would take turns with Dad driving when we went to New Jersey. Driving through York, Pennsylvania I blew through several stoplights on red, with Dad yelling at me. You see in York, the lights were horizontal, not vertical, and it was then that it was discovered that I was colorblind, and since I couldn't tell green from red, and the lights were horizontal, I drove right on through them, fortunately without accident.

My father taught me to drive, a stressful experience to say the least. We had an old Plymouth with a stick shift that reached to the floor. The first time out, Dad had me drive to the end of our street, Ridge Avenue, then turn right on Rankin Street which ran uphill. I stalled the car over and over again, with Dad getting more and more irritated with me.

Rankin Street was fairly steep for several blocks and in winter when it snowed the police would block it off so we kids could use it for sledding. It was so much fun. You could really get a lot of speed going down that hill. Then you would walk all the way back up and do it again.

Finally I got my license. Because we lived in the hilly part of Pennsylvania and received a lot of snow in winter, I had to learn how to put chains on the car. It was not an easy thing to learn, but I accomplished that too.

One time when I was driving at night on Ridge Avenue in the block next to ours, a dog ran out in front of my car. I hit and killed it. I stopped and tried to find whose dog it was. The first house I went to was where the dog lived. What family lived there? My brother-in-law's brother and family. I was so distraught that they made me feel that what had happened could not have been my fault. "That dog was always running into the street." And that was that.

THE DARK NIGHT OF THE SOUL BREAKS OUT

The somewhat idyllic life of my early years was about to come crashing down in two events that characterized the 1940's for me. The first began with strange symptoms. I can recall that there was an incident that occurred in 1943. I was heading home from playing with friends and feeling so tired that before I crossed the street to my house I had to sit down on the curb and lie back on the sidewalk before I had the strength to go on home. Still it was a struggle to continue after resting awhile.

The climax of what was happening to me took place later that summer when, after playing a board game with family members, I found that I had so much pain in my joints that I literally could not get out of the chair. The table was lifted off me and the game was put away. How I got to the bedroom on the second floor is a mystery.

After a visit to Dr. Thomas the verdict was in: rheumatic fever. In the mid-20th century rheumatic fever was looked at and treated similar to scarlet fever: isolation, complete bed rest and sulfa tablets. School began and this nine year old was in bed on the second floor of his home. Little did Dr. Thomas or anyone know this would be my life for the next nine months.

My friends were not permitted to visit for fear of contagion. Only one friend, Wanda, was allowed to come to play on occasion. We had fun when she came. We created costumes out of crepe paper and, although I was not supposed to get out of bed, I would slip out of bed to fix the fairy wings on my back or play with whatever the creation was that day. We played with paper dolls and I made scrapbooks. I also weaved dozens of square patches in many colors and eventually Mother crocheted them into an afghan that I prized.

The days became weeks, the weeks turned to months. Teachers provided lessons from school occasionally. There were some visits from my Sunday School teacher. These visits broke the boredom. Frequent trips to the public library by my mother and older sister brought all kinds of wonderful experiences, stories of children in countries all over the world, the Bobbsey Twins series and many adventure stories. The books came home in great stacks and I devoured them. Reading during that time was a wonderful introduction to worlds I did not know and brought me into a lifetime of books. Reading contributed to my desire to travel and experience other cultures.

My imagination was stirred by listening to daytime soap operas: One Man's Family, Ma Perkins, Lorenzo Jones and his Wife Belle and many others. My mother taught me to embroider and I embroidered dishtowels, pillowcases, and anything else I was given.

Mother and I listened to programs in the evening like Fibber McGee and Molly, The Aldrich Family which always began with the mother shouting out, "Henry, Henry Aldrich," to which he would reply, "Coming, Mother."

On rare occasions, Christmas morning being one, my Father carried me down the stairs for a family celebration. I was gaining weight from inactivity and the consumption of food, so the effort by my Father was exhausting but he never complained, at least to me.

By now I was ten and had missed the entire fourth year of school. However, since I had kept up with my studies. I moved on to fifth grade.

But things had changed. The friends I had had moved on to other circles that excluded me. I didn't know how to relate to those at school and they didn't know how to relate to me. I had become much more introverted and shy. Names started coming my way, "Chubby," or "Tubby," which gave me an identity that continues to this day. Even when I would lose considerable weight I still thought of myself as fat. Whether this contributed to my lack of skill at sports or not can never be known.

I could never swing a bat, hit a ball, throw a ball with any degree of force or accuracy, swim (despite taking lessons several times), shoot a basket or score a touchdown. In fact, swimming is a complete mystery. How someone can stay afloat in water and move forward when I would always sink baffles me! And those are the activities that tend to define boys at that age and even later.

In school, there was a year when we all took shop: electrical, plumbing, and woodwork training. I did all right in plumbing and electrical, but woodworking? I spent the entire time trying and failing to plane a piece of wood so when you put the el-square on it you could see no light at all. Obviously that was not a skill I had. I felt humiliated. While others were creating things out of wood, I was working all the time on that one piece of wood. I received a D in that class, the only time in my life I ever got a grade less than B.

Later in life I did build a desk for my son, Randy. It consisted of a plywood door for the top, a file cabinet I did not build to support one end, and shelves I did make to support the other end. It was ugly but served the purpose for which it was made. I also built a camp kitchen that was so heavy we never took it out of the car when camping. But it was something we used and enjoyed for several years.

I longed, as every boy does, to have a close relationship with my Father, but I didn't know how and I believe neither did my Dad. At times Dad would become so angry with me *(no doubt with some justification)* that he would take a broom handle, belt, or some other weapon to me. My mother would cry out for Dad to stop hitting me. I was never hurt badly, only my feelings. Mama's boy. Please Mama. Those feelings permeated my life for years.

Weight has been a lifelong struggle, perhaps stemming from the months of inactivity. There were many experiences that caused me to feel that my body was not good enough. Uncle Herb, mother's brother, often made comments when I would come home from college. "I see he is broad in the rear." (No firm glutes as young men were supposed to have.) Weight has been a major contributor in my lack of self-esteem and my penchant to feel bad about my body.

I have been on just about every diet plan during my life: Weight Watchers, Nutrisystem, South Beach, Stillman, the hot dog, banana and hard boiled egg diet, Jenny Craig, you name it. I have gained and lost hundreds of pounds during my life.

In 1970 my weight blossomed to 255 pounds. My doctor said, "Ray, if you continue to gain weight at the rate you are, do you realize what you will weigh in a few years?" That did it! I went home determined to lose weight. Of course I had just bought a new sport jacket, size 48 *(I always go on a diet after investing in larger size clothes.)*

My wife, June, joined me in the Stillman diet, just lean meats, only protein. That's all we ate, well, all I ate. During this time June would frequently make trips to the basement. Later I learned that June was cheating. She had stashed ice cream in the freezer in the basement and would go down there and eat ice cream from time to time. In a few months, about four or five, I had lost 90 pounds and June lost 60. People didn't even recognize me. I have never exceeded 220 pounds again.

Later, when attending high school reunions I would always try to lose weight so I would look great. I included a prayer by Erma Bombeck in a sermon on how we become slaves to things in our life, in this case, food. Before reunions she would pray:

> *Please God, have I ever called upon you for a 'biggie'? Now, Lord, all that I am asking, before I go into the room filled with the class of 1949, is it too much to make me look thin, to make me look sleek and slender? And, Lord, if you can't make me thin on such short notice, could you please make Eloise Heartfly look fat?*

I prayed that prayer too and it never worked unless I went on a diet.

Actually I did do something for my 20th high school reunion. I prepared by going on a diet and losing enough weight that I was able to wear a baby blue sport coat that fit me just perfectly. Of course by then I also was wearing a toupee I had started wearing in 1970. When I went into the reunion many of my classmates did not recognize me.

STRUGGLIING WITH THE BIG QUESTION

Who am I? That was a question that percolated beneath my exterior most of my life, especially my youth. I became a Mama's boy, enjoying various activities around the house, but longing to be part of all that was going on outside.

Dad was my image of a Man! I didn't fit into any of his categories: hunter, fisherman, carpenter, and whether true or not, I felt my Dad was not proud of me nor wanted me to share his life. When Dad would go hunting or fishing he never invited me to go with him, probably rightly thinking that I would not want to do anything like that. The truth is that had Dad asked me, I may well have said "Yes!" But maybe it would have been "No" unless Dad encouraged me.

I remember an incident when I was in Cub Scouts. I was to build a birdhouse. Dad was working with me in the basement where all the tools were. I was having trouble cutting and nailing the pieces together for this simple project. Finally, in frustration, Dad grabbed the tools and finished it himself. I felt worthless and rejected. Then he called me a sissy.

THE SALESMAN IN THE MEN'S STORE

Then came my encounter with a salesman at Miller's men's store. (No relation) It is difficult for me to write about this and I have given considerable thought to ignoring it, but this experience has had such a profound impact on my life that I cannot gloss over it. As I have mentioned, my battle with rheumatic fever left me with considerable emotional and self-image issues. Then something happened that fed on who I was.

It happened when I was about 12 or 13. I needed some clothes and my mother took me to Miller's clothing store in town. After selecting the trousers I wanted, I was taken into a fitting room. In this case it was to measure the inseam length for my trousers.

I stood on a stool and one of the Miller brothers proceeded to measure for length. A tape measure was used. One end had a three-inch hard board that was put into the crotch to get the inseam measure. In this case Mr. Miller's fingers moved into my crotch and did some manipulation with my genitals which produced an erection. He talked to me about things I had never thought of in my life. "How many boys liked me?" "How many girls had I made happy?" Stuff like that. It was embarrassing, a little exciting, but mostly disgusting. I did not know what to make of what had just happened. I was greatly aroused and that caused many layers of confusion for me.

I understand completely how, when a child or young person is molested and never says anything about it, why it becomes a secret. *How can you tell what happened?* It is your word against the adult. It is too embarrassing. I would never have thought to say anything to my Mother and certainly not my Father. Today I know that what happened was sexual molestation.

The fact that what happened produced some level of sexual excitement left me wondering about myself. Why did this happen? Did I give some signal that gave this man the idea that I would be open to what he did?

When this experience is added to my relationship with my Father, my confusion about what it meant to be a man, and my lack of a positive self-image, it became an issue for me that lasted for years. In fact, I never resolved the issues surrounding these experiences until I underwent some counseling in the 1970's. While in that safe space, I reconciled with my Father and began the journey to understand fully who I really am.

I want to say that experiences like I had did not make me gay. One's sexual orientation is established at birth, and is not a chosen lifestyle.

I did not have the kind of relationship with either of my parents that would have made possible a conversation about what was happening to me during those years of puberty. I was naïve and therefore vulnerable to the most dastardly of events. I thank God that I finally found people who helped me to move beyond what for years, even decades, held me hostage.

MOVING ON

Athletics has never been one of my skills. In baseball I could not make a throw that reached any base nor swing the bat and make contact; basketball wasn't a possibility, and football was never even considered.

Then there was swimming. One year a service club (Kiwanis) offered a week at a summer camp to the winner of an essay contest on citizenship. Quite to my surprise as well as considerable apprehension, mine was judged best. The result: a week at a summer camp in Michigan. The most memorable experience at Camp Minnetonka centered in the required swimming lessons. The final exam? To jump off the far reaches of an L-shaped pier that jutted into the lake, and swim to shore. When the instructor pointed at me and said, "Jump," I jumped.

When my breath ran out I began to flail away in the water. I would surface and hear someone say, "Should we throw him the safety ring?" But it was never thrown. I struggled and actually thought I would drown. But finally I made it to the shore. I did not have the strength to get out of the water for quite some time. It was humiliating.

I nearly drowned another time and this time drowning was a real possibility. It was 1972 and we were visiting my sister, Kathleen and her husband, Jerry, in Hawaii where he was stationed in the navy. We went to the beach. Jerry talked about the beauty of the coral and the fish a person could see while snorkeling. I said I would really like to see that. Jerry said, "Raymond, you should do it." But I didn't know how to snorkel. He said it was easy and that I could stand up any time I wanted. So I put on the snorkeling gear and entered the Pacific. I was quite distant from where the others were sitting on the beach. I went alone.

After a short time I decided to stand up. I was in water too deep for standing. I panicked and started moving my arms and legs with what seemed like little success and no idea how to get to safety. Somehow I made it to shore, but had to lie on the sand for a while to recover my breath and overcome the fear that had invaded me.

The skills I had revolved around academics, music and administration. Perhaps those months confined to bed when books became a source of exciting adventure for me lead me to enjoy literature. As a person who had always loved intellectual challenges, math, especially algebra, physics and science were a source of great delight.

A few piano lessons enabled me to read music, but for more than seven years it was the trumpet. It was the sale of the aprons that my mother made and sold that enabled her to buy me my first used trumpet. Mother was so proud that I was learning to play the trumpet and that my older sister, Mary Jane, was playing the piano. We practiced some piano-trumpet duets.

Then my mother arranged for the two of us to play a duet at a meeting of the Women's Society of Christian Service at our church. The composition was "In a Monastery Garden" by Albert W. Kekelb, a rather dreary song at best as the title suggests. I was so nervous and some of the notes did not come out well, but of course, the women all gave great support with rousing applause (although some may have said to themselves, "Never again!" I said that too).

I may have set a record for most years in a high school band, a total of six. I didn't actually play all those years. In the first year or two I served the function of adding numbers to the band for halftime performances at football games. In eighth grade I had progressed sufficiently that I was allowed to actually play my instrument.

The Arnold High School Band was good enough that we were invited on at least two occasions to perform at halftime at a Pittsburgh Steelers football game. We had never performed before such a large crowd and it was thrilling to be there.

Second chair trumpet in the concert band was as far as I could go. Triple-tonguing notes was beyond me. But those years instilled in me an appreciation for classical music. I remember so well when the concert band played Beethoven's "Egmont Overture." At first, because it starts with holding the opening notes for what seemed like a long time, I found it a bit boring. However, it has become one of my favorites in adulthood. Actually I didn't know who Beethoven was at that time.

That was the beginning of my interest in classical music. We never had classical music playing in our home. Mostly it would be hymns or some old songs, or Bing Crosby or Nelson Eddy singing "My Time is Your Time." Then I heard

"Beethoven's Fifth Symphony" I bought it, the first classical LP I owned. I played it over and over and over again, sometimes directing the orchestra when no one was around.

The fun part of playing trumpet came when, with a few friends, a small combo was formed with myself as lead trumpet. We were not very good, but did get a few gigs, mostly wedding receptions, mostly Polish receptions where after a half hour or so it didn't matter whether we were good or not. It all sounded good to many of the wedding guests because they were drunk. We did need to learn some polkas and we managed that too. Earning a few bucks playing the trumpet was great!

At one wedding reception, one of the drunken guests came over to the bandstand and handed me a beer. I was a teetotaler at that time and didn't want the beer. He insisted and in the process of his trying to force the beer into my hand, spilled it over my music. I thought, *When I get home I will be smelling like beer, so what will I say and who will believe me?* But, much to my relief, nothing happened.

Administration training came through my involvement with Key Club. We formed this organization under the direction of the local Kiwanis Club. I was elected president of the club and found myself working with other students who found enjoyment in working to better our community. That experience of leadership helped me in my later years in college and as a pastor.

When it came to academics, I excelled. Getting less than a B grade was a catastrophe. When I got a D in the shop class, the woodworking segment, I was devastated. That was the only time I made less than a B in all my classes throughout my academic career.

Apparently there were those who remembered me as a good student because at one reunion, one of my classmates, one of our football players, made the remark that I was the one who got him through certain classes. I have no memory of that, but felt happy to hear the compliment.

It is amazing what one learns about oneself at high school reunions. At one such, I was dancing with a female classmate who told me how she had had a crush on me. I think she had had too much to drink and thought I was someone else because I barely knew her name. When I was telling humorous stories at another reunion, someone commented that "Ray has said more this evening than he said throughout high school."

I did not date much, just special occasions and interestingly my parents never encouraged me to date. There was one girl I did date a couple times. I was taking a classmate to the prom so I invited her out on a date. I don't remember if it was a movie or something else. When I drove her home we sat in the car in front of her house. I thought, *I think I am supposed to do something, but I don't know what and if it's what I think it is, I don't think I want to.* She was a very nice girl, but she had hairy legs. It seems I was attracted to hairy legs on girls, because a girl I invited to a dance in college also had hairy legs. In West Virginia, this was not necessarily unusual.

It came as a surprise to many of the students and perhaps somewhat to myself when I was named the valedictorian of my high school class. I edged out one of my best friends that ended our friendship. As valedictorian it was necessary to write a speech for graduation and to give the speech without referring to notes. I was both nervous and proud to have this recognition and many commented on my delivery. Some even made the comment that I should become a pastor because I could speak so well.

Thus ended high school. There were many fond memories and some painful ones. But it was time to move on.

THE PITTSBURGH PIRATES

I became a fan of the Pittsburgh Pirates professional baseball team when my Aunt Violet and Uncle Clyde took me to my first game. The game was played in the old stadium called Forbes Field. The Pirates were losing so we left the game in the ninth inning to start for home. As we walked to our car in the parking lot, we heard the crowd erupt in a loud cheer. The relief pitcher, Kirby Higbe of all people, had hit a home run and the Pirates won the game. I was hooked.

Through all these years I have followed the Pirates, mostly in their terrible years, but on occasion, in their championship years. In the 1940s and 50s there was only radio to broadcast baseball games. I learned later that when the Pirates were playing away from home that their announcer, 'Rosey' Rosewell, was not at the game. Instead he was in a studio in Pittsburgh and received the information about the game by tickertape. He would then recreate the game so that listeners felt that he was actually seeing what was going on.

He was a colorful announcer, having his unique ways of describing the game. For instance, you might hear him say, "Get in out of the garden Aunt Minnie and open the window, here comes." There would follow the sound of crashing glass indicating the ball had hit a window. Then he would say, "She never made it." If the batter hit a double or triple, he called that a "dipsy-doodle."

In 1960 I was attending a clergy event at a retreat center several miles outside Chicago. That year the Pirates won the National League championship. In the World Series, the underdog Pirates were playing the hated New York Yankees. The Yankees were outscoring the Pirates by dozens of runs, but after six games the series was tied. I HAD to listen to that seventh and deciding game. So I skipped out of whatever meeting was taking place to listen to it on the radio.

Radio reception was very poor there, but I heard enough to realize that Bill Mazeroski had hit the game winning home run that enabled the Pirates to become the major league champions that year. I was ecstatic. Of course in Chicago no one shared my joy.

The Pirates had gone from the worst team in baseball to the best. With the help of players like Roberto Clemente and Willie Stargell as well as Bill Mazeroski, the Pirates had a number of excellent seasons.

When we moved to Chicago, I could never become a fan of the Cubs, because the Cubs and Pirates were in the same division of the National League. In fact, when I was growing up, the Cubs and Pirates seemed to fight it out to see who could be the worst team in baseball.

I talked a lot in sermons about my interest in sports as a spectator. There was one sermon on the topic, "Learning to Live When You Feel Inadequate." Introducing this sermon I told this story.

> *A prehistoric man climbed up a mountain to a guru.*
> *The mountain is steep and he was having a hard time*
> *climbing. When he reached the top he says:*
> *"O great guru, you are our only hope."*
> *"What is it my son?" asked the guru.*

> *"What must we do to perpetuate the species?"*
> *"You must go forth and multiply."*
> *On his way down the mountain he thinks,*
> *"I don't even know what I'm doing and I'm batting cleanup!"*

I know that's pretty sad, but the congregation loved it, and it gave me the opportunity to speak to the people on the topic of the morning and I believe they listened to the message more intently.

THE CHICAGO BULLS

The other team that provided many illustrations for sermons were the Chicago Bulls. June and I purchased a partial season ticket plan the first year the Bulls were in existence, 1966. We were there the night the Bulls beat the Boston Celtics, one of the greatest teams of all time, for the first time ever. In later years we were present for many games in which Michael Jordan played and astounded us with his athletic ability.

We raised our son Randy well. He was, like us, a great fan of the Chicago Bulls. When he graduated from law school, he and a friend bought five season tickets in the second balcony, center court. Our son saw to it that we got to attend many games.

The acoustics in the old Chicago Stadium were such that when the crowd was cheering at its loudest, my ears would often reverberate to the extent that I would feel somewhat dizzy.

Randy was superstitious about some things. I remember one time when we were watching the Bulls on television and they were winning, if one of us got out of our seat to get something he insisted that we sit in exactly the same seat when we came back until the game was over thus ensuring the Bulls victory.

During one year, as you entered the stadium you were given a slip of paper that was the color of an M & M. At halftime there was an M&M race that was shone on the scoreboard. June and I would walk around and around the concourse picking up slips that people had dropped hoping we would have some winners.

When we told the kids what we were doing, they were highly embarrassed. However, as a result of our 'unabashed diligence' in picking up the slips, we would get many free bags of M&Ms that June could give to the children at her school. At my retirement celebration in 1999 it was said that I was retiring in that year because that's the same year Michael Jordan was retiring. Maybe!

WORKING MY WAY TOWARD COLLEGE

Besides selling veggies and dishcloths from door to door I had other ways of earning money. First was a paper route that I started as soon as I qualified. I had a route some distance from where I lived but faithfully made the trek every afternoon to deliver the *Daily Dispatch*. The number of my customers increased to the point that the company was considering dividing my route in half. I objected and it never happened.

Collecting for the papers that I had delivered was done weekly by going door-to-door. Often my customers would give me a little tip, a dime or quarter. At Christmas they were more generous and I could end up with nearly a hundred dollars. One year, I bought my own Lionel train with that money. I bought it after Christmas when the trains went on sale.

One year there was a heavy, deep snow perhaps the year was 1949. I did not know if it would be possible for me to trudge through the deep snow for a mile or so in order to get the papers to deliver. That time Dad went with me to help out. This was an expression of his love for me that I missed at the time. But I was very grateful.

There was a small corner grocery store where I picked up my papers for delivery. The owner offered me a job stocking shelves and cleaning up his dog's feces in the enclosed area behind the store for forty cents an hour. Later it increased to fifty cents.

I was then promoted to work at the cash register. This was the old type of register where you punched the price keys for a product then pulled a handle before going to the next item. My math teacher shopped at that store and we would have a contest with him adding up the cost in his head while I was using the register, and he always came out correctly and faster than I could. He taught me how to do math in my head.

My next place of employment was at Silverman's Department Store, a very nice women's store. My aunt, who was the head cashier, got me the job. I was to deliver packages to the homes of those who had made purchases. I became acquainted with streets and areas of the city that I had never known before. When I was not in the delivery van I would help with folding and boxing clothes for delivery. My supervisor showed me how to properly fold garments so they would not wrinkle. I still try to fold my clothes that way but often don't accomplish that. I blame it on the fabrics, of course.

When someone bought something, the sales slip and the money was put into a round canister and sent through a pneumatic tube to the upper level where the purchase was processed and change sent back. It was like we do at the drive up windows at banks today, but it was new to me in the early 50's.

One day I was delivering packages and it was raining and dark. I was making a U-turn at an abandoned filling station (gas station) and because I could not see well, drove the van over a two-foot embankment. There was no damage to the van, but I was seriously shaken up.

One additional responsibility I was given was to drive Mr. Silverman's son to Hebrew School at a synagogue in Pittsburgh on Saturday mornings. All I had to do was to drive the lad to the synagogue, wait in the car, then drive him back, and I received my hourly wage. Not bad, I thought.

During summer break from college, I was hired at Glenn's Frozen Custard across the Allegheny River in Natrona Heights. This was a very popular stand in the summer. I started at ninety cents an hour and was given increases to a dollar and then a dollar ten during the three summers I worked there. I really liked the work. It was hard at times, but I loved the busy times because the time moved more quickly.

Because I usually gained some weight during the college year, I lost weight, truthfully, working at the custard stand. For my lunch or dinner I would have half a head of iceberg lettuce with no salt and a custard milk shake. I shed pounds fast.

My work week consisted of 72 hours every week. It was twelve hours a day six days a week. One night after midnight I was driving home and fell asleep at the wheel. I crashed into a car ahead of me that had stopped at a red light. My car was totally demolished, but the other car was not badly damaged. There was a couple and a small child in the car that I hit and they were not injured. I was so thankful for that.

My left hand hit the round metal bar on the steering wheel when I crashed. That round bar was the way you sounded the horn. It broke and that resulted in a major scar that I can still see on my hand. I was unconscious as a result of the accident and woke up in the hospital. Believe it or not the accident took place in front of the hospital. I spent just one night in the hospital, but a few days recovering at home.

The two summers after my junior and senior years in high school I worked at the Alcoa Research Lab in the neighboring town. It was boring, but the money was more than I made at other jobs.

I paid my way through college working at that job plus the money I had saved from my other jobs. As a result I had no debt when I graduated.

THE CALLING

For the two summers during my junior and senior years in high school year I worked at the Alcoa Lab, I worked in the spectrography lab scraping samples of pitted aluminum that came from products that were not holding up well. Scrape, scrape, scrape. Then I would run them through the spectrograph. I was not trained to read the results so scraping constituted most of

my work for two summers. There was not always enough work for me to do but I was told that I needed to look busy. That is something that has always been hard for me to do.

During Christmas breaks I had a job as a mail carrier to help with the huge amount of mail. One day one of the other carriers approached me and said I needed to slow down. I tried to figure out how to do that. Apparently when I finished too early it reflected on others poorly. I work conscientiously, but it is hard for me to feign work.

During that second summer of work at Alcoa, after my graduation from high school, I was eating my brown bag lunch on the tree-shaded lawn of the research center. I was alone and suddenly it became as clear to me, as it must have to those gathered on the Day of Pentecost, that God was speaking to me and what God said was to the effect: "I do not want you to spend your life in a scientific laboratory. I created you to minister to and care for my people. Your mission in life is to become a pastor. You need to change direction and do it now."

This was not the first time I had heard a call. When I was in junior high, perhaps seventh grade, I was attending a weeklong Methodist Church camp in the mountains outside Uniontown, Pennsylvania. This mountaintop camp overlooked the valley far below where U. S. Route 119 carried traffic from Morgantown, West Virginia to Greensburg, Pennsylvania.

It was there on that mountain graced with a huge metal cross that could be seen for miles around during the day in its white paint and at night with spotlights focused on its crossbeams that a vesper service was held in the waning light of day near that cross. Part of the worship service involved a call to serve the Lord in one of the many ways one could commit to. I made a commitment to become a missionary. My idea of a missionary at that time was someone who ventured into the deepest, darkest depths of Africa to care for people who were very needy. Quite the romantic view of missionary work.

But this time, in 1953, things were different. I now was a young adult. I heard that voice, not audible to the ear, but heard in the heart, and the confirmation of the call was the sense of great peace that came over me.

However, there was a problem, a significant problem. For several years my career goal had been to become a chemical engineer. I was prepared to enter into such studies. I had enrolled at Case Institute of Technology in Cleveland, Ohio (now Case Western Reserve). In fact, my Father, through his work in the Alcoa factory, knew someone who knew someone, who arranged for me to meet the head of the Alcoa Research Lab who was a graduate of Case. Through this contact I was granted a scholarship to Case. In fact Father was very proud that his son was going to become an engineer. It was such a huge step up from being a factory worker and my Father was extremely happy that he had had a role in my receiving that scholarship.

Now there was going to be a midsummer course adjustment. I feared sharing this decision with my parents, especially my Father. Instead, I went to my aunt and uncle, Violet and Clyde Kuhlman, my Mother's brother and his wife. They were like second parents to the three of us Miller kids. They had no children of their own. Sitting on their front porch on Leishman Avenue in Arnold, I told them what had happened. They were very quiet and then said, "Raymond, if that is what you feel you need to do we will support you in that decision." I needed to hear that. It was yet another sign of confirmation of the call.

They knew that it would not go well with my Father. But he needed to know as did my Mother and I needed to find a college to attend, and with it already being mid-July there was no time to lose. When I told my folks, my Mother was happy with that decision, but my Father was devastated. I, my Father's only son on a path to becoming an engineer, was rejecting that vocational path and the scholarship at Case which he had helped me obtain, and instead was choosing to become a pastor...how could he deal with his pain and disappointment?

Dad did so by closing me off. My Father had few words to say to me for several months. No conversation. No support. Nothing! It was devastating to me. Although I could have reversed course, I knew that

I was on the path God intended for me.

ALMA MATER OF THER MOUNTAINS

College! What to do about college? My cousin, a Methodist pastor, had attended Mount Union College in Ohio. He took me for a visit. It seemed immense (although not as immense as I probably thought at the time). Then my pastor, Dr. Howard Jamison, said he would take me to visit West Virginia Wesleyan College in Buckhannon, West Virginia, where he was on the Board of Trustees.

We drove down Route 119, past Jumonville, the Methodist camp I had attended, through Uniontown and Morgantown into the mountains of West Virginia. There were no interstate highways, just a two-lane road that went from smooth pavement to rough pavement, to a road with no guardrails along steep dropoffs. I fully expected that the road would turn to gravel or dirt before we got to Buckhannon, but it never got to that point.

Classes were not in session so the campus was vacated. We talked with the Dean of Students, Dr. Schoolcraft, and he was encouraging. Of course, I did not know at the time that WVWC was recruiting students heavily in the northeast, students who had not done well in other institutions in order to boost the size of the student body. Enrollment at Wesleyan was very low, numbering only around 400 students my freshman year. Therefore, my admittance was assured and a scholarship was given.

Mom and Dad drove me to school that first year, a mostly quiet ride with Dad still effectively shunning me. After all my stuff was moved into the new freshman dorm my folks headed home. There I was in some tiny town in the midst of the mountains of West Virginia. John Denver sang about, "Country roads, take me home to the place I belong, West Virginia, mountain mama, country roads, take me home." I wanted a highway to take me home to Arnold.

During my freshman year I lived in the freshman dorm that was being used for the first time. My roommate ran track and on occasion would ask if I would massage his legs after one of his workouts. Of course I would and enjoy doing it.

I quickly made friends with three other freshmen. We were virtually inseparable during that year. The freshman class elections we're coming and my friends decided I should run for president, which I did. Quite surprisingly I was elected president. I remember someone from the state of Michigan who was elected to an office and afterwards said," Now what do I do?" That is exactly how I felt. I didn't know what was expected of me but nevertheless the freshman class engaged in several activities and participated quite respectably.

One of the activities was a float for the homecoming parade. Our float consisted of three very large boxes on the bed of a truck, each one bearing the name of a detergent that was popular at that time. It went like this: *Duz* we win? *Vel* we better. *Lux* to us. Hardly Rose Bowl quality, but it was acceptable for a school of 400 in a town of 6,000.

The next year I was elected vice president and then I lost interest with my discovery of other activities I found more engaging.

There was a football game that first day on campus and we all went and had a great time. Unfortunately, as was usual in those years, our team was defeated.

The marching band at Wesleyan was rather pathetic, and that is being generous. After one year, I decided I had other ways to invest myself. Choir, Broadway musicals, and pledging a fraternity occupied my time.

The choir tours, even though they rarely left the state of West Virginia, nearby southwestern Pennsylvania and the panhandle of Maryland, nevertheless had memorable moments. On one tour several of us stayed at the home (mansion) of the owners of the Fostoria Glass Company, located in the northwest panhandle of West Virginia. The glass-topped table where we had breakfast impressed me. The private tennis courts, and then the question, "Which cars shall we use to take the students to meet the others?" *Cars?* I never knew people had more than one. That experience made me realize there was a world out there that I was completely unaware of.

WVWC had housed some troops during World War II and there were still barracks on campus. After living in the newly opened freshman dorm my first year, two of my friends and I moved into one of the apartments in the barracks. There were three rooms, a bedroom, a living room and a small kitchen. Two of us slept in the living room and the other in the bedroom. I slept in the living room along with my blonde roommate with whom I was infatuated. I had known my attraction to men since high school.) However, he had a girlfriend from back home who was also a student at Wesleyan so any dreams I had were for naught.

Although pets were not permitted, we had a rabbit in our apartment. That rabbit lived a charmed life. One day we had tied him outside at the foot of the three steps that led into our abode and when I went to check on him he had jumped through the opening in the steps several times and was hanging by his neck.

Another time when he was similarly restrained outside, a dog came running between two rows of barracks, and as he passed he smelled the rabbit and came to an abrupt stop. Fortunately, I was sitting on the steps and rescued our rabbit from becoming a plaything for that dog.

That rabbit was our morning wake up call. He would waken early and begin exercising, running across the room and crashing into the wall where the bell we had hung around his neck would ring. Over and over again he ran until we got up and fed him.

FRATERNITY LIFE

There were three fraternities on campus: Theta Chi, the academic frat, Kappa Delta, the drinking frat, and Alpha Sigma Phi.

I was recruited by Theta Chi, the top frat on campus and invited to pledge. I was thrilled that I was chosen as a pledge.

One of the required pledge activities was to hitchhike to an out-of-state university that had a Theta Chi chapter. We were each given two dollars by the fraternity. That was all the money we were supposed to take with us. However, we cheated by taking a little extra money stashed away in our gear.

It was mid-winter and a friend, Cliff, and I decided to hitchhike to Bucknell University along the Susquehanna River in the middle of Pennsylvania. Of course we couldn't choose a place over the border into southern Pennsylvania or eastern Ohio. No we chose to go on US Route 50 across the mountains IN THE WINTER!

The day we left there was a snowstorm. We got rides to US 50 and headed east across the mountains. It was miserably cold and snowy. There was little traffic. Finally, a car stopped to give us a ride. The driver was a little strange. He was driving an old car with the window on the passenger side broken out and covered with plastic. He said that he sometimes drove back and forth on the highway to transport hitchhikers.

When we stopped at a restaurant for a break, we felt that as we entered there were some who cast glances suggesting something not quite right. But our journey was without incident and the driver got us over the mountains on snow-packed roads to Oakland, Maryland.

Continuing north on US 15 we finally arrived at Bucknell in late evening on Saturday. The fraternity was having a party, lots of alcohol, and we were invited even though they did not make us feel particularly welcome. But the two of us, teetotalers at the time, had no interest in a beer party so we just went to bed and prepared for our journey back.

It seems strange that there is no memory of the trip back to Wesleyan. In fact, whether we used public transportation part of the way or not is a mystery. Shortly after this excursion, both Cliff and I decided to de-pledge. The brothers were far more sophisticated than we were (at least we thought so). It just didn't seem to be the kind of life either of us was interested in.

Fraternity life did not disappear completely for me. Sometime later, several of us decided to form a local fraternity that we called Phi Sigma Epsilon. We intentionally made it interracial, with low dues but with many activities. We designed a symbol for our group and asked my Mother to make a banner bearing that insignia. It was made of a silky, shiny material that was hard to handle. I believe she said to herself, "Never again." We had pins made using that same symbol worn by all the members (unless used to 'pin' one's sweetheart).

We Phi Sigs were not considered to be equal to the nationals that existed on campus, but we filled a missing niche in the campus life. There was also success and recognition that came with the winning of the annual May Day Sing (groups from sororities, fraternities and independents prepared two songs each for the competition). There was also the creation of an entry for the Sadie Hawkins Day celebration, also Homecoming events.

I served on the Inter-fraternity Council and was elected president one year. Years later our local decided to go with national Phi Sigma Epsilon and purchased a house off-campus.

There was an organization on campus called the Methodist Student Movement. Members of that group formed teams that would travel to little churches in the mountains to help with whatever was needed, often with a youth group that might consist of two or three youth.

Driving to one such church on a Sunday evening after dark, the lights on my car suddenly went out. There was a mountain on one side and a steep cliff on the other with no guardrail. I managed to get stopped and somehow we got the lights working again. A little scary! *A LOT SCARY!*

The student union at Wesleyan was in what had once been a military Quonset hut. For a couple years I worked as a soda jerk. During that time I learned that students from New England called milkshakes fraps, and pop, soda.

Studies did not come easy. I had to work hard and was particularly annoyed rooming with someone who was a speed-reader. We would both be reading and I would hear the pages turning while I was still struggling through one page in the text. But with hard work I managed to achieve. When graduation day came I received cum laude honors.

One of the required freshman courses was: Creative Writing, taught by Miss Crisman. We wrote multiple papers and when mine were returned there were always positive comments. She encouraged me to do more writing and said that I had a talent for that. Her encouragement became instrumental in my love for writing, whether sermons, letters, or other forms of communication.

ENCOUNTERING SEGREGATION

Being a border state, integration of African Americans had not yet taken place. In fact, black students had been admitted to Wesleyan for only two years and these students were not permitted to live in campus dorms, eat in campus dining rooms, nor participate in any social activities.

I had never experienced the kind of racism and segregation that existed in West Virginia. My most vivid memory came as a jolt out of the blue one Easter when several of us decided to drive over the Susquehanna Mountains and spend the holiday in Washington, D.C. An African American student's father, an officer in the military, was stationed in D.C. She was looking for a way to get to D.C. and I said, "Sure! You can come with us."

We stopped shortly after crossing into Virginia for something to eat. The girl said she was not hungry and would stay in the car. I asked why she wouldn't come in with us and then it came as a bombshell. Segregation! She could not come in and be served, and to save us some embarrassment, she decided she would stay in the car. None of us ate. When we got into D.C. we encountered even more threatening examples of racism. I was on four lane roads. Young white dudes would ride by and shout out remarks about a black girl being in a car with a bunch of white guys, shouting racial epithets. I was shaken by this experience. Awareness of what it was like to be black in the United States in the 1950's began to dawn on me. That was an important learning and began to shape my attitude towards persons of color.

On campus, a movement got underway my freshman year to force the Board of Trustees to permit all students to live on campus, eat in dining rooms and attend social functions. The Board listened and by my sophomore year those restrictions were lifted.

IN THE VICINITY OF PRESIDENTS

I have been in the vicinity of several Presidents. The first time occurred when several of us college students went to D.C. for the weekend. On Sunday morning, we were heading to the National Cathedral when suddenly we saw many police around the entrance to the National Presbyterian Church. We knew that was where President Eisenhower attended worship. Quickly we found a parking place and went into the church. Soon the President entered and sat about 15 rows in front of us. When the service was over, the President stood to leave. We had been told to remain seated until the President had left. There were dozens of men who stood, all Secret Service who were there to protect the President.

Then we found ourselves in Wrigley Field, home of the Chicago Cubs. President Ronald Reagan was attending the game and was to throw out the first ball. When he went to the pitcher's mound, many in the crowd booed. I was not a fan of President Reagan, but I was embarrassed because, whether you like the person who is President or not, I believe the office should be respected. (My attitude about this changed in 2016-2020 when Donald Trump was president.)

Then there was opening day for baseball, 1964, when the traditional first game was played between the New York Yankees and the Washington Senators and the President would throw out the first ball. It was not long after the assassination of President

John F Kennedy. No one knew if President Johnson would be there. But as we made our way across the field to the stadium, we heard the rumors. "Yes, he is coming." He did indeed. When he stood at his seat in the stands to throw the ball, Secret Service men (there were only men in the Secret Service at that time) stood with him. All we saw was his hand with the ball. Security was tight, as you would expect.

The fourth was not with a President, but one who would be President. I was a Barack Obama supporter before he was chosen to be the Democratic Party's nominee in 1968. We were living in Colorado by this time. I made fund-raising calls, (first to my son so I would have a positive experience, before continuing to others I did not know). I walked the streets passing out literature, up three flights of stairs, then down, then up again and down, over and over again. That was quite a commitment for a 73 year old. Obama was coming to Fort Collins to speak at The Oval at Colorado State University. We got the word that if we visited 100 homes in one week we would get VIP positions at the rally. Of course I was going to qualify.

On the day of the rally I went to the campus of CSU. People were waiting in long lines to get in. As a VIP attendee I was permitted to go in as soon as I got there. We all were standing and I was in the second line of standees, immediately in front of the dais.

Then the Obama motorcade pulled up and he walked in. The enthusiasm and electricity in the air was palpable.

So much for basking in the glory of politics.

BACK TO COLLEGE LIFE

One of the great surprises for me at graduation was to receive the Wesleyan Key. This was awarded to graduates who had accumulated a certain number of points for participation in various school functions. When my name was announced. I was elated, for this is considered a treasured achievement at Wesleyan.

Dating was virtually non-existent for me in college. I had some coed friends, but none that I ever considered dating, and those I might have wanted to date, I thought would not want to date me. There was one girl who caught my eye, the daughter of my philosophy professor, Dr. Franqui. She was a beautiful girl, of Puerto Rican heritage, but I was afraid to ask her for a date because she was the professor's daughter. Hence, I never asked and never found out if she would have gone out with me.

The times I did have dates were for school dances and 'everyone' was going, so I got up the nerve to ask someone to go with me, often someone who may not have gotten a date otherwise. That is just who I was: shy, unsure of myself, and afraid to risk rejection. Of course, now I feel that girls would have been falling all over themselves to go out with me *(a little humor here)*.

I did actually date a girl named Norma Davis. She was a musician. The piano was her forte and I was attracted to Norma, not only because she had a pleasing appearance, but maybe even more so with her musical ability. I was sure I was in love with Norma and believed she would be a perfect pastor's wife. One

Sunday, during a school break, I traveled to her home, a couple hours from where I lived. There in the living room of the church parsonage (her father was a Methodist pastor) I asked Norma to marry me and she said, "No!" It's not easy being turned down when one believes firmly that the answer would be "Yes.'" I guess I learned that you should never take that step until you are sure the answer will be Yes. But I was desperate to feel normal.

Little did I know in those years that God had someone more wonderful than any I had ever met who was to be my companion in life for more than forty years. It has always been difficult for me to believe in and trust God with my life and its unfolding. Only in retrospect do I see how I have been led again and again, even against my will, to the better life God had in store for me.

Those four years at West Virginia Wesleyan still burn bright in my memory.

HEADING TO SEMINARY

As graduation day was coming, I needed to decide what school of theology I would attend. I ruled out Drew in northern New Jersey because my cousin had gone there and I didn't want to follow in his footsteps. Boston University was too academic for one planning to be a parish pastor. Wesley in Washington, D.C. was too new. Same for St. Paul's Theological Seminary in Ohio. I never considered those located in the south or west. At last I chose Garrett Biblical Institute (now Garrett-Evangelical Theological Seminary) in Evanston, Illinois. Little did I realize how that decision would chart much of the rest of my life.

Garrett, on the shores of Lake Michigan north of Chicago, was an unknown quantity and quality for me. The excitement of going beyond the state of Ohio into the far reaches of the Midwest captured my imagination.

As I prepared to drive my old ugly green Pontiac to Illinois, across Ohio and Indiana, I got much advice from friends and acquaintances. "Don't go through Chicago. They have roads that have three and four lanes of traffic in each direction. You have cars passing on both sides of you. Avoid Chicago." And "I know someone who lives in Chicago. Maybe you will meet him." *Sure, among millions a chance meeting was likely!*

US Route 30, the Lincoln Highway, became my way to the west. One overnight was all I could afford. I listened to the advice of the fear-mongers and drove completely around Chicago to get to Evanston. It took hours of additional time. Of course that was ridiculous, but coming from the Pittsburgh area where there was nothing more than a four-lane highway, I believed driving through Chicago would be taking my life in my hands. Later when I was driving on Lake Shore Drive, the road I was warned about, with cars passing on both sides, I realized what a mistake it was to listen to reports from people who may never have been as far west as Chicago and may have been repeating what others had told them.

Garrett Bible Institute provided studies in theology, Bible, church history, Greek, Hebrew, preaching, pastoral counseling, and all the classes that are designed to prepare one to be a pastor, teacher or other religious professional. I studied hard and worked my way through the classes doing as well as I did in high school and college. New Testament was my major focus with Dr. Ernest Saunders as my advisor. Theology was my most difficult course of study. I could not keep the various theologians and philosophers sorted out. To this day I consider myself to be an inadequate theologian, if that involves being able to quote Tillich, Heschel, Bonhoeffer and other great theologians of the time.

The way I learned how to be a pastor, was by being a pastor. The way I learned how to deliver a sermon, was by preaching, and listening to preachers who were excellent. The way I learned pastoral counseling, was by spending time with people who had issues to deal with, listening, and providing guidance where I felt it appropriate.

I remember when I was to conduct my first funeral, I had no idea how to do that. We had never had any instruction on weddings, funerals, and some of the other practical aspects of pastoral ministry.

At Garrett, the final part of one's education experience was the oral exam. Three professors who would be unknown to you until you walked into the room for the oral would be the questioners. I nearly collapsed when I saw that one of my profs was the Professor of Theology with whose courses I had had the most difficulty. As a result, although making mostly A's and a few B's in courses through my four years at Garrett, I stumbled badly with a brain that froze from nervousness and insecurity. When the three called me into the room again for their evaluation, they expressed surprise and some disappointment with my oral, but because of my academic record, passed me and enabled my graduation. Whew!

YOUTH PASTOR

Although I had received a generous scholarship, it was still necessary to find some kind of employment to help me with my expenses. There were job opportunities listed on the jobs' board at the seminary. I interviewed for a position at an orphanage north of Evanston, and considered other options. Then it was posted: Youth Director at Austin Methodist Church on the west side of Chicago. Youth director! What qualifications did I have for youth director? I had been active in my youth group growing up, had served as a counselor a few times at church camps, but youth director in a large Methodist Church in Chicago?

Nevertheless, I scheduled an interview. The Rev. Dr. Norman Miller (no relative), the senior pastor, came for the interview. I may have been the only one to interview for this position, but regardless, I was offered the job. Salary would be $160 per month. Housing was provided for weekends at the home of an elderly gentleman who enjoyed having someone in the house.

On Friday when I was making my way from Evanston to the Austin neighborhood of Chicago, I passed the first McDonalds I had ever seen with a sign that told how many millions of hamburgers had been sold in their stores nationwide. I rarely stopped. Instead for lunch I would have a peanut butter sandwich and a bowl of soup for forty cents at the YMCA across from the church.

That very year I decided on a practice that continued throughout my life, committing a tithe (which to my thinking was ten percent of my income) to the church, roughly four dollars a week.

The Austin Church had a secretary who ran the church. Edna Stinogel, a spinster who had been in the church office for so many years I don't think anyone knew how many. She was a take-charge person and if you were on her good side, you were blessed. Thankfully I managed to stay on that side.

It was necessary to find someone to help with the youth work and I received suggestions from several people. But initially, it was me: teaching the high school Sunday School class and working with two large youth groups, something I had never done before.

Mrs. Watts, the superintendent of the youth department of Sunday School, kept telling me about a young woman who would be graduating from the University of Illinois in Champaign-Urbana after the first of the year. Junetta Rabito was her name, a name I thought rather odd. It was a merger of two names: Jun from her brother who died before she was born and Etta, her grandmother's name. With no middle name she chose her maiden name for her middle name. So she was Junetta Rabito Urzi. Again and again I was told how active she had been in the youth program and how qualified she would be to help.

Both of her parents came to the United States at the age of five. The families were from the same town in southeastern Sicily, but did not know each other until they were both in Chicago.

Most Italians are Roman Catholic. So June's mother was Catholic. The story goes that when June was a little girl she went with a friend to a Methodist Church on Mother's Day. When she came home she brought a flower given at church for children to take to their mothers. Her mother was so moved by that gift that she began going to an Italian Methodist Church and remained a Methodist the rest of her life.

When Junetta came home for Christmas break, I met her. One thing I quickly learned about June was that she loved hats. She bought hats, not from J C Penney or Sears but from Marshall Field's. One that she wore for an Easter Sunday looked to me like a battle helmet. Another large hat looked like a flower garden (a hat kept in a large round hat box until we moved to Colorado when, with much lamentation, it went to Goodwill.) Apparently they were very stylish. What did I know?

June, as I came to know her, was a blessing. We worked hard on the youth program and it went well. Every Friday, I would arrive at her home on Race Avenue, a few blocks east of the church. We would work on plans for the youth meetings when she arrived home from teaching her kindergarten classes. Her first teaching assignment was on the near west side of Chicago where she had about 50 students in the morning session, and another 50 in the afternoon. Often her mother would provide dinner for me, including homemade spaghetti, lasagna, ravioli, homemade cannoli and much, much more.

I learned later that June had always said she wanted to marry a pastor. So between her desire to marry a pastor and her mother's cooking, and my growing love for her, the stage was set.

June became more than a youth counselor. Being with her was always something I looked forward to. We had a lot of fun and enjoyed working together. It was not a romantic relationship as often understood, a falling in love, perhaps in part because I did not really know how to express myself or even knew what I wanted to express.

We never dated, in large part because my life was occupied with classes five days a week and youth ministry on the weekends. When I think about it now I remember that almost every night I would call June from Evanston and we would talk for up to an hour. June was my best friend. That should have said something, but I still did not know how I really felt as far as marriage goes. Plus conflicts had arisen in me.

One time I did ask June to go to Riverside Park, an amusement park in Chicago. She said that she told her mother she did not know whether this was a date or if the youth group was going with us. It wasn't a smashing success, because we discovered that we did not like the same kinds of rides and so mostly walked around.

June was a trooper as a youth counselor. We took the youth group horseback riding in Chicago near the Lincoln Park zoo. In preparation for that, June had taken riding lessons. That day she was given a very tame horse. In fact, the horse was so tame that her mount got into the middle of Clark Street, a very busy north-south street on the near north side of Chicago and would not go any farther. She kicked the horse and the horse simply kept turning around wanting to return to the stables. Finally she gave up and let the horse have its way.

Meanwhile, I am in Lincoln Park riding my horse along with the youth wondering where June was. I couldn't leave the group, and certainly was not a sufficiently experienced rider to return looking for her. When we got back to the stables, there she was, riding her horse around in a circle in the stables.

As our relationship grew, I did ask her to go to a hockey game with me, the Chicago Blackhawks. Despite the fact that she had had wisdom teeth pulled the day before, she went with me suffering all the way. This was indication of the kind of support to my life and ministry she made through all our years, and hopefully, I became more sensitive to her needs as well.

We initiated a young adult group that grew in numbers and whose members became among our best friends. The meetings took place after the youth groups on Sunday evenings. One day

I asked another woman in the group to go out and I guess June was really upset about that. That *date* was a flop!

My participation in worship services was expected, reading scripture and leading other acts of the liturgy. One Sunday, when it was time for the reading of scripture, to my horror, I had forgotten to mark the place in the huge lectern Bible. The reading was from one of Paul's shorter letters, perhaps Philippians. My mind blanked and I could not think what came before or after Philippians. I knew it was in the latter part of the New Testament and found myself turning one page at a time looking for Philippians that, in that Bible, was on one or two pages. It was a humiliating experience.

There was yet another time of embarrassment One Easter I was to participate in the Easter Sunrise Service and sometime after the service was already underway, a knock came on my door to get me up. I had overslept and was late. I was so embarrassed about missing the service but was assured that it was no problem. This was not to be the only time I slept through the beginning of a worship service. We'll save that for later.

At the end of my first year in seminary I went to Johnstown, Pennsylvania, to be ordained a deacon. I was called before all of the clergy in my conference. In front of the congregation the bishop asked me one question, "Are you married?"

I replied, "No."

He looked me in the eyes and stated, "You need to get married." What a great exchange. Of course I had always thought I would get married, but I didn't expect the bishop to say that in public.

AN INTERLUDE

Two years of seminary were complete with so many credits that I could have finished in one additional quarter. However, doubts had begun to arise about whether the pastoral ministry was really for me. I was still searching for my way and it was not clear what that *way* was to be.

Perhaps it had something to do with my Mother's great desire that her son become a pastor. That was not reason enough for continuing on to ordination. Perhaps there were other factors, some of which had plagued me throughout my life. Was I really *good enough* to be a pastor? Could I do it? If I didn't continue on, what would I do?

Another issue, however, may have been paramount, sexual attractions. I will discuss this later. There were so many questions and I did not have the answers, but the passion to become a pastor did not seem to be there. Had seminary stripped me of that passion?

Faced with these issues I decided not to resume my seminary education in the fall of 1959. Since this was during the Vietnam War and the draft was still in effect, when I left school I immediately became draft eligible, 1A. After consulting with my pastor who was himself a major in the Illinois National Guard, a Chaplain, I knew my options were either to enlist in the Guard for six months active duty followed by many years in the reserves, or wait to be drafted, which would be a two or three year commitment. I chose the Guard.

In October I boarded a bus loaded with others heading for boot camp at Fort Leonard Wood in Missouri. Fort Leonard Wood had a reputation for being the worst place one could go for basic training. I had no idea what awaited me.

On reflection I realize this was one of the wisest decisions I had made. I needed time to think about what I believed God truly wanted for me, and what my relationship with June was to be. It was perfect! In basic training it was best not to think, just to do whatever you were told to do. There was a kind of freedom in that. The stress of school and work was gone and all I had to do was to get up at ungodly hours when the drill sergeant came in the barracks and had us stand at attention in the middle of the night, and follow orders.

One essential was to learn how to fire an M1 rifle. I did not excel in that, but did well enough to become a Marksman, the lowest passing rank. We did night maneuvers, during which I had to crawl on my stomach under machine gun fire at night, under barbed wire, through ditches, in the mud. We were not sure if there were live rounds being fired overhead, but none of us decided to stand up to find out), nor did we know if we would encounter snakes in the ditches.

After basic training I was assigned to Fort

Sill, Oklahoma for artillery training, a major upgrade from Fort Leonard Wood. One part of the experience at Fort Sill was the bivouac, spending several days camping in the outdoors and receiving more specialized training. It was winter in Oklahoma. My bunkmate and I planned to tent together. I was so excited. He had already given me back massages so who knows what else. But before we left for this exercise he became ill with some bug and did not go. I will never know what might have been.

There had been that time during WW II when I feared being in the military, but my six months of active duty proved that I could take my place among men and hold my own. And I did that. I was rather proud to have been able to accomplish what I did during that time.

Six months may not be a long time, but during that time period I made two life-determining decisions. First, I decided that I wanted to return to seminary and complete my education and eventually become ordained in the Methodist Church. Secondly, and probably even more importantly, I realized my deep love for June. We corresponded almost daily and I looked forward to her letters and kept them secure. When there were not 50 youth hanging around, I had time to realize just how much I loved June and wanted her to be my wife.

However I was having some sexual experiences with men, some of which placed me in a precarious position. Had I been found out, I would have received a *dishonorable* discharge. It seems I was always tempting fate.

I left active duty in March and in April asked June to marry me and she said "Yes." Wow! There was someone who wanted to share my life and who wanted me to share her life. We decided on a wedding for July 30 of that year, 1960. But so much happened between April and July.

Someone has written:

> *When I was in my very early twenties I married a wonderfully talented woman...I mistakenly took our wonderful friendship as a sign of romance and decided that what I needed to do was to marry her. In time I convinced myself that would be the solution to all my shame about being gay. In fact, it was going to cure me, as I wouldn't be gay anymore.*
>
> *The Velvet Rage: Overcoming the Pain of Growing Up Gay in a Straight Man's World*
> —Alan Downs

Sometimes I have wondered if I thought that would happen with me if I married June. But it didn't work. I lived with shame through all of my life to the age of 79.

In a sermon titled "The Preciousness of Life," (CLUMC, January 22, 1995) I quoted something I had read about the pastor of the Boston Avenue United Methodist Church in Oklahoma City. He said:

> *When I was growing up my mother would come into my bedroom every night before I went to sleep and she would say "When I look in your eyes I just feel there is something special in you. God made you for some special purpose.*

That is the gift God gave to me in June. Her love made me feel I had been made for something special. I felt important. Her love built up my sense of self-worth and self-esteem.

LIFE AFTER NATIONAL GUARD

When I left active duty in March, 1960, I received a call to serve for a short time as pastor of the Halsted Street Institutional Church on the near Southside of Chicago, just south of Maxwell Street, the famous Jewish outdoor market. Within a few months this little congregation was going to merge with a Presbyterian congregation and would no longer exist.

The area in which the church was located was in transition. At one time Al Capone had been active in this area, and one elderly gentleman in the congregation, a dentist, told me that he had worked on the teeth of some of Al Capone's gang. It had become a Lithuanian neighborhood, and now Puerto Ricans were moving in.

There was considerable crime, but I decided I wanted to sleep in the church on Saturday night so I would not have to drive from Evanston on Sunday morning. The congregation was concerned about my safety. Nevertheless they helped me fix a place to sleep, a room on one of the upper floors.

One night I was awakened by loud noises. I thought someone had broken into the church. But as I listened I could tell that the noise was coming from some place on the other side of the wall of my bedroom. It turned out that there was some kind of manufacturing company that occupied that space. No one had told me. My heart finally stopped racing and I was able to go back to sleep.

The only negative that happened was one Saturday night when, after I had retired, I heard a loud noise coming from the street below. I looked out and saw my Dodge station wagon entangled with another vehicle. The owner of that car said he had no car insurance, but assured me he would pay for the damages. As I have often done, I took him at his word. We did not report this accident to the police. Damages amounted to around $400. I received one payment and that was it.

Life was so good. A woman had agreed to be my wife; I had made a commitment to pastoral ministry; I had a church to serve. Marriage came on July 30, 1960 in the Austin Methodist Church on the west side of Chicago near Oak Park, the church where I had been youth pastor. I prepared for this special day by

spending two weeks at summer camp with my Guard unit and returned to begin as full-time pastor of a church.

Two things occurred during that time at summer camp. The first was that somewhere along the way between Chicago and Camp McCoy in Wisconsin I was told I was to drive one of the trucks hauling one of the 105 howitzers. I had never driven that truck nor pulled anything like a howitzer, but I did it.

The other thing was that one morning when inspection was taking place by the officer in charge of our unit, he noticed that at the foot of my bed was a footlocker on which there was the inscription, Major Miller. He looked at the Company Commander and said, "Why do you have an officer living here with the enlisted men?" The officer had no idea that that locker was there with

My parents on my wedding day

that inscription. I had borrowed it from the senior pastor of the church in Austin where I had served as youth pastor. With that explanation the crisis was over.

My preparation for the wedding on the morning of the day of the wedding was to prepare the bulletins for the church for the Sundays I would be away on honeymoon. These were prepared on the old wax stencils. I was nervous and felt pressure to get them done, so made many mistakes and had to spend a lot of time repairing the stencils.

Then I needed to go to the drugstore and buy condoms. You didn't just go in and pick them off the shelf, you asked the pharmacist for them. I was so embarrassed and was so naïve. I had never bought condoms, had never needed them.

It was probably well that I was not present for the final preparations for the wedding because, with my penchant for having too many opinions about everything, my future wife and her family were spared my input.

My family who attended included my sister Mary Jane, my parents, and Uncle Clyde and Aunt Violet.

We extended personal invitations to family and close friends and then invited the entire congregation. More than 400 people pressed into the church for our wedding. Two memorable attendees were Mr. and Mrs. Glen Hefner, parents of Hugh Hefner of *Playboy* fame who were members of that church.

June was escorted down the aisle by her Uncle Charlie because her father had died in 1957. June's mother always said that she was sure that her husband, Guy, had met me at the doors of the church when they were leaving after worship. Of course if that happened it was before he or I knew that I would become part of his family.

So many problems were associated with our wedding. First, the church had decided to redo the entire lower level of the building where our reception was going to be held. So we put in a lot of effort to decorate and try to cover as much of the destruction of the walls as we could.

Next, we learned that a friend of my fiancés family who was a baker was to prepare the wedding cake. Unfortunately he had died. When the cake arrived it was festooned with large, gaudy artificial flowers that June abhorred. She and the pastor's wife removed the flowers and fixed the icing so it was presentable.

The reception was to be buffet style, and we had decided that contrary to tradition, the guests would come through the receiving line and go immediately to the buffet. The caterer misunderstood and could not understand why the bridal couple was not eating first. The reason was that we had more guests than could be accommodated in the fellowship hall and our hope was that those who ate first would relinquish their seats for the later ones.

Then came the disaster with wedding pictures. Another family friend was hired as photographer. After enduring the endless posing for pictures, we learned that the film in the camera was defective. As a result, few pictures.

But despite all of these extraordinary circumstances, we were married. At least I think we went though the wedding ceremony. I was so nervous that I don't remember much of the ceremony. One interesting feature about our wedding was that the pastor, the organist and the groom were all named Miller, but none were related.

I have counseled couples preparing for marriage upset about the wedding arrangements and tried to help them realize that it isn't really the wedding that is important, but the marriage. I doubt that many couples ever heard what I was saying.

THE HONEYMOON

Then came the honeymoon. But first, according to Italian tradition, we went to the bride's home to change clothes, also to open all the envelopes given as gifts to see how much money each guest had given. I thought this was not a good idea on the night of one's wedding day, but that's what happened.

Our departure from the house included a car that was definitely not ready for the first few miles of travel: stones in hub caps, cans tied on the back, streamers, a note in the gas cap so gas attendants (which there were in those days, people who actually put the gas into the car) would know we were newlyweds and offer congratulations, rice in envelopes on the reverse side of the sun visor. The next day when we lowered them to shut out the sun we were showered with more rice that was then scattered throughout the car, and then rice that we discovered later that night in our luggage.

Our destination was a resort in the Laurentian Mountains about 70 miles north of Montreal. I had mapped the route and when we were traveling north toward Grey Rocks Inn, the road turned to dirt. That became an experience on many of our travels in the future, a dirt road on a numbered *highway*.

Actually, because of that route, when it was lunchtime we stopped at a little restaurant in a small town that was totally French speaking. Since we neither spoke nor understood French, we ordered hamburgers. The young son of the owner soon ran from the café and returned a little later with a package, the hamburger for grilling. Who orders a hamburger in a French café?

The resort was wonderful, an experience in luxury I had never known. We had assigned tables for meals. The cuisine was French and the grounds were fantastic. I was truly out of my element and a bit overwhelmed by it. Obviously, June had made these reservations.

One day we rode horses, a wonderful ride, just the two of us with a guide. We rode up and down hills, through streams. It was marvelous until we were headed back to the barn. Suddenly, June's horse, Old Minnie, took off on her own, galloping back toward the barn. I had no horsemanship skills to help, and as I rode behind, I saw June slip out of one stirrup and slide to the side of the horse. Fortunately she hung on and made it back to the barn without falling off. The owners could not believe that Old Minnie had done that. Old Minnie was the one horse given to June they were sure would be very tranquil. The only injury, other than embarrassment, were bruises which were still there when we got home, causing her mother to accuse me of spousal-abuse (in fun).

There was that one other fun activity we did while in the Laurentians and that was to take the one and only sea plane ride we would ever take. What made this memorable was that the pilot came dressed in swim trunks. We weren't sure what that meant but it was a wonderful flight.

Neither June nor I had any heterosexual experience to bring to our marriage. We were both virgins. No one had ever talked with me about sex in marriage and so it took us some time to figure things out, but we did and discovered the joy of sex with the one you love.

On our way back through Vermont, on Route 100 that was unpaved for many miles, we happened to stop at a restaurant where it was obvious a party of some significance was going to be hosted. Tables had been set with beautiful coverings, china and silverware and gorgeous centerpieces. We were told that a prominent politician, perhaps the governor, was hosting a dinner or party. I was so uneasy about being in such a place that I could not enjoy my meal and wanted to get out of there fast.

That is the way I have often felt during my life. Being the son of a working class father, I had a hard time finding comfort being in the presence of people of greater wealth and knowledge than I believed I possessed. Later on, serving as an associate pastor in the Beverly Hills area in southwestern Chicago placed me in a situation where wealth had characterized the people who lived there. Many were executives of the meat packing industry.

I visited one of the members of that church and sat in her living room in which a grand piano did not look large. Later she hosted at least a hundred people in her home as a reception for her daughter when she married. This was not a world that I had experienced before.

On our way back to Chicago we stopped at my home to see my Mother and Father. That was the last time I saw or talked with my Father. He died suddenly four weeks later.

THE LITTLE CHURCH IN THE CITY
Memorial Methodist Church
1960-1963

The church to which I was appointed in July 1960 was a small church on the near northwest side of Chicago that had once been a German language Methodist Church. It's name? Memorial Methodist Church (not sure what was being memorialized). It was located near Armitage and Central Park Avenues. The area was predominantly Bohemian and Roman Catholic. The children in the neighborhood called me "Father," and I responded to them without correction. In fact, it was rather fun.

The neighborhood boys came to the church for Cub and Boy Scouts. These kids could come to the basement for Scouts, but they were forbidden to go upstairs to the sanctuary and they adhered to that *religiously*.

It was my practice in those early years of my ministry to go door-to-door meeting people, introducing myself, and inviting them to come to the Methodist Church. Some actually came and while not in huge numbers, the membership and worship attendance actually increased.

On November 29, 1997 in a sermon titled, "How Do I Become a Christian?" I told this story:

> *A pastor was making calls on parishioners on a Saturday. He rang the bell at one house, and*

> *although it was obvious that there was someone at home no one came to the door. Finally he took one of his calling cards and on the back wrote, Revelation 3:20, "I stand at the door and knock, if you answer, I will come in and eat with you and you with me." The next day in the offering plate, the card was returned with another Bible verse: Genesis 3:10, "I heard your voice in the garden, but I was afraid, because I was naked and I hid from you."*

I heard stories of pastors who would knock on a door and when the homeowner answered that person was naked, but I never had that experience, thank goodness!

The parsonage was next door to the church, the first floor of a two-flat. Life in the three years we lived there were both wonderful and strange. Paul Russell, one of the two leading men of the congregation, was the handyman of the church. He could do almost anything. He had key-access to the parsonage and would enter at times without telling us. We would hear noise coming from the basement and hope it was Paul.

One time Paul was doing something in the basement and suddenly his drill punctured the floor in the kitchen above. To say the least we were startled.

June was terribly afraid of mice. One night while we were sitting in the kitchen, she spotted a cute little critter scamper across the floor. She screamed and shouted, "Get that mouse out of here!" So I got the broom and started looking for the mouse to end its life. After chasing it around the kitchen for a while I saw it go out onto the enclosed back porch.

I moved the freezer out there to look for it, moved all the other stuff we had there but never found the mouse. I decided it must have either had a heart attack out of fear, or found its way outside where it was safe. This would be the first of our mouse stories.

Eight years later we were just beginning to unpack after being moved into the Beverly Hills area of Chicago. A woman from across the street came to welcome us and brought a lovely plate of homemade cookies. I took them to the kitchen and placed them on the table, and went back to converse with our neighbor. When we came back to the kitchen, the mice were having a party on the table. They resented our intrusion on their party. We could see it on their faces. We lied to our neighbor and told her how delicious the cookies were, transferring that message to her from the mice.

That house was infested with mice. We set traps, placed mouse poison in places where our dog could not get to it and finally discovered a nest behind the stove. When we eliminated that, the situation came under control.

Back to Memorial Methodist Church. A song by Nat King Cole comes to mind: *Unforgettable!* Yes! That word characterized the three years we lived on the near north side of Chicago. First we entered a local drawing for a turkey at Thanksgiving time. Unbelievably, we won that turkey! At that time it was almost like winning the lottery.

Also unforgettable was buying our first dog, Dodie, from a pet store. Before long we realized she was a sick puppy. Visits to the vet did little. We gave her a little whiskey, which the vet said should help her refrain from the spasms she had, but it did no good. Dodie was my first dog, the fulfillment of a desire I had had since a kid. After sitting up with her many nights, holding her in my arms, with tears flowing and my heart breaking, it became clear that she was not going to regain her health and we put her to sleep.

Not deterred, we decided never again to shop for a dog in a pet store. So we went the pure bred route. A Golden Retriever it was to be. We answered an ad in the newspaper and found a beautiful Golden Retriever puppy, the runt of the litter, in a western suburb of Chicago. The breeder was very particular about who bought her pups. Because we had had a sick dog, she insisted that before we could have one of her pups we had to wait several weeks, thoroughly clean the house, scrubbing it down, ridding ourselves of anything associated with Dodie.

Finally the day came when we could bring her home. Her AKC name was Lady Natasha, but we called her Ruffles. A wonderful dog came to live with us just six weeks before another unforgettable experience.

THE FAMILY EXPANDS…
WELCOME JOHN RANDAL MILLER

Our first child, a boy, John Randal Miller, was born on March 25, 1962. *(Obviously we had figured the sex-thing out.)* We were not totally prepared because Randy decided he was ready to experience the world outside the womb three weeks before his scheduled time.

His timing was rather auspicious. He decided to begin the process of being born while June was at a bridal shower at the church. She had baked a *wedding cake* for the shower. While there, her water broke. She came home and said we should hurry to the hospital, St. Elizabeth Hospital in Chicago. What's the hurry?

I was never allowed to forget my participation at the time of his birth. St. Elizabeth's had many Nuns who RAN the maternity ward. I was put in a room, the father's room. Because it was three weeks before the due date, as I was driving June to the hospital, I thought that undoubtedly I would be bringing her home shortly. I had no idea what it meant when the water bag broke. There were no classes for expectant fathers in those days.

I waited and waited and finally, because there were no other expectant fathers in the room and no TV I fell asleep. Apparently, during her labor, the doctor asked if June wanted me to come and wait with her *(fathers were not permitted to be present at the time of delivery)*. She said 'Yes". He came back a few minutes later and told June I was asleep, did she want him to waken me. She responded, "No." As a result I slept through the birth of our son.

AND OUR NEW DOG…RUFFLES

Meanwhile Ruffles was at home, totally un-house-broken. So I had cleaning up to do when I got home. Then there was shopping for the baby things we had put off getting and painting the bassinet that was to be the bed for our son, a bed that had also been the first bed for my wife, this and that to be done because I had procrastinated. Everything was last minute or and that characterized my later life as well.

Ruffles was a very sweet, mild-mannered dog. He liked to sleep on our bed between June and me putting his back against June and pushing me with his legs. He also liked to crawl under the bed. As he got older and bigger, getting him out from under the bed was a problem. I tried banging a metal pie pan on the floor to scare him out. The bed had wooden slats and we were afraid the slats would move or break when there was excessive movement on the bed, which occurred fairly regularly and we would crush Ruffles. One night he was under the bed. No matter what we tried, he would not come out. Finally, I took the bed apart to get him out.

Ruffles was so good with Randy. She was protective of him and when he was learning to stand, he would grab her ear and pull himself up and Ruffles would just squint her eyes and sit there patiently.

Unforgettable!

Yet another experience that lived with both of us through the years was that which occurred a few days before Christmas, 1962, the year Randy was born. Frequently I would walk to the drug store on Armitage Avenue, just a block away, and buy formula for Randy. In December, every time I went into the store to make a purchase, I would look at the Christmas music boxes that were for sale, wind one or two and listen to the lovely sounds of the music box. One in particular caught my attention, three choir boys and the music was "Ave Maria."

I always listened to that music box. How I would have loved to buy it, but there was no money for a music box. Then shortly before Christmas I entered the store and saw that the three choirboys were gone. Someone had purchased *my* music box. Well, I couldn't buy it anyway.

On Christmas Eve I went to the pharmacy owned by a lovely Jewish couple, and before I left the store, she said, "Pastor, one minute." She reached under the counter and brought out a beautifully wrapped package, handed it to me and said, "Merry Christmas." I knew what it was but I couldn't believe it.

Our Jewish pharmacists presented us with a gift that has graced my Christmas decor every one of the nearly 60 years since and I listen to "Ave Maria." Perhaps that is why I can never hear that music without thinking of the three choirboys, that music box, the three choirboys, and the Jewish couple who gave it to us. Remembering this always brings tears of joy to my eyes.

In the summer of 1962 when Randy was just four months old we (well, maybe it was I) made the decision that we should make a camping trip completely around Lake Michigan. We had bought a tent and I wanted to use that tent. June's mother decided she should go with us to protect her infant grandson.

Every night there was rain. Every night I put a bucket of water on our Coleman stove and used that to sterilize the baby bottles.

The water never boiled. There were all kinds of flying insects circling the pot of water with the bottles. Mom thought that was terrible. "I'm going to kill her grandson."

Every night she would say, "Let's go to a motel and I will pay for it." But being the stubborn person I was and am, I said, "No, we are going to sleep in the campground."

For the final night's meal Mom said she wanted to buy steaks to grill. She and June went to the store to shop. When she came back she had three large steaks, far more meat than we could possibly eat, but that was Mom, always being sure there was at least enough and some leftover.

That night I relented and we slept in a motel.

On our way home as we drove down the east side of Lake Michigan we found roadside stands selling freshly picked and washed cherries, a specialty in Michigan. We ate and ate and then discovered that eating a lot of cherries could cause diarrhea. Who knew? We learned.

According to the wisdom of the day among Methodist pastors, after three years at a small church it was time to move on and begin to climb the church ladder. So I requested a new appointment.

LIVING IN THE MAFIA CITY
1963-1968

In 1963 we moved, to Melrose Park, a western suburb of Chicago. The movers were taking our belongings into the parsonage when one of them said: "Aren't you afraid to be moving here?

I asked, "Why?"

He responded, "Because many of the mafia live here." Really?

Melrose Park Methodist Church had been a Swedish Methodist Church at one time. There were still some Swede leftovers from those years. An annual fundraiser for the women's group was making and selling Swedish sausage. If you have never had Swedish sausage, let me tell you, it looks rather sick. It is a potato sausage, very light in color, not the color sausage is *supposed* to be, or that I was accustomed to.

Swedish sausage isn't grilled. It is boiled. It has a rather bland taste and takes some getting used to. Eventually we even began to enjoy eating it.

Several events marked our years living in Melrose Park. June was pregnant and we were excitedly looking forward to the arrival of our second child. She was a few months pregnant and had gone to the hospital for a checkup. The hospital was in walking distance from our home. I was in a meeting when I received a call from the hospital telling me that I needed to go there immediately.

Then, a while later she became pregnant again and this time gave birth to a baby girl we named Jacqueline Grace (Grace being her maternal grandmother's name). It was our second blessing of a healthy child. It was 1966.

A major snowstorm hit Chicago during our years there. It snowed so hard that Chicago was virtually shut down for a few days. We could walk down the middle of Lake Street, a major artery that was near our home because there was no traffic.

I remember taking Randy to a neighborhood grocery pulling him on a sled. As I pulled him along, he slid off the sled and was sitting there in his snowsuit, unable to move, much like Randy in the movie, *A Christmas Story*.

The snow was piled so high in our backyard that our dog Ruffles got over the fence and disappeared. We searched for her everywhere and could not find her. Finally, a couple days later someone called to say they had found her. She was several miles from home. We were relieved to know she was all right and welcomed her back home with her family.

On Sunday I didn't expect many, if any, people would come to worship because of the snow. Amazingly, about fifty were there. Our organist could not make it, so I decided to use my limited ability on the piano to accompany the hymns on the reed organ that required air to be pumped using one's feet.

After the service, as I was greeting at the door, a woman whom I did not know said she was the organist at another church in town but couldn't get there so came to the Methodist church that was in walking distance. I asked why she didn't offer to play the organ. She said she thought of it, but decided I could handle it. I was terribly embarrassed.

When we went to church on Sunday we would put Ruffles in the kitchen that had sliding doors. Ruffles had learned how to slide the doors open. One Sunday when we were walking home from church we saw Ruffles on the white couch, head resting on the back of the sofa looking out the picture window. As soon as she saw us she disappeared. When we came in the house she was under the kitchen table, the tip of her tail wagging, looking at us like, "I've been here all the time."

Ruffles, being a retriever, liked to bring us gifts when she went out into the yard. One time I heard June scream. I ran to see what had happened. Ruffles had brought June a special gift, a dead squirrel. Another time it was a small bird that she held in her soft mouth that was neither dead nor injured. We managed to rescue the bird.

After five years, Ruffles became sick. Examinations with the vet determined she had a liver condition that was not uncommon with Golden Retrievers. The vet said he could operate, but could not guarantee that that would do any good.

We decided we had to let her go. I held her. The injection was administered and within a few minutes there was no life. Tears filled my eyes and flowed. My precious dog was gone. This was the first of several times holding a beloved friend as the fluid coursed through their veins and stilled their hearts. My heart was not stilled. Thinking of Dodie, Ruffles, Whiskers, Pepper, Obie and Calvin bring fond memories, but also sadness that they are no longer with me.

One of the most memorable experiences that took place at Melrose Park was when I decided to take the youth group to New York City. Seven youth and a few parents went. We traveled in cars, stopping in Pennsylvania at my sister's home overnight before proceeding on to New York.

Entering New York through a tunnel I hit a pigeon and killed it. The youth were aghast. "The pastor killed a pigeon!" Now I was a murderer.

I used a travel guide, *New York on $5 a Day*. I mapped out the entire trip which included: staying in a flea-bag hotel near

Times Square that was cheap, a necessity, several meals at Tads Steak House for $1.79 each, tickets to see *Fiddler on the Roof* seated in the last row of the balcony, the Rockettes at Radio City Music Hall, the UN, visiting with representatives of Israel and Egypt during the six day war, and touring. I had charged the youth ninety dollars and when we got home I gave each of them a refund of fifteen dollars. Can you imagine?

It was then time to move again, this time into an associate pastor position at Trinity Methodist Church in the Beverly Hills section of Chicago once again in charge of the youth.

THE ECUMENICAL INSTITUTE

One day I heard a clergy colleague talking about something he had attended that he said energized him and gave direction for his ministry: The Ecumenical Institute. The teaching at the Institute was that the local church was the place where the transformation of the world could take place because these were little conclaves of people scattered about in nearly every community, large or small.

So I signed up. It was a three-day event, only clergy in attendance. The location was in one of the worst neighborhoods on the near west side of Chicago. There, in buildings that were once a seminary that had moved to the suburbs, we gathered.

At breakfast before we ate, but after the food had been served, a speech was given about how a pig had died in order that we could have ham for breakfast that morning. Therefore, since one life was given up so that our lives could be sustained, we have a responsibility to live our lives with gratitude for the life given and live for all humanity. I have never forgotten that teaching.

In our group sessions, held in a room with a single light bulb. We studied sentence-by-sentence Paul Tillich's sermon, 'You Are Accepted.' In that sermon he talked about how we experience *separation from ourselves, others, our world, and from the Ground of our Being* (his term for what we might call God). His text was from Romans: 5:20: 'But where sin abounded, grace did much more abound.' He called that separation "sin"

He spoke of how everyone, at times, has felt *lonely*, has felt a separation from the rest of life. This, he said, is the experience of being   Then he moved on to grace. He wrote: *Sometimes at that moment of experiencing our separation from ourselves and all creation, a wave of light breaks into our darkness, and it is as though a voice were saying, YOU ARE ACCEPTED...DO NOT TRY TO DO ANYTHING NOW...SIMPLY accept the fact that you are accepted!*

That was a powerful message. There is nothing we need to do, nothing we can do to earn God's love. It is just given and given to all of us without strings attached.

The most difficult exercise then took place. Each of us was asked to respond to the question, 'Is Hitler accepted? that is to say is Hitler forgiven by God?' The only answer possible is to say is, 'Yes' even though none of us wanted to respond so. What happened to Hell for evildoers? I wanted to hang on to that and condemn Hitler to Hell because of the massacre of Jews, homosexuals and others he thought were deviants.

That's how most of us had been taught, with that legalistic theology that said if you're evil and you commit evil acts, you will suffer the consequences of Hell. The problem for us is: Who among us has not committed evil? Are there different levels of evil or is evil evil?

I was stunned and confused by this teaching. It was something I had never encountered before. But there was something freeing as well.

We are loved by God always!.

I found this teaching truly powerful, an understanding that made so much sense.

NEARLY OPTING OUT OF MINISTRY
Trinity United Methodist
1968-1971

Becoming an associate pastor after having served for eight years as the lead pastor was a hard adjustment. The senior pastor was Rev. Howard Benson. He and I got along well. However, with so many executives in the meat packing industry who also had positions in the leadership of the church, I felt I was treated as though I was an insignificant employee at their business. I was never dealt with directly, but always through Howard. I was never invited nor welcomed at a meeting of the personnel board.

During these years Jackie developed an obsession, visiting bathrooms. If we stopped at a gas station or went into a restaurant, Jackie always had to go to the bathroom, just to see it. One day she disappeared and we couldn't find her. I knocked on the neighbor's door and asked if she had seen her. "Oh yes. She wanted to see our bathroom so I am showing it to her."

Jackie's other hobby was to rearrange the kitchen cabinets, something she did well.

Trinity United Methodist Church is located in the Beverly Hills part of Chicago, what had once been one of the most exclusive places to live in the city. In the past the congregation would choose their pastor from across the country, not the usual Methodist way, which is by appointment to a church by the bishop. This speaks to what had once been the exclusiveness and power of this congregation.

The architecture was Gothic-style, cement pillars lining the outside aisles, no carpeting in the aisles, stained glass windows, quite dim. I felt it was rather austere yet beautiful.

One thing this *cathedral* lent itself to was pageantry, especially at Christmas. Howard and I designed a Christmas Eve service that included a procession of large, beautiful banners that opened the service. There was the traditional candle lighting and in that setting was particularly elegant. Those Christmas Eve services sparked my interest in designing worship that was both true to the faith and spoke to the emotions.

I was the youth pastor and one of the events I became involved in was providing the venue, a large fellowship hall, for a community teen dance. Four hundred teenagers showed up that night. There were sponsors, however, who, when a little scuffling broke out among a few of the teens, quite suddenly announced that the dance was over and everyone should leave, a huge mistake.

The result of 400 youth exiting the church at the same time, unhappy the dance been shut down, led to what amounted to a riot in the street. Police had to be called. I thought there would be an inquisition charging me with tainting the reputation of this 'magnificent' congregation and that I would be burned at the stake *(figuratively, I hoped)*, but it was never mentioned, not to me at least.

OUR THIRD DOG

We had gotten our third dog. We named her Whiskers, a Cockapoo (part cocker spaniel, part poodle). One time Aunt Violet and Uncle Clyde were visiting us for the Christmas-New Year's season. On New Year's Eve they wanted to have a toast to the New Year. I joined in although I had never had hard liquor. We had let Whiskers outside and when I went to bring her in I called, *"Whiskey, Whiskey!"* The alcohol had gotten to me.

Whiskers looked like the Benji dog that was on television at that time, cute with curly hair. One summer we decided to go camping to central New York State. We stopped at my Mother's overnight. One of her friends walked in the front door without knocking, something Mother said she had never done before. Whiskers took exception to this *intruder* and bit the lady. I had to take the lady to the hospital for a tetanus shot.

That was the first of three such instances on that trip. We discovered that Whiskers, though she looked like a cuddly dog, was only so with us.

On one occasion we took her to the beauty parlor for a bath and trim. When we went to pick her up they brought out this skinny dog that looked nothing like her. I said, "That's not our dog." They said, "She seems to know you," because she was jumping all over us. They had had to shave her because her hair was so matted. I think Whiskers was embarrassed because of the shave, but of course her hair grew back.

One evening a few years later, we had gone to a movie. When we returned we found that a brick had been thrown through one of the windows in the den. There was blood on the window frame and we decided that Whiskers, though small, had a vicious bark and had scared the would-be robber.

CHANGE WAS IN THE AIR

Sometime around 1970 I began to have a serious psychological problem. It was evidenced when I was asked to officiate at a wedding. In the course of the liturgy I would become so nervous that my voice would shake, sometimes it would actually leave me. It was so embarrassing to me and I am sure disturbing to the couple getting married. I tried using tranquilizers but that didn't work. I didn't know what to do but I knew that if I was to continue being a pastor that I needed to be able to officiate at weddings without becoming a basket case.

There were many things happening in my life at that time. I was extremely unhappy as an associate pastor at Trinity United Methodist. The Senior Pastor who succeeded Howard Benson was strange. Nearly every Sunday in his sermon there would come the time when he would use an illustration about a time when, through his prayers, someone had been miraculously healed. I believe that a healing can take place that is beyond our understanding, but so many? I felt nauseated listening to his sermons. I knew that if I had to remain there one more year I would need to look for another profession. But what? What does a person trained to be a pastor qualify for in the market place? I thought about an admissions counselor at a college. Actually I couldn't think of any real possibility. I was between a rock and a hard place.

But then I received a phone call from the District Superintendent. "Ray, we would like you to become the pastor of First United

Methodist Church in Harvey. What do you think?" Without consulting my wife I said, "I'd like that." Just like that! That was a church I had always thought I wanted to serve.

GROWING HAIR?

Well, not exactly 'growing' hair but I was losing my hair at an early age. By the time I was 35 I was showing a lot of bald that was not cool in the '70s. June made a suggestion to get a hairpiece, also called a rug or toupee. I preferred *hairpiece*.

The first one I got looked like a rug. When I look at pictures I can't believe I actually wore it. But it covered the bald. It was held in place with a kind of glue that irritated my skin and made bandaids necessary where there was irritation, which meant the hairpiece was not securely fastened.

At the same time we went on the unhealthy Stillman diet, popular then, which led me to shed 90 pounds. Between the weight loss and the hairpiece, people literally did not know me. Some at the church had to look twice to see that it was in fact me.

When we moved to Harvey, Illinois in 1971 the first big event was the annual carnival in the parking lot of the church. Among the games and food was a dunk tank. You know how that works. Someone sits on a collapsible seat inside this cage with a tank full of water beneath. People throw balls at a target, which, when hit deposits the one sitting in the cage into the water. I was told that the pastor always went into the cage. I didn't want to do it, primarily because of the hairpiece. But I didn't win that one, so into the cage I went praying that no one would hit the target. Of course!

I had a lot of bandaids under my hairpiece and knew it was not secure. When they hit the target, down I went and as I went under the water my hairpiece came off, and when I surfaced I came up right under the hairpiece but it was cockeyed on my head. I didn't want people to know I had a hairpiece so as quickly as I could I headed into the church to dry off and get my 'hair' settled correctly on my head.

I don't think people were fooled by my attempts to pretend there was no rug on my head. However, as years went by I invested more and more in the hairpieces I bought and they started looking better. In fact, when we were in Crystal Lake in the 1990's, one woman exiting worship said, "I love the way your hair looks. What barber do you see?" I quickly said, "Oh, well, I go to someone in Chicago," which was true.

I wore that hairpiece until the day I retired. When we left Crystal Lake for our new home in Colorado, as we exited the city, I took that hairpiece off and threw it in the back seat and that was the end of that chapter. The demise of the hairpiece. Such freedom!

HARVEY YEARS AND DEPRESSION
1971-1981

I was enthusiastic about the move to Harvey. My career was not endangered. I did not have to look for other employment. And when we got to Harvey the problem with weddings suddenly ceased.

However, another problem surfaced not long after that move. I found myself falling into periods of depression, deep depression. I consulted with the District Superintendent and he suggested I schedule an appointment with Dr. Robert Moore at Chicago Theological Seminary 1973. I did so.

He diagnosed an unresolved issue related to my relationship with my Father. During our counseling sessions, I came to realize that the problem with weddings stemmed from the fact that I had assisted in the wedding of my younger sister just a day after we buried my Father, who had died very suddenly earlier that week. That was the root of that problem

Bob helped me to see that I had been very angry with my Father when he died, leaving me before we could develop the kind of relationship I wanted so desperately. I could not forgive my Father for dying so soon.

Dr. Moore had me visualize my Father sitting in a chair across from me and telling my Dad just how I felt and forgiving him for dying. I could also tell my Dad that I was sorry that I had not been the son he would have liked me to be.

The next exercise was to listen to what my Father was saying to me. I heard my Father *(not audibly, of course, but in my inner being)* say that he loved me, and was proud of me. Believe it or not, that settled the issue with my Dad and instead of harboring ill feelings I was able to go on in life knowing that my Father actually had loved me and loved me still.

But the depression continued. Dr. Moore suggested Zoloft to help stabilize my moods and it seemed to help. I continued on this medication for about 40 years. I did not know that long-term use could render a person impotent, something with which I was afflicted in later years. Why hadn't someone warned me?

Harvey years were my first *Camelot* years. I loved being pastor in that church. The community was changing racially. Before we moved there housing had been built on the west side of Harvey that would accommodate hundreds of black families from Chicago. It was part of the movement to try to integrate whites and blacks. It didn't work.

Much of the white population became frightened with so many black people moving in so quickly along with the crime that did ensue, and chose to flee. The black population moved east. In fact, the day we moved into the parsonage, a black family, ironically named Miller, moved in across the street.

One night we heard a police siren and the police car stopped in front of our house. Gunfire was heard shooting between our house and the neighbors. I started to go out to see what was happening but June ordered me to stay inside the house. We never found out what caused that incident. Dixie Mall, located near the new housing apartments on the west side of the city gradually closed due to some crime, but mostly due to fear by whites who ceased shopping there.

I never felt unsafe during the ten years we lived in Harvey, even when I went out at night. I loved living in Harvey with a community of wonderful people. I believed that people of different races could live together harmoniously and that became my mission. One day a black family attended worship, Bob Harris, his wife and two sons. I decided to visit them in their home not far from the church. They realized, of course, that they were the only black worshipers and told me that they did not want to cause a problem.

I assured them that they were very welcome in the Harvey Methodist Church (the full name was the Zella Gamble Methodist Episcopal Church) and I encouraged them to continue to worship with us and they did. The day came when they became members.

Most of the congregation welcomed them warmly, but a few were less so. I remember one woman who, if she found herself in a situation where she might have had to shake hands with the Harris family would turn her back. She was the exception.

To calm the fears of the white members I attended every meeting of every group and when conversation turned to people thinking of moving, I would encourage them to stay, or, if they moved to continue to be part of the congregation, which many did, probably because of the fantastic pastor they had. Maybe not!

We built the program of the church to make the congregation more visible in the community. A mid-week youth program became very popular and brought black children as well as white, and eventually their parents to the church.

It was at Harvey that we built friendships that would last a lifetime. A couples group was there, adjunct to the rest of the church. They called themselves The Birthday Group. One of their activities was to celebrate each person's birthday, supposedly as a surprise, therefore not necessarily on the actual birth date. There were eight couples and when one couple moved away, we were invited to take their place.

On my birthday, a big surprise greeted me. We had gone to Hawaii in the summer of 1972 to visit my sister and brother-in-law stationed there. He had chosen a career in the Navy. We were able to leave the kids with my sister for a week so June and I could take a tour of the islands of Kauai, Maui and the Big Island, Hawaii. During that week when we were on the island of Hawaii we saw the nesting sites of the frigate birds with their seven-foot wingspan and the red-tailed boobies.

After coming home we had a program for the congregation showing slides, among which were some of these birds. Our friends thought it very funny that I had made such a fuss about frigate birds and the boobies.

So on my birthday in 1973, when I opened the drapes in the living room, there facing me was a huge white bird made of chicken wire and Kleenex. Hanging from the bill of the bird was a little sign that said Happy Birthday. Then the phone calls began. I answered and the voice on the other end would say, "Frigate bird, frigate bird," and then hang up. Then another call, and another and another. One of the most memorable birthdays I ever had.

All of our experiences in Harvey were not wonderful. There was Bill. I first met Bill when he arrived in Harvey after riding in a boxcar from his home state of New York. He got off in Harvey because, at that time, it was a hub for the Illinois Central railroad. His mother had called me because I was the pastor of the United Methodist Church. She asked me to try to find Bill and help him.

When I found him at the Western Union office in Harvey where his mother had wired him some money, Bill was such a pathetic looking creature, and obviously had so many problems that I felt I wanted to do something to help him. His clothes smelled of urine and he smelled from lack of soap and water on his body. He was withdrawn and spoke few words, but I was determined.

There was a book that spoke about how some pastors are plagued by a *Messiah Complex*. That was me at that time. I believed I could help and heal people through my own efforts, of course because God was working through me. I made their problems my problems. I was going to bring Bill back from addiction to alcohol and drugs, get him cleaned up, help him get a job and return him to the world as a contributing member of society. What a star in my crown that would be. One person saved!

June and I took him to the store and bought him a new pair of pants, some shirts, underclothes, the works. We dressed him up and when he had on his new duds he looked pretty normal. But underneath those clothes, underneath that appearance of normality, nothing had changed.

Although we got him a room at the YMCA where he could sleep in a bed rather than under a railroad car, although we brought him to church and encouraged to try singing in the choir, although we more or less adopted him into our family and included him in some of our family activities, nothing had really changed for Bill. He used the corner of his room at the Y to urinate instead of the men's room; he alternated between being friendly and talking with intelligence and significant knowledge to reacting violently toward me, at one time even threatening to kill me.

On Good Friday night Bill threw a brick through one of the church's stained glass windows and through the protective glass with such force it put a chip in a pew in the last row of the sanctuary.

The next day when he showed up I took him to a mental hospital and explained what had been happening, including that he had threatened to kill me. They admitted him, but within twenty-four hours he was at our front door, Easter Sunday. I didn't know that they could only keep him if he agreed to it.

What I didn't realize was that Bill's mind had been fried with extensive use of drugs. In my lack of knowledge about what drugs did to the body and mind, I thought that simply changing his environment and showering love upon him would make him a different person. What I failed to take into account was that you can offer anything to anyone, but unless they are willing and able to accept what you're offering, it is futile.

I would like to tell you that Bill accepted the love that was extended to him, that his life was changed, that he became a committed follower of Jesus Christ and was restored to society. I cannot tell you that because the last I heard of Bill, he had returned to New York, had threatened to kill his mother, had gone into a mental hospital, then walked out and had not been heard from. So much for being a messiah. That was not my job.

THERE'S A BANDIT IN THE HOUSE

June had always told me that she did not like cats, so what a surprise when one day she came home from school with a baby kitten. It seems her principal had found these kittens and taken them to school to see if anyone would like to have one. June took one look at them and decided that she would like to bring one home. I could not believe it.

As time went on all of us fell in love with this big black-and-white cat we called Bandit. At Christmastime that year I had set up a ladder in order to hang greenery over one of the archways. I was busy hanging ornaments on the greenery over an arch. I left the room and when I came back little Bandit had climbed to the top of the ladder and with one paw was hitting one of the ornaments, watching the sparkling orb move back and forth back and forth.

As I mentioned before, at Christmas time I created this elaborate village and train display. It took hours and hours to complete it. One day I came home, went into the living room and saw that Bandit was under the tree. I was so shocked I yelled which caused her to scamper and in the process produced chaos under the tree. She had actually gotten under the tree without moving anything but my yelling caused the damage.

We often had an open house during the Christmas holidays for our extended family and members of the church. This particular Christmas Bandit had gotten onto the shelf of our teacart in the dining room and was well hidden. As people walked by she reached out her paw and swiped at that person. it was really funny.

Our mail arrived by being pushed through a slot in the front door. One day the doorbell rang. It was the mail carrier. He said, "I don't know what it is, but the next time that paw comes out through that slot I am going to kill whatever it is. Apparently Bandit had discovered how the mail arrived and would wait by the door until the mail carrier came, then reached through the slot and waved her paw.

Bandit stayed with us until we were relocated to Glenview. We found a wonderful welcoming family for her. That was our last feline experience.

BARNEY MILLER

After the death of our precious Whiskers, we adopted a dog at a shelter, a yellow lab. We named him Barney. After we brought him home we discovered that Barney's eyes would turn red. We thought he was possessed. He was uncontrollable. We tried keeping him in the kitchen when we left but on two occasions he chewed the wall paneling while we were gone and it had to be replaced.

One of the humorous experiences related to Barney occurred when I took him to the vet. When it was time for him to go home, they would call out, "Barney, Barney Miller," so I would step up. At that time in the 70's there was a TV series called Barney Miller. People in the waiting room were amused.

One time I was coming home, driving June's Plymouth Scamp, hurrying, trying to get home quickly to conduct a funeral. At an intersection right in front of our children's elementary school, I started through the intersection not seeing a car coming on my right. There was an accident.

Of course we had to file a police report and by the time I got home I was so nervous about getting ready for the funeral that the gate to our backyard was left open and Barney raced out of the yard into the street. A car hit him. He was not run over, but he was stuck under the car. His tail was caught in an axle. The car was jacked up and Barney was brought out.

A friend took him to a veterinarian to be checked out and everything seemed to be fine, but a few days later we noticed that he kept biting his tail so we took him to the vet again. This time the vet told us that Barney's tail had been broken and it would have to be amputated.

It was with regret that we decided we could not keep Barney. We returned him to the shelter and knew that there would probably be no other person who would adopt a yellow lab with no tail.

LUMINARIAS

At Christmastime, 1978, the church decided to use luminaries, little candles sitting in sand in small paper bags to light not only the walks leading to the church doors on Christmas Eve, but to also line the flat roof on the education building with these candles.

Randy and others were on the roof lighting the candles. The thought occurred to me that the fire department would not be pleased with the possibility of fire caused by these burning candles. But it was stunning and no fire occurred

THIRD OF JULY

In the '70s I had read that there was going to be a concert in Grant Park with fireworks from barges anchored on Lake Michigan and a concert by the Chicago Symphony the evening of July third. I thought that would be something great to do, great music under the stars and fireworks from barges on Lake Michigan. So we packed a picnic and headed downtown.

It was a WOW! experience, beautiful and awesome with the orchestra concluding their pre-fireworks concert with Tchaikovsky's 1812 Overture. As the orchestra reached the point where cannon were fired, the fireworks began. The orchestra continued playing, including "Semper Fidelis" by John Phillip Susa. Everyone was standing, many singing along with the music.

I know that today this happens at practically every fireworks, usually on July fourth, but for me, this was the first time I had been to such an extravaganza. On the way home we heard on the radio that there had been 300,000 people in the park that night. I could hardly believe it. Had I known there were going to be that many people I would not have gone. However, our experience was so wonderful that we went back every year until we left Illinois for Colorado. We missed attending this annual celebration.

Eventually, *The Taste of Chicago* was held on streets adjacent to the park that increased the number of people who came. On one occasion I went to *The Taste* and the crowd was so thick I couldn't move. Because I am somewhat claustrophobic it was a frightening experience for me and I never went to *The Taste* again when the crowds were so dense.

Friends were with us one time, one celebrating her birthday. I decided it would be fun to sing *Happy Birthday* to celebrate her special day. I approached the people sitting around us and asked if they would join in singing *Happy Birthday*. There must have been a hundred people or more singing Happy Birthday to our friend. She was embarrassed, astounded, and thrilled.

We could leave our blanket and go to the *Taste of Chicago*, or the restroom, come back and find that nothing had been touched. This, in the middle of one of the great cities in the country, gave me a lot of pride to think that this could happen even in this day.

YMCA AND MACHO MAN

Our friends, Fairy (that was her name, Fairy Bee) and Bob Pearson, heard about disco lessons to be taught at a recreation center. The four of us decided to take the classes. The first session began with the famous dance performed by John Travolta in *Saturday Night Fever*. None of us mastered that dance, of course.

Later on we were taught ways to disco that we could actually do. It was so much fun, something I enjoyed, and while previous to this I had been self-conscious on the dance floor, learning disco set me free to dance, something I continued to enjoy for years.

When the classes were over we decided we wanted to find discos where we could dance. The daughter of Fairy and Bob told us of a wonderful restaurant where we could have dinner and dance. It was called Marie's. So we drove to that address in Chicago, but there was no Marie's restaurant at that address. It was now called Coconuts. Nevertheless we decided to go in.

After being seated for dinner, the waiter came to our table dressed in long tight pants, no shirt, with red straps attached to the pants crossing in front and back. He was gorgeous. Of course I was enjoying having him as our waiter and truthfully the food was excellent.

At one point Bob went to the men's room and when he came back he said, "Ray, you need to go to the men's room."

Immediately upon entering I saw what he meant. The men's room was decorated in pink with a lovely vase of flowers on the table and a pink upholstered chair.

You don't have to be Einstein to understand exactly where we were.

After we ate we went to the dance floor and began dancing and having a great time. As the evening went on however, the lights on the dance floor gradually were getting dimmer and dimmer and finally only came on occasionally, and the clientele on the dance floor changed also. There were guys dressed in various costumes and some in stages of undress. It was at this point that we decided it was time to leave and return home. Had I been alone I would have loved to stay longer, but it wasn't possible under the circumstances. This was an evening never to be forgotten.

Later we went to another disco in Chicago where the entrance was made of a shiny silver metalic-like material. We entered a hallway that was also made of the same material. We couldn't find the door with the dim lighting and the shiny walls, and only did so by walking along the hallway, pushing on the wall until a door opened. We were among the few there. Disco was going out of style, like wearing knickers in the 40s, and Nehru shirts and suits in the 60s, but we had fun.

WEDDINGS

Weddings play a big role in the life of a pastor. There have been memorable weddings during the years of my ministry. The first came at the first church I served. That old former German Methodist Episcopal Church had air flowing upwards from a grate in the middle aisle.

It was a winter wedding and as the bride came down the aisle the furnace began to blow hot air up through the duct. As the bride walked across the grate, her gown and veil both were filled with air that ballooned the dress and lifted the veil. It was hilarious.

Harvey was the site of the most memorable weddings I conducted. I was preparing for a very formal wedding with the groom in white tux. I was in the upstairs bathroom of the parsonage when the doorbell rang. I told Jackie, maybe five years old at the time, to tell whomever it is that I am getting ready for a wedding and can't come to the door now.

She came back upstairs a few minutes later and said, "Daddy, the man says you need to come to the door."

When I went to the back door, two men were standing there. They flipped out their FBI IDs and asked if I was officiating a wedding that day for a particular young man. I replied, "Yes."

They announced, "He is wanted by the FBI for desertion from the Army. We want to arrest him when he comes for the wedding."

I suggested, "Can't you go to his home and arrest him there?"

"Where does he live?" I told them and they said, "No, he doesn't live there. That is a false address. Where will he go when he comes to the church?"

"To my office."

"We want to station one of us in your office and the other will be outside the church. Do we have your permission to be in your office?" What could I say?

The arrest was made and he was taken to the city jail to await transfer to Fort Leavenworth. I went to the bride's home that was close by. It was pouring rain. I told her and her family what had happened and learned that the bride was aware he had deserted. After a few minutes the parents asked, "If we can get permission, are you willing to marry them at the city jail?"

After thinking a bit, I replied, "If I was willing to perform the wedding in the church then I guess I would be willing to perform it in the city jail." And that is what happened.

The bridal party and parents were the only ones present in a room guarded at every door by an armed policeman or FBI officer. They were permitted to bring the wedding cake and had a small reception. Then he was taken back to his cell. This young man was taken to Fort Leavenworth and given a dishonorable discharge. Later I saw him around town. He had started a house painting business and all seemed to be well with him.

Another memorable wedding took place in a hospital. It had not been planned that way, but after the rehearsal, the bride developed severe kidney pain, kidney stones. So instead of an elaborate wedding in the church, it took place in a small chapel with only parents, best man and maid of honor. The bride came in a wheelchair with an intravenous bottle attached and a veil. After the ceremony the groom went off to the reception. What could he do? The bride went back to her hospital room. The next day a photo appeared in the local paper with a brief article about the wedding.

The saddest wedding took place in Glenview, Illinois in the '80s where I was pastor. The bride had confessed doubts about the marriage and I had said she should postpone or cancel the wedding. She replied, "But my parents have already spent a lot of money on the reception."

I counseled, "It would be better to lose money on a reception than to find yourself in a marriage you didn't want."

The wedding took place and two weeks later the bride moved back home and said she didn't want to be married.

FAMILY WEDDINGS

Our daughter, Jackie, got married in February. We were having a particularly cold winter. The wedding party was dressed in colors that were appropriate for the season. It was a beautiful wedding.

However, the day before the wedding my sister Kathleen flew in from Florida and we were having a snowstorm. At one point as I was driving to O'Hare Field to pick her up there was a complete whiteout. I could not see more than a couple of feet in front of me. It was very scary but I managed to get my sister back to our house.

When Randy married Melissa in California in March 2003, once again there was a major snowstorm. By then June and I were living in Colorado. We were scheduled to fly there on Wednesday, arriving a couple days early so we could do some sightseeing before everyone gathered for the pre-wedding celebrations.

We decided to get a room at a motel near Denver International Airport so we would already be there ready to check-in at the airport the next morning. When we were leaving the house there were already several inches of snow on the ground, perhaps as much as a foot or more. When I backed out of the driveway and tried to get out of the cul-de-sac where we lived, the car became stuck in the snow. It wouldn't go forward nor backward. The wheels just spun in the snow and ice.

Fortunately there were neighbors who saw our dilemma and came out and pushed us until we got to the next cross street where we could get some traction. Why I continued on I do not know. Well, the reason: we were flying out the next day.

The ride to the airport was on streets, roads, and interstates that were snow packed, and more significantly, icy. On a toll road when we came to a tollbooth I actually slid past the tollbooth and had to back up in order to pay the toll.

Driving at about 25 miles an hour I finally, miraculously, made it to the exit to the motel. On the way, there were cars stranded alongside the road. I did fine until I pulled into the entrance to the motel where I got stuck. Some men in the lobby of the motel pushed my car into a parking space.

Obviously the airport was shut down and there would be no flights the next day at all. In her anxiety and desire to get to California on time, June suggested that we drive there. Of course, Interstate 70 across Colorado was completely impassable. Our only alternative was to wait until the airport opened once again, which occurred two days later.

We got to California in time for all of the pre-wedding activities and the wedding and that was what was most important.

Melissa had two children, Paighton and Delaney. My grand children increased to five and I Ioved it. I added three more when Jackie married Steve Gates in 2017: Chloe, Mia and Nick. Add in Juniette, born on August 25, 2006, my grandchildren now number seven.

WHERE DO YOU STAND WHEN YOU PREACH?

At an event of the United Methodist Southern District of Chicago for United Methodist clergy, the senior pastor of the First United Methodist Church of Colorado Springs was our guest leader. He talked about his life and ministry in this large church with more than 5,000 members. Among the things he told us was that he tried to remove barriers between the congregants and himself.

For instance, he felt the pulpit was one such barrier. The pastor behind the pulpit, he said, put a wall between the pastor and the congregants that could possibly hinder the congregation from applying the message to their lives.

His solution? Deliver the sermon from the center of the chancel away from the pulpit. I pondered this as a possibility for myself. I knew that one day I would step out from behind the pulpit and deliver the sermon, but I just didn't know when.

Without pre-planning, one Sunday morning during worship, I did just that. I was so nervous that I literally shook. I held my sermon notes rolled up in one hand just in case. The response from the congregation was so positive that I never went back behind the pulpit again. Eventually I gave up the rolled up notes and became even more relaxed with my delivery.

The only time there was a problem came on a Palm Sunday in Glenview in the '80s. The District Superintendent, my boss so to speak, was in attendance. I don't know if that is what caused me to blank out, but I totally forgot what I had said and where I was going in the sermon. I had my notes on the pulpit, went there, found my train of thought and proceeded. I was so embarrassed. However, a couple parishioners, trying to make me feel better, commented that they now knew I was human.

THE 100 YEAR OLD PARSONAGE

The parsonage in Harvey was a hundred year old two-story house with walkup attic and full basement. It had been well cared for by the congregation and we loved living there. It was a house with character. The beautiful wooden trim around the archways, the huge mirror at the foot of the stairs, surrounded by the same wood, spoke of old-time elegance.

Hot water radiators heated the house. A wood-burning fireplace, a kitchen that had been enlarged by enclosing the back porch, three bedrooms upstairs and one bathroom were characteristics. The bathroom had character too. The only way to get the light on in the bathroom was to throw the switch and hit the wall. If you didn't hit the wall the light did not come on.

We had lots of unexpected visitors in that house. Birds would sit on the chimney and the fumes from the furnace would cause them to lose consciousness and they would fall into the basement.

We also had a bat visitor. Now how do you get a bat out of the house? We tried opening the doors and shooing it, but the bat was on the second floor and wasn't responsive to our 'shooing' efforts.

Next came the fish net but I couldn't snag it in the net either. Then I saw a canoe paddle Randy had on the wall in his bedroom. As a last ditch effort I grabbed that oar and started swinging it at the bat. And miracle of miracles, this guy who could not hit a baseball with a bat, hit a bat with an oar. I scooped up the bat and took him out to the alley. I thought he was dead, but the next morning the bat was nowhere to be seen. He must have just been stunned.

YUKON OR BUST

The ten years in Harvey, Illinois produced so many memories. It was while living there, in July 1975 that we set out on an adventure that gave us the most memorable family vacation ever, driving to Alaska. I had done extensive research in preparation, purchased the mileage marker book that detailed everything along the 1,200 mile Alaska Highway from Dawson Creek, British Columbia to the Alaska border and on into Alaska.

Camping was to be our mode of travel in our 11-year-old car with an odometer that read 105,000 miles driven. An extra tire was strapped to the roof. Care had been taken to outfit the car to be sure it would carry us safely on this long journey of 3,500 miles. Except that while the book said to protect the gas tank with rubber or other cushioning so that on the 1,200 miles of gravel road it would not be punctured, the mechanic said we did not need extra protection because it was already well protected. I took his word for it but June was not so sure.

Off we set, an enthusiastic send-off with dozens of church members cheering us as we drove out of the church parking lot.

All went well until we crossed into Minnesota. I had noticed that when we stopped it was becoming more difficult to get the car started again. After staying at a KOA campground and struggling to get the car running, I pulled into the next town and had a mechanic check it out. There was a defect that would require hours to repair. So we waited it out, grateful that we had not gotten stranded on the highway.

With the car running well again we set off to North Dakota, then through Saskatchewan and Alberta, finally arriving at Dawson Creek, British Columbia where the Alcan Highway began. As we left Dawson Creek a sign said that in one hundred miles the pavement would end. We were excited. Everyday brought something new.

Most campgrounds were primitive, so we had to carry water and try to take care of our bathroom needs as best we could, mostly stopping at a gas station or little restaurant where there might be a bathroom.

At times it rained and we would take long lunch breaks to dry out the tent and other items that had gotten wet.

Many nights we slept in the station wagon and at times I would awaken early, like 4:30 or 5, and start driving while the others slept. Ten or twelve hours a day were common. We had been warned about driving too fast because the gravel would heat the tires and cause blowouts so I usually traveled no more than 35 miles an hour.

The landscape changed every day. We crossed the border into the Yukon Territory and back into British Columbia then back into the Yukon. It made me remember the radio program, *Sergeant Preston and the Yukon*. We were in true wilderness.

One night we settled into an isolated campground. I noticed a horse standing among the trees looking at us. I thought it had a weird look in its eyes. It actually frightened me. I wasn't sure if we were safe there or if that horse might do some damage to our campsite and us. I had never been in such a remote part of the world and it was a bit unsettling. But as it turned out, all was well.

Somewhere along the way, I looked at the dashboard and noticed that the fuel gauge was on zero. Because I filled the tank frequently, I knew that something was wrong. A hole in the gas tank! I kept thinking, that June would be so upset because I took the mechanic's word that the tank did not need more protection. But then, after driving a while, shaking from anxiety, I noticed the heat gauge was also not working. So something must have happened with the electrical system and there was no hole in the gas tank. You have no idea how relieved I felt. So now it was, fill the tank every 100 miles and pray that the car did not overheat.

The largest town we came across, Watson Lake, had about 500 residents. When we arrived in Whitehorse, the capital of the Yukon, population 10,000 with about 10 miles of paved highway, it seemed wonderful to be back in civilization. But Alaska was growing nearer every day.

Along the way we saw black bears waiting for handouts at certain rest stops. Spring rains had washed out portions of the highway causing single lane traffic and a very rough, boulder-strewn roadway. Travel there was slow. We crossed bridges, with supports seriously damaged, at five miles an hour, one car at a time.

Finally we reached the Alaska border where multiple pictures were taken, including one showing the dirt and mud-covered station wagon. Now we were on paved roads again. However, because heat from cars that traveled on the roads would melt some of the permafrost causing the roadways to sink here and there, it made for some roller coaster driving.

We arrived in Fairbanks ten days after leaving Harvey. After a week and a half of eating freeze-dried foods, when we saw the Golden Arches, we headed to McDonalds for a hamburger.

Everything in Fairbanks was jammed. The oil pipeline from Prudhoe Bay was under construction and there were thousands more in Fairbanks than the population of 25,000 could accommodate.

I tried to find someone to repair the car and was told they could do so in ten days. Finally a 'mechanic' at a gas station said he could repair it for us. As I watched him take more and more pieces out from under the hood I started to have misgivings about this person. No, he assured me, he could repair it. He finally had it all back together, but now the gauges still didn't work correctly. He had messed up the electrical system so that when I wanted to use the turn signals, the windshield washers came on, etc.

About a month after we got home, I noticed something wet coming from under the car. The gas tank had a leak. But we were home.

One of the special excursions we had arranged for our trip to Alaska was a 24-hour tour to the top of world, Barrow, Alaska, situated on the shores of the Arctic Ocean. It was a different world. We stayed at the "Top of The World Hotel," a hotel constructed in Washington, taken apart and transported by ship to Barrow. There was recycled water in the toilet, heavy drapes to keep out the light because it was the season of the midnight sun.

For me, sleep didn't come that night because I kept going outside to see if, in fact, the sun never did set. The sun could be seen, at least part of it, throughout the night. On the shores of the Arctic were huge chunks of ice, indigenous children playing, and a town that seemed it never slept. One man told me they sleep in winter.

At a restaurant June had whale and I ate reindeer. Reindeer is much tastier than whale, more like beef. The kids had hamburgers. For souvenirs Jackie got the pelt of an arctic fox and I got a piece of scrimshaw.

When we arrived back at the airport in Fairbanks and went to our car, we discovered that someone had broken into the car. The only damage was that this weirdo had gotten into the suitcase with Jackie's clothes and torn up her underwear. This really freaked her out, as you might imagine.

Leaving Fairbanks, we traveled to Denali National Park (then still known as McKinley). Our reservation was at a campground 80 miles from the park's entrance, the farthest in it was possible to drive.

The drive was slow. We were always watching for wildlife. I'm not very good at that, partly because of colorblindness, but we were following a car in which the occupants were very good spotting the wild inhabitants of the park. Every time they pulled over and stopped, I did too, and looked in the direction they were looking.

Caribou were in abundance. Then we saw it, a grizzly bear. It was to the right of our car up an embankment. As she got nearer we became very quiet as the grizzly crossed the road between our two vehicles. We could see how massive the grizzly was with paws that could have easily smashed the windshield. But off she went without paying any attention to us at all.

That night as we pitched our tent we could see grizzlies far off in the distance. Jackie became ill that night, nauseous, and very stressed. This could have been the result of the break-in of our car at the Fairbanks airport, but also perhaps by being in a campground so far from the entrance. We were to have been there three nights, but by morning it was clear that we needed to get her and us out of the park. So we slowly made our way back to the more civilized part of Alaska.

We had made arrangements to stay in a dormitory at what was then Alaska Methodist University, now part of the University of Alaska. We had beds and a place to shower. It was heaven.

I had been growing a beard for the ten days we were driving to Alaska. With hot water coming out of the faucet I decided the beard had to go but I would keep the mustache. I knew nothing about how to trim a mustache but I kept it anyway. On the first Sunday back at the church after the worship service one woman came up to me and said, "You look like a walrus." That did it. I went home and shaved off that mustache.

While in Anchorage we visited the site of the hugely destructive earthquake of 1964 and the park where there had once been a neighborhood, now just mounds of sunken earth created by the quake. We visited Portage Glacier and also attended an indigenous program at the museum.

It was time to leave Anchorage and begin to make our way back to Whitehorse where we took the narrow gauge railway to Skagway. In those days a highway was being constructed through the Chilkoot Pass, traversed long before by miners on their way to search for gold.

Although the distance between Whitehorse and Skagway is not far as the crow flies, it took the entire day, stopping at midpoint for lunch at the place where the trains going in each direction could pass one another.

We had a day in Skagway before embarking on the Alaska Marine Highway System that would get us to Prince Rupert, British Columbia. It was Sunday and we decided to take a small prop plane to see the glaciers. The pilot said he had just come from church and we thought that was a good sign.

The flight, with the other three behind the pilot and me next to him, was spectacular, almost too much so. It seemed he flew far too close to the mountains to show us mountain goats and then, looking down to the water he said, "Do you see the seals there?" We hesitated. Big mistake, because he decided to take us down to see them up close. Like a corkscrew the plane descended with all of us starting to become sick from the circular motion, but perhaps more so from fear. But the view of the face of the glacier and the hundreds of seals was spectacular.

We boarded our ship on which we had booked a stateroom for the two-day passage to Prince Rupert, British Columbia. Along the way, the ship stopped many times taking on and discharging passengers, vehicles, and supplies. Little League teams got on board at one stop and off the next where they were to play a game. We had enough time at Ketchikan for a quick organized tour that included the Totem Pole Park. Ketchikan has approximately 150 inches of rain per year, but during the time we were on tour there was no rain.

Between Ketchikan and Prince Rupert, we entered into an unsheltered part of the Pacific. The water became fairly rough and all four of us were feeling queasy. At long last we were able to disembark into British Columbia.

The adventure was not over however. From Prince Rupert we visited the stunning Lake Louise, then rode a tram to the top of Whistler Mountain near Banff. On the way down, Jackie picked up a piece of the shale rock to take home. A woman waiting to ride the tram commented, "If everyone took a piece of rock, soon there would be nothing left." Really?

At the Columbia Ice Fields the ride out on the ice in a Snocat was another experience we will never forget. Seeing the water spouts shooting up out of holes in the ice was spectacular. Then it was on to spend a day at Glacier National Park, then Yellowstone, then the Black Hills where we stood and looked in amazement at Mount Rushmore.

From there we traveled East across South Dakota into Minnesota and because we were quite ready to get home, continued non-stop for many hours until we arrived back in Harvey. A Great! Unforgettable! Vacation!

TRYING TO BE BRITISH

That wasn't the end of our journeys in the 70s. In 1978 I applied for and was accepted into the Methodist Ministerial Exchange program, trading churches, parsonages and autos with a pastor from Sheffield, England.

The day we arrived in London, we had just gotten to our lodging and were walking back toward Victoria Station to have lunch when we became aware of the crowds on the sidewalks and the Bobbies keeping order. We heard someone say that the Queen was coming. She was not coming to welcome us but the President of Romania. Queen Elizabeth II did indeed come in her open carriage with all the pomp that is associated with British royalty. A true thrill.

I started my driving lesson on the 'wrong side' of the road (the left side is more accurate) in London where I rented a car to get the family to Sheffield. Driving from the car rental to the B&B where we lodged I heard people shouting. They were shouting at me because I was driving on the right side of the road that was the wrong side in England. I should have been driving on the left side instead. I quickly made the adjustment and realized I needed to concentrate on driving, which I did without further incident.

June wanted to try driving, so once when we were in the country she had her chance. It lasted about three minutes because her first turn left put us on a collision course with a car coming toward us in the lane to our right, which is where June had our car positioned!

This was the time of year when the Annual Conference for British Methodism took place. As a foreign clergyperson, I was to attend the opening ceremony, and ceremony it was. All of the foreign visitors were seated on the dais behind the president of the conference. At one point we were to be presented to the president. Therefore, we needed to be seated in correct order so that when our name was announced we would be in front of the president of the conference.

There were many pastoral opportunities while in Sheffield: visiting in a hospital where the patient was in a ward with several other patients; conducting two weddings and learning that the expectation was for a sermon as part of the ceremony; conducting services of Holy Communion at an Ashram House, and at a restaurant where people gathered fortnightly for communion, people who would not go to a church building for worship.

My assignment was with four churches, three Methodist and one Anglican, which were part of the Inner City Parish, plus several experimental ministries. One of the congregations met in a very large church building where the congregation of 16 gathered in a Sunday school room for worship. That was a church that rented their facility to a black congregation.

After we came home we learned that the National Front, the ultra right wing in England, broke into the church and totally desecrated it with Nazi symbols, destroying much of the interior, obviously a protest against blacks. We then learned that this was such a scandal throughout England that contributions came in from throughout the British Isles that enabled that church to be restored.

Another of the Methodist churches was also in a large building. At one time this congregation had had a wonderful music program with a choir that made recordings and traveled extensively, but now had only about twenty-four attendees at worship. What was strange was that people sat in this huge sanctuary exactly where they had always sat, with choir members seated in the same places in the choir loft where they had sat when there had been a choir.

The third Methodist church was one with real life. On the site of that church there had been a Gothic style edifice. During World War II a bomb penetrated the roof and destroyed the entire interior. When restoration funds were made available, instead of reconstructing that building, the money was used to build something entirely new: a smaller worship space with two wings for apartments, several of which were designated for low-income families and one that was the parsonage for the pastor. I found that to be a very creative and faithful way to use the funds they received.

During our stay, June and Randy took the train to London for sightseeing. When they were ready to return home, they asked directions to the rail station from a woman they met along the street. Before she answered however, she mentioned, looking at Randy, that he had been a Native American in a previous life. She could see that through her 'third eye.'

When they left the woman, June started following the directions the woman had given and Randy asked, "You're really going to go the way she said?" They did and easily located the train.

One day we were invited for dinner at the home of two parishioners. At one point June asked "Where the bathroom?" The hostess said in her very British accent, "Oh, do you want to take a bath?" You see, in many British homes the toilet and basin were in one room and the bathtub in an adjacent one.

It was the practice for the Lord Mayor to host a tea for American visitors to Sheffield in an elaborate room at the City

Hall on the fourth of July. The American flag was flown over city hall on that day as well. Instead of offering only tea, a concession was made on this day and coffee was also served for the Americans.

Prior to the tea we met with the Lord Mayor in his chambers, arranged for by a member of one of the churches I served who was a member of the city council.

We had so many experiences while there, including a radio interview and pub tour with members of the church. Prior to going to England I had not had even a bottle of beer so had to practice before we left home to see which I could handle best. It was ale. Then there was a bus trip to northern Wales to the North Sea where we saw people relaxing on the beach wrapped in warm clothing to ward off the cold breezes coming off the Sea. It was summer and they were going to go to the beach, regardless.

Every week we had two days off from church duties so each week we drove off in a different direction from Sheffield. One time we went to Stratford and attended a play by Shakespeare. Perhaps it was, *The Taming of the Shrew*. There we had our lunch of cheese and bread along the river Avon where a bevy of swans swam. It was so beautiful.

Another time we traveled to Sherwood Forest and Windsor Castle. Then there was the trip to Epworth, the place where John and Charles Wesley, founders of the Methodist movement, grew up. Like John, I stood on the grave cover of his father's tomb where he had preached a sermon after being cast out of the church. I had no sermon to preach. My family appreciated that.

We went to Scarborough and remembered the Beatles song about Scarborough Fair. Another time we took the train to Edinburgh where a man on the street asked if we would like to go to a gay bar. Why he asked, I don't know, unless he was just out drumming up business for that bar. We went in but quickly left. (At a later time I may have enjoyed going to that bar.)

After our commitment in Sheffield was over, we said our goodbyes and headed to Wales where it rained much of the time, then took the ferry across the Irish Sea to Ireland, landing near Waterford.

We lugged our suitcases off the ferry stuffed with dozens of Sheffield knives, a product for which the city of Sheffield is known. We also had purchased several sets of duvets for our beds, like the ones we were using in Sheffield. Duh! We could have bought all of those items in the U.S. instead of carrying it all home with us. Our time in Ireland was wonderful, but again the weather was cloudy with drizzle and fog.

The journey across Ireland included the obligatory visit to the Blarney Stone. However the weather was such that much of the time we were unable to see the gorgeous landscape I had read about.

For our lodging on the final night in the British Isles we stayed in a castle. It was a beautiful castle with lovely gardens. We were given lodging in the turret where we enjoyed sleeping in our round room.

It was time to fly home from Shannon. We got to the airport and learned that the flight was going to be delayed a few hours due to a slowdown for many flights because of some kind of protest in France. While we waited, we tried Irish coffee for the first time.

When we boarded we were given two free drinks as compensation for the long delay. I took them both. I thought they would put me to sleep but instead I became drunk and all I could think of was that I was going to get off the plane in Chicago drunk and there would be church members at the airport greeting us as we returned home. Neither proved to be true: I was not drunk and there were no church members at the airport.

THE NOTEL MOTEL

June and I were on a trip out west to Washington, Oregon, and California. The personnel committee at the church in Harvey decided the church should provide a car for the pastor. I was given the responsibility of choosing the car. I chose an Oldsmobile with a diesel engine thinking it would be more economical. However there were multiple problems with our car that necessitated stops for help from auto mechanics.

One night we decided to stop in Eugene, Oregon. It was on a one-way street that we found a Budgetel Motel and checked in. Now it was time to find something to eat so we set off ending up on the street running one-way the opposite way behind our motel.

Then we saw it in flashing lights, "Notel Motel." It was the same motel we had checked into as Budgetel but it was also an hourly-rate motel on the other side. June was freaked out, and didn't want to stay there, but since we had already paid and were tired we stayed. She insisted that I back the car up close to the door to our room as a safety measure.

On an earlier trip out west to Yellowstone when Randy was two, we stopped at an historic site to see one of the cabins that had been preserved from pioneer days.

As we walked down the path to the cabin, Randy had his 'nubie' (pacifier) in his mouth and was carrying his 'blankie' pressed against his cheek. A woman commented that that was so cute, the boy with the pacifier and his blanket and she gave a small laugh.

When we got back to the car, Randy bit and broke his pacifier. We had no idea where to find another pacifier in that desolate part of the country, but it turned out not to be necessary. From that day on he would have nothing more to do with a pacifier nor his blankie.

On that same trip, we were camping at a private campground in Cody, Wyoming. A chuck wagon dinner with entertainment would be held nearby. We decided to go. We were partway through the meal when a strong windstorm blew in. The dishes were being blown off the tables, so we decided to return to the campground. When we arrived there we found that our tent was on the ground. The wind had gotten underneath the tent and ripped the floor so that it could not be used again on this trip. The owner of the campground allowed us to sleep in a small room with no windows and one door. That ended camping for that year.

EXCHANGE STUDENTS

One of our friends in Harvey was involved with the foreign exchange student program at Thornton High School. She and her husband along with at least two other couples from the church hosted students from other countries. Jean thought we should do so too.

Thus into our home came Spiros from Thesoloniki, Greece. Spiros was 15 with the attitude that there was nothing in the United States that they did not have in Greece. We were to have had him for a few months, but ended up having him for the entire year.

Our oldest, Randy, was only 13 years old so we did not know how it is with high school age youth. But we learned the hard way.

The year Spiros spent at Thornton High School was a year that counted on his academic record unlike that for most exchange students. Of course Spiros knew everything already in the courses he had taken in Greece, or so he said. Then we started getting calls from the school: "Spiros has an odor that needs to be corrected"." We never did figure out where that odor came from because we knew he showered every day, but he did perspire profusely.

Next was, "Spiros is not passing in his studies." Then Spiros became part of the high school musical. He had a role that involved dancing. He would come home from practice around 10:30 or 11:00 and throw himself on the floor. Ohh, his legs hurt from all the dancing. It seemed strange to us that the school would keep him out so late on a school night.

So, I called the school and talked with the drama teacher. No practice lasted past nine o'clock. So where had Spiros been between 9 and 11:00? He finally confessed that he and friends went to a burger place after practice. We were at our wits end.

We probably should have asked for him to be sent to another family, but we toughed it out, gluttons for punishment. The day came when he was to return home, a day in July of 1977. A war was going on between Greece and Cyprus at that time. We were concerned. "Please let us know you got home safely. Will you do that?"

"Yes, Dad."

So he left and as we left the airport we said to each other, "We survived!" We did hear from him a year or so later very early on a Christmas Eve morning. We were still in bed. The phone rang. I answered. The voice on the other end of the line said, "Hello Dad." I said to June, "Aren't the kids home?"

It was Spiros. He talked as if we had just spoken the day before. We should come to Greece. He would be coming to the United States. But we never heard from him again. At least we knew he was alive.

So, why would we take another student? Who knows, but we did. Mireja, who went by the nickname Yeya, came to our home. She was from Columbia and we were to have her for only three or four months. She was a delight. We enjoyed having her and there were no problems.

Oh yes, our kids, including Mireja, were at their grandmother's house along with a cousin when a snowstorm dumped so much snow they were unable to return home. A love affair broke out between Yeya and the cousin. Eventually they married and had four sons.

We were called again the next year. Would we take Claudio who was from Chile? It was not working out with the family he was living with. So Claudio came in 1978. Claudio spoke very little English and was shy about using what he knew so we used a lot of sign language and other means to communicate. Claudio was a joy to have in our home, but when he returned to Chile we never heard from him.

Tony came next in 1979. Tony was from Cuatzalcoalcos, Mexico, in the state of Veracruz. We loved Tony. He became like a son.

During the winter of 1979 a major snowstorm hit northern Illinois. Roofs were collapsing from the weight of the snow. It was difficult to get around and the shelves of stores were becoming empty. Tony heard all of this on the news. Think about this: he had never seen snow, and now it was piling up in feet.

"Dad, I'll shovel the snow off the roof."

"No, Tony, our roof is sloped and will not collapse."

"Mom, I'll go to the store to get food."

"No, Tony, we have plenty of food."

He would sit in his bedroom looking out the window at what was happening and I know he worried.

After Tony went home, he called and said that he really missed TV dinners. We had those on occasion. Apparently they were not available in Mexico. Tony kept in touch with us and we with him. We visited him, his wife Nora and their daughter, Constanza, for Tony's 40th birthday in AUGUST, the wrong time to go to Cuatzalcualcos. It was HOT and HUMID. We thought we would die.

The family treated us wonderfully and provided many experiences, including attending a wedding of family? Or friend? Of course, Tony said weddings always start late so we shouldn't go at the stated time. When we finally got to church it was locked.

We had missed the wedding. On to the reception, however, Tony wasn't sure exactly where the reception was to take place. After a few phone calls getting directions we arrived. The reception lasted all night until after breakfast the next morning. We didn't last that long; someone drove us home.

LEARNING TO FISH

Other than the unhappy experiences fishing in New Jersey, I had never fished again. However, in 1976 several men from the Harvey church were going to go to Canada to fish and they needed one more guy to go with them. I became the designated one.

This was to be lake fishing from a small boat. As one who never learned to swim I had anxiety about it, but agreed to go. All the way there one of the men talked about how he could already feel the fish pulling on his line. He was so excited to be going, but his patter became somewhat irritating.

The men were taking turns driving, but for some reason my turn never came. Possibly the reputation ascribed to many clergy of having a heavy foot?

We took a boat from the dock to an island where our cabin was located and hired a guide the first day. I will admit that the first time I caught a fish I was 'hooked' as they say. I called home and raved about the experience. "We need to go fishing as a family, maybe later this summer."

The week passed fairly quickly, but as when any six guys are thrown together, certain feelings would get rubbed the wrong way. But all in all it was fun.

On the way home we stopped at a restaurant for dinner. Without paying any attention to what anyone was ordering, when the food was delivered to the table, we discovered that all of us had ordered liver and onions. The waitress said she had never had that happen before.

While in Canada something was happening in Harvey that I was not made aware of until I got home. Randy was in the hospital. June had been taking him to the high school for a basketball camp and one day as Randy was crossing the street another car swung past our car and struck Randy. He suffered a break in the lower leg where the growth line is located. At least he was not dead. The doctor told us that more surgery would probably be necessary as he grew. He recovered and fortunately never had to have any follow up surgery.

FISHING ON LEECH LAKE

Despite that incident we made plans to go to Minnesota to fish on Leech Lake, a huge lake in north central Minnesota. Randy was in a cast from his ankle to his thigh. Spiros was with us. June's Mother went along to care for Jackie while we were fishing.

We hired a guide that first day. From then on I ran the boat. I was not experienced at running a boat, but I did the best I could and we did catch some fish. I looked to see where other fishermen were working the lake and would go there, thinking that might be a good spot.

One day I got brave enough, or stupid enough, to take the boat across the lake to a little cove where there was a restaurant reachable only from the water. We had lunch and started for home. I noticed the boat was rocking a little at the dock. But when we got into the lake the water was not rocking, there were waves, large waves, created by strong winds coming from the north. There were no other boats to be seen.

Our boat would go up in the front then down and the motor would come out of the water. Thump, thump, the boat sounded as it hit the water. I fixed my attention on a point that I thought was near the entrance to Agency Bay where we were staying. I kept to that course.

There we were, Randy with a cast, Spiros our exchange student, June and myself. If we capsized we would all drown and what would people say? Actually I don't think I was thinking that at all. I was glued to that point across the lake. Miraculously, none of us drowned. We got into Agency Bay where we were staying and there we found the water was as smooth as glass. Fortunately, Grandma had no idea what was happening to us, or she would have been terribly worried.

The years in Harvey were wonderful. My children went through elementary school there. Randy was the only white boy on the junior high basketball team and Jackie was the only white girl on the junior high pom-pom squad.

Randy graduated from Thornton High School doing well with his studies and having had a great career in music and theatre, including portraying Elvis Presley in that wonderful white Elvis Presley costume with fringes, a costume that June made for him. It was a performance met with thunderous applause.

Randy decided to try out for the freshman football team at Thornton High School, however, he developed pneumonia and never returned to practice.

He told us that he wanted to study law because he wanted to become the mayor of Chicago, then president of the United States. He went to Illinois Wesleyan University for his undergraduate studies, then to Washington University in St. Louis to study law. So far he hasn't become mayor nor president of the USA but he has excelled in his profession as a lawyer. He did actually become a president, president of the franchise Boston Market.

As I mentioned, Jackie was the only white girl on the pom pom squad in middle school. One day she had not come home from practice. June went to the school to see if she was still there. There were kids playing in the field next to the school. June said, "Do you know if Jackie is still there?" "Is she the one with curly hair?" We have thought that response interesting instead of asking if she was the white girl.

In addition to excelling in both Junior and Senior High in her studies, she played the flute in the high school band, then became a drum major and was a member of one of the girls' music groups while we were still living. She graduated 20th in her class of 400 at Glenbrook South High School in Glenview, Illinois where she finished her high school education.

Jackie graduated from the University of Illinois in Champaign-Urbana with a degree in actuarial science and has had a great career in her profession, working with companies to build their benefit programs.

IT'S JUST LIKE THE ROOKIES!

We encountered police on several occasions while living in Harvey. The second floor of the education wing of the church was being rented to Thornton Community College for extension classes. One night the phone rang around midnight. We had had this happen before. Since it was Saturday and I needed my rest so I could be fresh for Sunday morning, I asked June if she would go over and meet the cops as they walked through the building. Dressed in her nightgown and robe and with large curlers in her hair she went into the church.

She didn't see any police at first and started to check around. When she went into the storage room where our life-size Nativity figures were stored she found a cop who, upon hearing her, turned and pointed his gun at her and shouted for her to stop. He was shaking because he was already on edge because when he had entered that room he thought the Nativity figures were real people. Then here was June in her curlers.

After the church was thoroughly searched and an inventory made of what had been stolen, June heard one of the young cops shout, "This is just like *The Rookies* on TV," a program that was popular at that time. Right, only this was real!

One day I was driving from a hospital on one side of the city to a hospital on the other side. I was speeding, yes speeding down 155th Boulevard right past our house. I didn't get any farther than that. A police car with sirens blaring pulled me over.

"Do you know how fast you were driving?"

I lost it! "You pull me over when I am making visits on my parishioners in the hospitals, but on Saturday nights when I need my sleep so I can lead worship on Sunday, cars race up and down the street making so much noise that I cannot sleep."

I couldn't believe I had done that. I could have been arrested and charged with verbal assault on an officer, but instead the officer said, "Pastor, be calm. Go on to the hospital, but watch your speed." Whew, I dodged the bullet.

Another time I was going to a different hospital and was stopped for speeding. The cop asked where I was going. I said, "I'm on my way to

Sherman Hospital where one of my parishioners is dying." (Only partly true, because no one was dying, but he was really ill.) He let me go. Where have I learned to lie like that?

There was another time I was coming home from the hospital, stopped at a stoplight, and when the light turned green I started forward, however the car ahead of me had not started moving yet AND there was a police car right behind me. That time I got a ticket and paid for the damage to the other car.

LIVING THE SECRET GAY LIFE

While living in Harvey I learned of a place in Hammond, Indiana, where gay men hung out for sex. I don't know how I found this place, perhaps an ad in the Want Ad section of the newspaper. One day I went there to see what it was. Over the next few years I had occasional experiences there when my gay sexual desires became intense. Nearly always I left there feeling shame and hating myself, nevertheless returning another day.

One day a guy I had just met gave me his phone number that I put in my wallet. June had looked in my wallet and found the number. Because she must have thought I was having an affair with a woman, she called the number and when a man answered she hung up. She asked me about that number and I just said it was someone I knew but I was not continuing our friendship, something like that. She never asked again. Did she know?

FUNERALS

Funerals are part of a pastor's job description. In a sermon I named "Near to the Heart of God" (Crystal Lake, March 10, 1996), I began with this bit of humor:

The pastor was calling on parishioners who lived in the country. He was sitting in the parlor with his hostess when her small son and his friend came dashing in carrying a dead rat. Excitedly the boy said to his mother, "Don't worry, Mother, he's dead. We hit him and bashed him and stomped him until, then he noticed the minister for the first time, and added in a lowered voice, until God called him home."

Funerals provided another learning experience. We were on vacation when I got word that Bob Harris, the first black man to unite with the church in Harvey, had died. We were not to be home for about a week, but the family decided they would wait for the funeral until I got home and was in charge.

Another was for the husband of one of our black members, a far more black family than the Harris family. Let me explain. At the funeral service, the widow was led out of the service several times, overcome, as I am sure she was. But I learned that it was expected that a spouse would publicly show grief that way.

At the cemetery when I began the words, "We commit his body to the grave," the funeral director reached in and released the lock on the bands holding the casket and it started to lower, which caused his wife to become hysterical. I was quite startled because I did not know that would happen.

One of the most embarrassing experiences of my life took place on a day when I had three funerals. None of these families was known to me, but I had counseled with each one. At the third funeral, I accidentally began using the name of one of the deceased persons from an earlier funeral. I caught myself, but the damage was done.

Then there was a funeral for a woman who had no family or friends. Her next-door neighbors came to arrange for the funeral. They said she was a nasty woman. Although they too did not like the woman, they had done some small things to help her out at times, so they were the only ones to handle the funeral. They made it very clear that they had not liked her. That couple were the only ones at the service. What do you say at such a funeral? Just some platitudes, and maybe that she was loved by God, which was true.

COMMUNITY INVOLVEMENT

My community involvement in Harvey was significant. I was elected to be a member of the Elementary School District Board and did what every pastor should do on Easter Eve, sit in the school board offices waiting for the election returns. In addition I was appointed to serve on the Harvey library board, and was president of the Harvey Area Community Organization. Our work focused mainly on realtors who were redlining parts of Harvey, only showing certain neighborhoods to blacks where they could make huge profits. I'm not sure our efforts which included picketing some realtor offices made any difference in their practice but we were making a stand against these racial practices.

MOTHER'S DEATH

On March 8, 1980 I received a call from Kathleen in Florida. She told me that Mother was fading. She had suffered from congestive heart failure for a number of years. I got to Florida as quickly as I could and went directly to the hospital to her room. She was still quite lucid. We talked. It was obvious that she was having difficulty breathing. She wanted to sit on the side of the bed and I helped her do that. Then she asked if I would rub her back because it was so sore which I did. Sometime after midnight I decided to leave and get some rest at Kathleen's. During the night or early morning mother died. I regretted that I had not stayed with her until her final breath. Mary Jane did not arrive until later that day so did not have an opportunity to spend any time at all with mother before the end.

There was a song that kept going through my head as I headed to Pennsylvania where mother's body would be laid to rest. The song was: "Sometimes I feel like a motherless child, a long way from home."There would be no more letters telling me she wished I lived closer, no more phone calls, no more time to spend together. I grieved because now there were no parents left.

In Harvey my lasting legacy is found on a plaque where my name is inscribed outside the Gwendolyn Brooks Junior high school (she was the poet laureate of Illinois at that time), built during my time on the board. But like so many names that appear on such plaques no one will ever notice and if they do no one will know to whom that name refers.

After ten years I felt it was time to move on. The Harvey church had become a multiracial congregation with blacks in significant leadership roles, a strong community presence, solid financial undergirding and a growing membership.

A young black couple I had married gave me a parting gift of a cassette tape they had made for me. With it was a note that said, "Never forget where you have come from." I believe they were saying that I should remember my years in a racially diverse community and I never have forgotten. I loved the people there. Harvey was my first Camelot experience.

HEADING NORTH
Glenview United Methodist Church
1981-1989

The opportunity to move came with an invitation to become the senior pastor of the Glenview United Methodist Church, a fairly wealthy northern suburb of Chicago. I accepted and as I did so the district superintendent said, "Do you think you can handle it?"

What? I should have asked, "Do *YOU* think I can handle it and if not, why are you asking me to go?"

Although I have no proof I believe that several others had been offered this position and turned it down. The reason some may have been hesitant to accept that appointment was because the departing pastor was very popular and the transition could be difficult. But being who I am, I said sure I would meet with their personnel committee.

The meeting with the committee proved to be the most bizarre interview I ever had. I was asked to bring tapes of some of my sermons, which I did. I sat there with the committee while they played parts of several of my sermons. I looked at faces that showed no emotion whatsoever. It was very uncomfortable.

Then I was asked to leave the room while the committee discussed my possible appointment to their church. I waited a long time, but when they called me back in, they said they had approved me to be their pastor.

Fears must have arisen among some in the congregation when they heard I was to be the pastor. The church had a reputation for producing a major musical event every January/February. Musicals like *Damn Yankees, Music Man, Our Town* and others with full orchestra were performed four times to sellout crowds. For some reason, the fear by those involved in the theatre productions must have been that they believed I would put a stop to the productions.

I had no intention of doing so, but unlike my predecessor, I did not believe the church classes and ministries should go into hibernation during the theatre season. Directors could not stomach anything happening in the church during theatre time. That time was sacred. They feared I would violate that!

Moving from the lower middle class community of Harvey to the much more affluent city of Glenview affected me such, that with all the grand homes and manicured lawns, as I drove around the city I sometimes felt a little nauseous, as though I had eaten too much ice cream.

The move was especially difficult for Jackie. She cried because she was leaving her friends and her activities at school as well as teachers. Shortly after moving she asked if one of her friends could visit one day. I brought her friend to Glenview, a black girl, to a lily-white city. I wondered what people would think of a black girl at the parsonage, but truthfully I didn't care.

There were two seminary professors who were part of the congregation, the professor of pastoral counseling who had taught my course of study, and the professor of preaching. It was a bit intimidating, however, the preaching professor came to see me soon after I arrived and told me that he came to the church to worship, not to judge sermons. He proved to be very supportive of my ministry.

The pastoral care professor became terminally ill and died while I was there, so I provided pastoral care and conducted his funeral, and I know he and his wife appreciated the support I provided during those difficult days.

THE WALK TO EMMAUS

All seemed to be going fine. But during the middle of my time in Glenview I became acquainted with and involved in a movement that was active in many churches called Cursillo. In the United Methodist Church it is known as the Walk to Emmaus, a 72-hour immersion in the faith.

My participation in the Walk was life changing.

On Saturday night, we were to walk two by two to the chapel for a time of meditation and reflection on what we had experienced throughout the weekend. Everyone seemed to have someone they knew to walk with to the chapel. I didn't have such a person.

One of the leaders for the weekend was a particularly attractive man. I had a hard time keeping my eyes from focusing on him. Then just as we started to walk to the chapel that man, the attractive man, stepped in to walk with me. I was in seventh heaven. We sat together in the darkened chapel, heard a few instructions, and sat in silence meditating on what the weekend had meant to us.

Some of the men and their companions moved to the communion rail and knelt for prayer. Finally, the man next to me asked if I wanted to go forward to pray.

We knelt and he put his arm around my shoulders. I felt something wonderful come over me. I don't know if it was having been chosen by this man, or having him put his arm around my shoulders so I felt close to him, or an experience of God's overwhelming love for ME, or perhaps a feeling of acceptance even though I knew I was gay and that was all right.. Maybe it was a combination of all of these.

He prayed for me, that I would feel God's love for me. Then we returned to our pew. There was a joy in my soul that I had never felt before. I felt lightness that carried over to the next morning.

I was literally floating when I left the Catholic Retreat Center for home on Sunday evening. We did not have an Emmaus Community in the Northern Illinois Conference so I publicly committed myself to initiating such when I got home.

The next few years were amazing. Many members of that congregation attended Walks. I was the lead clergy member on about a dozen of the first Emmaus teams in Northern Illinois. Here was a ministry that I could really go with, and I did so with gusto.

But that became a problem with some of the parishioners who felt that those who were Emmaus grads were forming a cult. It is true that there was a special bond among those of us who had had that experience. Some folks who had not attended a Walk felt left out and resented it.

DOCTOR MILLER

As I neared the end of my years in Harvey, I decided to begin the three-year course of study for a Doctor of Ministry degree. The Doctor of Ministry is not so much an academic degree as it is a professional degree designed to help a person improve one's ministry. I chose to do so at McCormick Theological Seminary, located at the University of Chicago in the Hyde Park neighborhood.

I chose the pastoral ministry course of study. Instead of it taking three years, I was in the program for about five years because of my move from Harvey to Glenview and the necessity of delaying some of the courses of study.

In 1985 I marched down the aisle at Rockefeller Chapel on the campus of the University of Chicago to receive my hood signifying that I had completed the studies for the Doctor of Ministry and to receive my diploma.

I never referred to myself as Dr. Miller nor did I invite other people to do so. I never listed myself in the worship bulletins as Dr. Miller. I was still just plain Ray and I wanted to be that way.

INTRUDER IN THE HOUSE

One morning when we were living in Glenview, we woke up, went downstairs and discovered there was an intruder in our house. There were little footprints all over the furniture including the white sofa but there was nothing to be seen. We knew it was a critter, so we closed the upstairs bedrooms and the bathroom and sealed off as much of the downstairs as we could. We were sure we were going to be able to find that creature, whatever it was.

Whenever we would leave the house and come home we saw more footprints. However, we never saw anything other than footprints. This was such a mysterious event for us that it even made its way into one of my sermons.

We tried setting traps thinking that it must be in the chimney somewhere, but the traps didn't work. We called animal welfare and they brought us a trap and said that we should put a piece of plywood in front of the opening of the fireplace, after putting some bait in the trap, then whatever it was would go in and be trapped.

Of course that was a very sensible thing to do and it worked. As we should have realized it was a squirrel that had been sitting on the chimney and had fallen down into our living room. Anytime it heard us coming into the living room it went into the chimney and rested on the flue, hence we could not see it.

With the mystery solved we went on with our daily lives after getting the sofa cleaned, as well as footprints that were in many places. It was a rather fun interlude in our lives.

JUST GO IN AND
HAVE A HOT TODDY

It was winter and we decided to take a vacation at Lake Tahoe, Nevada. We flew to Reno, rented a car and drove over Mount Rose. On the east side of the mountain there was no sign of any precipitation whatsoever, but as we crested the mountain we saw that there had been a recent snowstorm. Ice had coated the trees and each needle was glistening. It was truly magical.

If you are in Tahoe in the winter, what do you do? Take ski lessons. We decided to take ski lessons. The lessons were conducted in the morning. The group then went up the lift to practice what had been learned. The instructor said to me, "I think you should stay and practice on the beginner's slope." To June he said, "Why don't you go into the lodge and have a hot toddy." Which she happily did.

Later when the group was taking the lift again for their second run I decided to go with them and ski down with them. It was a major mistake. First, I fell getting off the lift. Then I fell over and over again as I tried to make my way down the slope. The instructor was very worried that I would hurt myself. But eventually I got to the bottom and that was the end of skiing for that day and for many months to come.

In the 1990's I was appointed to the Crystal Lake United Methodist Church. The youth pastor at our church was an excellent skier. He was part of the ski patrol at a small ski area in southern Wisconsin called Wilmot. I told him I would like to learn to ski and he invited me to come to Wilmot where he would help me learn. This was in March, which of course was the end of ski season, and the slopes were icy.

I was having a good time, falling many times, nevertheless getting to the bottom and going up to ski some more. I was having so much fun. On one of my runs downhill I fell forward. I wasn't hurt but I realize that the middle finger on my right hand would bend at the second knuckle and then would only be restored to its proper place I pushing it. Didn't hurt but when I got home I went to see an orthopedic doctor who told me I had torn a very sensitive ligament in my middle finger. The healing took several weeks of physical therapy, squeezing rubber balls, massage and Electrotherapy. Ultimately it healed.

I encouraged the Glenview congregation to hold a fund-raising dinner and auction. June and I offered a gourmet dinner for eight. It went for $120. The evening of the dinner June had made a beautiful dinner, truly gourmet. One of the dishes was a spinach souffleé. It was in the oven when I saw the oven door open slowly and fall down The hinges had broken and the door would not stay closed.

What to do? Duct tape. I taped the door to each side of the stove. Good idea! Except as the tape warmed from the oven the adhesive began to soften and the door came open again.

At this point June and I began laughing, a full belly laugh. We tried to be as quiet as possible, but it was just funny. The only solution was for me to hold the oven door closed until the soufflé was done. After that the meal proceeded well. Of course we had to tell our guests what had happened. That was the entertainment for that evening.

WHITEWATER RAFTING

One summer we were driving to Asheville, North Carolina for a small reunion with my two sisters and their husbands. As we drove through West Virginia we spotted rafters on the New River, a river Lady Bird Johnson had rafted. We stopped to watch them. It looked like so much fun. We decided we would like to try it ourselves. So the next morning, before we continued our journey to Asheville, we found a place where we could access the water and did our first rafting trip. The rapids were very easy and we had a wonderful time.

During our stay in North Carolina we talked about this experience with Kathleen and Jerry. They said they would be willing to go with us on another rafting trip. We found a place where we could raft on the French Broad River. Again it was exhilarating and we had a great time. That's how rafting got into our bones.

Subsequently we rafted on the Salt River in Arizona, the Poudre River west of Fort Collins, Colorado and the Arkansas out of Buena Vista, Colorado. Ross (you'll hear about him later) and I also rafted through the Royal Gorge, which was listed as having number six rapids, the most difficult and dangerous. However, in July when we were on the water, the river was lower with the summer runoff having ended weeks before. We found there were no rapids more dangerous than what we had done before. Besides the thrill of rafting, the scenery through canyons and along the rivers was absolutely stunning.

SURPRISE

Not only were surprise birthday parties held by members of the Birthday Group, but June and I surprised each other on some of our birthdays.

I turned fifty in 1985. I wondered if there would be any special party arranged for me for this milestone. Nothing had been said. The afternoon of March third, Randy asked me if I wanted to play handball and of course I said, "Yes." So off we went.

When we returned, the entire lower level had been decorated, dozens of people were there and the celebration began.

On another occasion June had led me to believe that she and a couple of friends were going to take me to a very exclusive French restaurant that required reservations months in advance. She told me that I needed to have a lot of money and on the appointed day that I should wear my three-piece suit. I was really concerned about the cost, but did as she said.

On the way, Barbara asked June if she had made the reservation. June said, "No." She thought Barbara was going to make it. Nevertheless we drove to the restaurant and Tom went in. "No," they had no room.

We tried another restaurant in another part of town. They had no room. This went on another time or two. Finally they said we would have to go to McDonalds. We went in and there we found dozens of people, mostly from the church, in a section that had been decorated with balloons and streamers and all shouted,

"Happy Birthday." It was so much fun, but I had to pay for my own burger!

June's birthday was coming. December 30 was her day. Two other couples and I planned this surprise. Early on the morning of her birthday, I slipped out of bed, dressed, and unlocked the front door then went back to bed.

Around 7:00 AM the two couples came into the house, up to the bedroom, turned on the lights and shouted "Happy Birthday!" Then they whisked her off to one of their houses where we had a wonderful breakfast. They had originally said they wanted to take June to a restaurant for breakfast, but I could not agree to that for I knew that June would feel humiliated to be in public in her nightgown and without makeup or having arranged her hair. But it was a great and memorable birthday.

For another of June's birthdays I made a reservation at a 5-star hotel in downtown Chicago. Tom Wibbels, the music director, gave us a vintage bottle of red wine to take with us. On arrival at the hotel, when our bags were delivered to the room, we discovered the bottle of wine had broken and stained our clothes. The hotel offered to wash our clothes, but we weren't sure they would be back before we were scheduled to go to one of the best steak houses in the country.

So we took a short walk in bitter cold temperatures to Marshall Field's in Water Tower Place to get some clothes, just in case. Our clothes did get back before we left for the evening so we could wear our own duds. The next day necessitated another rip to Field's to return what we had bought.

I had planned to take June on a carriage ride around the city. Despite the cold, we did it, with horse blankets drawn around us to keep us as warm as possible.

SPIRITUAL GIFTS

The Walk to Emmaus peaked my interest in the spiritual gifts Paul talks about in first Corinthians 12:8-10: wisdom, knowledge, faith, miracles, prophecy, speaking in tongues, and the interpretation of tongues.

I invited someone skilled in helping people discover their spiritual gifts, gifts bestowed by the Holy Spirit, to come to the church and lead us in a process to discover our own gifts.

Much to my surprise my highest spiritual gift was teaching. It surprised me because I had always thought I was a failure whenever I taught a class. But if this was my best gift, I decided to work at honing that gift and thus had many years leading people in the discovery of faith experiences. My other gifts that were identified were preaching and giving, neither of which surprised me.

As a result one of the most wonderful experiences in my ministry in Glenview was being trained in and teaching the Bethel Bible Studies. Another member of the church and I traveled to Wisconsin for the two-week training. It was intense. The leaders of this training were all Lutheran pastors of Scandinavian descent. Hence we heard a lot of Scandinavian stories and humor.

They told us that Norwegians are not known for expressing their feelings very freely. For instance, one of the leaders told about a Norwegian farmer, who loved his wife and appreciated her so much that one day he almost told her so.

Subsequent to the training we then recruited seventeen persons to be part of the first study, a year-long study of the Old Testament. A one-hour lecture was part of the program. The classes lasted two and a half hours every week. There was homework and some memorization. The Old Testament came alive as never before.

The seventeen who started stayed to the end of that study, although several at times some thought they would drop out. It was too difficult, they said. But other members of the class encouraged them to stay.

There were weeks when prior to the class I would feel so tired that I didn't know how I could carry out my responsibilities with the class, but the moment I stepped into the classroom I felt a spirit fill me with energy and enthusiasm that was truly marvelous.

THE SINGING WAITERS

June and I went, with two couples with whom we had developed a great friendship, to a German restaurant in Chicago where they had singing waiters. As we ate dinner the three of us men began talking about how it was possible that the Chicago Cubs would clinch the division title with a win the next night in Pittsburgh.

It was 1985 and it had been years since the Cubs had been in the position to win anything like a pennant. The conversation evolved to the point where the three of us decided that we were going to drive to Pittsburgh the next morning, attend the game, then turn around and drive back home. And that's what we did. I went for the fun of it, because I was not and never have been a fan of the Chicago Cubs.

I was a pastor, another was principal of a school, and the third was an official in his company. We did not want our places of employment to know where we were on that particular day. We debated during the drive how we were going to let our spouses know that we had arrived safely without revealing who we were. Remember, these were the days before cell phones. We were like college boys as we came up with a plan.

The idea struck one of us that we would try to get a message to Harry Caray, the announcer for the Cubs, that would say, "The singing waiters arrived in Pittsburgh safely and want their wives to know." He actually made the announcement on the radio and then said, "I have no idea what this means, but perhaps the wives know."

DISCOVERING THE JOY OF JOGGING

To maintain my health I began running. Jogging is probably a truer term. On my lunch hour I frequently drove the couple miles east from the Glenview Church to a park where there was a running/biking trail. I was never fast, but would sometimes manage to clock seven miles on the run.

As a result I entered a couple of organized runs. One was in St. Louis where Randy was in law school. There were races all over the country to raise funds to refurbish the Statue of Liberty. I decided to enter the one in Forrest Park. Randy ran too, but did not register. He was there to keep me going. It was a 5K race and I crossed the finish line, not the first, but who cares. It just felt so good to finish.

Another 5K took place in Glenview on a Sunday morning. It happened to be a Sunday when the choir was singing a cantata, thus I didn't have to deliver a sermon. I calculated that I could participate in the race and still be back, changed and ready for the worship service that morning. Again it was 5K and I completed the run, and made it to church on time.

Later on when living in Crystal Lake, I entered another run beginning and ending at McHenry County College. This involved some hilly portions. Medals were given for each age level. I was in the old-men's category. I received the third place medal, but there were only four in my age category. But a medal is a medal.

SALLY AND HER NUMBERS GAME

June was always my protector, cautioning me about times spent counseling with women. I had come to learn that there were those who sometimes saw their pastor as their savior from unhappy circumstances in their lives, sometimes seeing the pastor as a father figure. June would remind me that being alone with a woman could put me in a compromising situation that could make my life difficult.

One such woman entered my life in the 1980's. I will refer to her as S. She needed to talk to me. We made an appointment and I asked my secretary, as I always did, to be aware that my office door was never completely closed and to walk past the office on occasion to witness that nothing untoward was going on.

She came to my office and showed me a paper that was covered with numbers and said, "See?"

I replied, "What do you see S?"

"Well, don't you see?"

"I see a page full of numbers, but that's all that I see. What do you see?" We talked some and the time was up.

She came several times, sometimes to talk about the problems with her husband, whom I knew as a stable man and concerned about his wife.

Finally, I realized that something needed to be done. Here was an intelligent woman who was a professional counselor and teacher who clearly was in need of far more than pastoral counseling.

In consultation with her husband, we arranged an intervention in their home. There were several of us present, some family members and a couple staff persons. She would only talk to me.

I opened with, "S, we believe that you need to go to the hospital for a little while to get some help so you can get on with your life. Are you willing to go?"

"No! There's nothing wrong with me!" We talked more and because she seemed to trust me, I was finally able to convince her to go. She gathered a few items to take with her and we left.

"I will not ride in the car with him," indicating her husband. At last she agreed for me to drive her there. I only did so with the agreement that her husband would follow immediately behind me in his car. Thus we made our way to the hospital where she was admitted.

She was there a while and I visited on occasion. Eventually she was discharged and seemed to be living a good life once again. She said she was grateful.

Several years later while I was the pastor in Crystal Lake I received a letter from her in which she castigated me for having ruined her life and her career by placing her in the psychiatric ward at the hospital. She made some threats about suits.

I consulted with an attorney in the church and he advised me to do nothing. "See if you hear from her again. Don't respond." I followed his advice and never heard from the 'numbers lady' again.

LIGHTS OUT! MANILA

June and I signed up for a mission trip to the Philippines to be led by one of our Filipino pastors. For one week we worked at a Methodist Student Center in the city of Echagua in the northeastern part of Luzon. We had a wonderful time. Besides our work sprucing up the Center, we visited rural villages where we planted trees, took plastic chairs to some of the churches in the area, visited the magnificent rice paddies that cascaded down the mountain sides, and rode a water buffalo to the delight of natives.

Then we were to go to the home of one of the district superintendents to do some work on his house. We returned to Manila where we could take a ferry across to the island where the DS lived. While in Manila, we walked to the huge shopping mall with stores mostly like we had at home. While there something happened to the electrical grid in that part of the city and the lights even in the mall went dark. I had already returned to our quarters, but June was there with several others of our group. They had to make their way back through the darkness of Manila.

ANOTHER MISTAKE

Once again, I made a huge mistake. I had discovered the power of the gifts of the spirit and embraced people who spoke in tongues, believed in spiritual healing, etc. One of my Emmaus friends, a member of the church, had a brother, an Episcopal priest, who was charismatic. We invited him to come for a weekend event at the church. During that time he spoke about and practiced the spiritual gifts. There were those who were appalled, especially with regards to speaking in tongues.

Thus began the demise of my ministry in Glenview. Despite strong worship attendance, financial support, a foundation of Biblical instruction, a group of about thirty families decided I must go.

They met secretly, began to be absent at worship, and started withholding their financial support. Secret meetings with the District Superintendent, my boss so to speak, were held. Some of these people, some who had been close friends who had even gone with us on a cruise to celebrate our 25th wedding anniversary, began writing letters to the bishop accusing me of having an affair (later you will see how ridiculous this charge was), being part of a cult, etc. It was very hurtful. The hurt I experienced lasted for years. I couldn't figure out why they had never spoken to me about how they were experiencing my ministry. The District Superintendent listened to these people and never talked with me one-on-one, nor did the bishop. But the die was cast.

I was asked to become District Superintendent of a district that was in the far northwest part of Illinois. Because June was a teacher in the Chicago Public Schools that was impossible. At last I was told I would be appointed to First United Methodist Church in Crystal Lake, about fifty miles northwest of Chicago.

Although I had often thought that was a church I would have liked to serve, it felt like a demotion: smaller Sunday School, lower worship attendance, smaller budget and I would have to take a cut in salary. This fueled my sense of being a failure, of not measuring up, of not being appreciated, which plagued me all my life.

But as it turned out this was a perfect fit for me and for that congregation.

CRYSTAL LAKE, MY SECOND CAMELOT
1989-1999

Things in Crystal Lake began with a crash, literally. We moved into the parsonage on Saturday, July 3. Most of our personal belongings, including our clothes, were in boxes in the garage. I needed to find a shirt and tie to wear on Sunday morning. I went into the garage and June followed. The door from the garage into the family room closed behind us. AND LOCKED. We did not have a house key with us. It was late at night and we didn't know what to do.

I knew there was a house key kept in the church office but how to get to it? I had no key with me to the church either.

The associate pastor lived nearby so I walked to his house and rang the bell and rang the bell and rang the bell! It was after 10 p.m. At last he came to the door in his underwear. He did have a church key but not one to my office. At least I could get inside the church.

I stood outside my office and pondered. There was a glass panel that ran along the side of the door. *Soooo…what to do?* I found something hard like a brick and broke the window that allowed me to reach through the window and around to the lock. I was in! Whew!

The next morning I tried to disguise the broken window as best I could and no one said anything.

Hopefully a person becomes wiser as one grows older. I like to think that that has happened for me. The pastor who was leaving the Crystal Lake church was beloved by many of the people, but others had complaints: he could not remember people's names, he did not show much emotion, was too intellectual some said. Others appreciated many of these same qualities.

Plus the pastor previous to the current outgoing one had literally died in front of the congregation, deteriorating physically week-by-week as he continued to lead worship and preach sermons, finally from a chair. He was much beloved by the people.

I decided that for my first sermon I needed to acknowledge the gifts of these prior pastors and express myself as appreciative of them and of the privilege of *following in their footsteps*. The sermon was warmly received.

To show their appreciation, a parade was arranged that went right down Dole Avenue past the church. Thousands came out for the parade. Of course it happened to be the fourth of July.

(A side bar.) Dole Avenue had originally had rail tracks that ran from the lake to the major train line into Chicago. This was because, in winter, ice was carved from the lake, crystal clear Crystal Lake and taken to Chicago to provide the ability to have a means for cooling foods during the summer months. Of course this was before refrigeration came into use.

My ten plus years in Crystal Lake were wonderful. The congregation grew. Worship attendance increased from an average of 270 to 675. The sanctuary was becoming too small and if we were to continue to grow more worship space was needed.

After a thorough study, a proposal was made to build a new sanctuary and remodel and expand other parts of the existing building. The cost would be something over three million dollars. A major decision needed to be made about spending that kind of money that would involve considerable debt.

At a meeting of the congregation it seemed that the proposal would be defeated until one man, a beloved member who had been originally opposed, stood and pointed out that the congregation of the church through the years had made major decisions about moving and building and that this was another such time. He said he supported the proposal. That carried the day with only about four opposing votes.

OVERSLEEPING AGAIN

One Sunday a baptism was to take place at the early service. I was officiating at the baptism. Around 8:45 my phone rang. I answered and someone on the other end of the line asked if I was all right and if I was coming to church. The service had already started. I had overslept! I hurriedly dressed and ran to the church, put on my robe and walked up the side aisle shortly before the baptism was scheduled. The first words out of my mouth sounded like I had just awoken, but not one person said anything. No one seemed to notice. I think they had gotten accustomed to having a pastor who was often doing the unexpected.

WORSHIP STYLES

When I arrived at Crystal Lake there were two worship services, one at 8:15 and the other at 10:30. In summer the early service was held outside in a lovely chapel area with trees, flowers, an altar, a public address system and everything needed for worship.

During the time I spent at the United Methodist Church in Crystal Lake, my understanding of worship in the contemporary world evolved as a result of attending conferences at large churches of various denominations. From the more formal worship of Glenview, I found myself in the more relaxed atmosphere of Crystal Lake, especially in the summer for the early service in the outdoors where attire was often a suit or sport coat rather than a clergy robe.

As the congregation grew and I learned more about how to structure worship in a larger church, we initiated a Saturday night service that was very informal with a music combo instead of organ. This service never became large but at times would number 60-80 in attendance.

One of the most exciting decisions we made was to create a worship team consisting of the head of our drama group, the musician, and the worship leaders. We had already been utilizing brief skits in worship, many humorous, that were helpful in the development of the message for that day. I provided the group with the sermon topics for three or four weeks in advance and they would go to work looking for music, looking for drama, looking for videos or any other medium that would be helpful.

When we met the next week we shared what we had come up with. Having the things they brought to the meeting helped me shape the sermon that I would preach on that Sunday. I believe this worked very well for the worship life in that church.

Finally, after we moved into the new worship space, we started a very contemporary service in addition to the two we already had on Sunday. The music was very contemporary, often loud, and the entire service was very informal.

So I tried to dress appropriately for each worship time: sweater or sport coat at 8:15, robe at 10:30, sweater or shirt at 11:45 and anything casual on Saturday night. I found myself changing attire on Sunday morning for each service according to what I felt was appropriate. As time went on the contemporary service on Sunday morning became the one that showed the most growth.

The lack of formality in some services caused some people to become unhappy and a few left for other churches. Then there was a couple that left because we had a woman associate pastor assigned. Another couple left because they thought one of my Independence Day sermons suggested the U.S. was not perfect, another became extremely distraught even to tears because we did not have printed bulletins with the order of worship for a couple of Sundays, and another because we began a very dramatic Easter service with the sanctuary looking as it did on Good Friday.

That Easter service took a lot of advanced planning. After the associate pastor and I had a dialogue similar to what we thought the disciples might have had on the first Easter morning when they were bewildered and discouraged, someone came hurrying in and made the announcement that Jesus was not in the tomb.

We ran out of the sanctuary as though going to the tomb to see for ourselves.

Then we shouted, "He is alive. He has risen." Immediately the organ began with "Christ the Lord is risen today," the choir processed with each choir member carrying an Easter lily to put in its proper place, while others brought the banners and still others the candles and lit them so that within a matter of minutes the sanctuary was transformed from Good Friday and it's somber decor to the joy of Easter. While the majority of people at worship that day found it to be an extremely moving Easter worship, there were those few who were ready to complain. Such is life.

A NEW MUSICIAN AND A BIG DECISION

We were looking for an organist and music director for the church. The pipe organ was a model not easy to play so candidates were scarce. There were three to be interviewed. Two of them had inadequate skills for the music program we wanted and needed. The third was a man, Tom Wibbels.

Tom was a skilled organist. He had experience as a theater organist as well as a church musician and had been director of a church music program. We decided to hire Tom.

He came to my office and I offered him the position. He said, "Pastor, there is something I need you to know before I accept the invitation. I do not want to create a problem for you."

"What is it, Tom?"

"I am gay. I've had a partner for eleven years. If that is a problem I completely understand."

I was somewhat shocked and responded, "Let me talk with the Staff Parish Committee and get back to you."

I called the chairman and we talked.

He said, "What do you think, Ray?"

I replied, "I think Tom has great talent and would grow our music program."

Rick decided, "Let's go with it, but we don't need to say anything about his being gay." (Well, why would we?)

BUT, that summer we needed a new youth director. Once again there were slim pickings. One young man, a recent graduate of Moody Bible Institute, a fundamentalist college, seemed the best candidate and we offered him the job. Things didn't go well with the youth program, and when he found out we had a gay music director he was over the top.

"How can you have a gay staff person?" He began to broadcast this among the congregation. He was trying to create division and we decided he had to go after about a month. But the poison had been spread.

Having wised-up after the experience in Glenview and all the secrecy that went on, I decided to deal with this head-on. I announced a meeting of the congregation to discuss this matter. A number of people came and we talked about the situation. Tom had told me that his relationship with his partner was platonic. I don't know if this was true or not but I wasn't interested in finding out what went on in their bedroom any more than in any other bedroom.

The result of the meeting was that nothing would change. Tom would stay and it seemed everyone was happy. The music program blossomed, and Tom introduced many special musical events. Perhaps the one that is most memorable was a concert with full orchestra and a large choir that he called 'Whispers of Hope that was also to help fund AIDS research.

He asked what I thought about having a friend of his perform who did an impersonation of Elton John. He would play and sing two or three numbers. I said, "Let's go for it." The sanctuary was packed with at least 500 people. The concert was high quality and 'Elton John' was a hit.

Tom was very cooperative with me and wanted to do what I wanted, but he also introduced new ideas, most of which were excellent and ones we implemented. The only issue was that

Tom wanted excellence and at times demanded more of the choir than some wanted to give. But people recognized the gift Tom brought to our worship and stayed with it.

It was Tom who asked me to bring the message at the World AIDS Day Memorial Service in 1996 and again in 1997. I met people at these events whose stories broke my heart.

THE YOUTH PASTOR

After the horrendous experience of hiring a young man who had just graduated from Moody Bible Institute, we set out once again in the search for a youth pastor. We had an inquiry from a young man in one of the Carolinas. After a phone interview by the search committee, we decided to bring him to Crystal Lake for a face-to-face meeting. I met him at the airport.

As soon as I saw him I knew he was the one, on two points. First, he had the looks of a person to whom youth could relate. Plus, he was good-looking, fit and caused my heart to jump. All the way back to Crystal Lake my sense that this was the one kept being confirmed.

The committee met with him and both he and the committee decided to think it over. He was married with one child and would need housing and health insurance and would need to be full time. It was going to cost a lot of money, but at last the decision was made to invite him to be the youth pastor.

I made the call and talked with him. After a short time he said that he could not come to Crystal Lake. I couldn't believe it. This was the right person, I was sure of it, but we hung up. I sat at my desk in tears.

Then I did something I can't believe I did. I called him back. That is never done, but I did it. He said, "I'm glad you called back because as soon as I hung up, my wife said, "We have made a big mistake." He was going to be the youth pastor. I was thrilled.

He proved to be the right choice, for the youth program blossomed under his leadership, but he did more than that. He became an important part of the growth of worship services, finally being in charge of the most contemporary service we had. He was gifted.

So every day I could see this handsome young man and think that that is exactly the kind of person I had always wanted to be and never was.

BUT THE WHEELS ARE SMALL

June and a friend had gone to a Women's Conference about 150 miles from home. June was driving a small Renault. On the way home she had taken a wrong turn and she realized she was going in the wrong direction.

To make up time she began driving fast. Her companion said, "June, don't you think you are going too fast? You are way over the speed limit."

June responded, "Oh, we aren't going as fast as the speedometer says because this car has small wheels,"

To which her friend replied, "Don't you think the manufacturer took that into consideration?" They slowed a bit and got home safely!

I had decided to deliver sermons on two hot topics of the day *(still hot topics in the 2020s), abortion and homosexuality.* There would be an opportunity for members to discuss these topics after worship. I told June my plan. She begged me not to have a sermon on homosexuality and I acquiesced. I've often wondered about her strong opposition to the sermon on homosexuality. Perhaps it had to do with fear of repercussions, or perhaps she had suspicions about me. I'll never know.

TAKING CARE OF MY BODY—AGAIN!

I have done more physical activity since turning 50 than ever before. I've mentioned running while in Glenview. Then, one day I went to the bike shop along the bike trail that ran through Crystal Lake, and rented inline skates. Complete with the pads and helmet I set out, shaky at first, but gradually getting the hang of it. It was wonderful. I have always wanted to be six feet tall and on skates I made it.

I skated as often as I could, finally skating from Crystal Lake to Elgin on the bike trail, approximately 15 or 16 miles each way. My glutes were tight and I was getting in good shape.

So I was running, skating, then I added serious biking. I read in the paper that a benefit ride was going to take place in July, 1998, a route covering 500 miles from Minneapolis to Chicago in six days. It was a benefit ride for companies working to find a cure for AIDS. I went to the information meeting and signed up, and I didn't even have a proper bike.

A friend loaned me his bike to use until I got one, and another friend, the youth pastor, began training me, showing me how to ride a road bike and the rules of biking etiquette. I was hooked, especially after I got my own Trek bike.

I trained and trained. I trained in rain, after snowfall, trying to increase the miles I rode. I knew there would be one or two 100-mile days on the benefit ride. I rode all over northern Illinois and southern Wisconsin. I finally rode one hundred miles in a day then another hundred miles the following day.

There was a time when I was riding on county roads in Wisconsin and became disoriented. I wasn't sure how to get home. There were no gas stations or stores along the road I was on. Finally, in desperation I stopped at a house and rang the bell. The young woman who came to the door must have thought she had a crazy person facing her. I said, "Can you tell me which direction to go to get to Illinois?"

Believe it or not she said she wasn't sure, but she pointed in a direction and suggested, "I think you need to go that way." She was right, thank goodness.

As a participant in the ride I was supposed to raise funds for the AIDS project and I did. I received commitments for over $18,000, the most of any of the 1,800 riders. I learned somewhere along the way that you should never hesitate to ask. People can always say 'No.' And some did, but I had support from doctors, friends, other pastors, church members, family and everyone I could think of to ask.

THE RIDE

On a July Sunday I flew to Minneapolis. June and our friend Sherry Walker drove there to cheer me on. My bike went with hundreds of others in a truck. Bikes, riders, friends and family assembled in the convention center for instructions.

Monday morning the ride began. Eighteen hundred riders exited the center. This was the scariest part of the ride for me. We were so bunched up that accidents were going to happen and did. Riders were pushed off to the side and down they went. Finally, we got into more open space and could ride with a greater sense of freedom.

Five hundred miles lay ahead. What the heck was I doing? But truthfully, I didn't have concern. I had trained hard. I had ridden a few thousand miles in preparation. My body was in good shape, my bike was like part of me, and riding in the fresh morning air felt marvelous.

The route was easy to follow. Support teams had marked the roads with arrows that clearly indicated how we were to go. I rode at a speed that was comfortable for me. I was neither the fastest nor the slowest, probably averaging 15 or 16 miles an hour.

There were rest stops along the way with snacks to provide renewal, cool cucumber slices to put on eyes to refresh, and on occasion brief massages. I spent little time at the rest stops because my goal was the day's destination.

Day one was fairly easy riding. I arrived at the overnight stop and checked my bike in at the bike corral. Next was to get gear from the baggage-carrying trucks, erect the tent and clean up. There were support trucks that offered showers, a mess hall tent and places for every possible need.

My roommate was Jeff Shoemaker, also from Crystal Lake. We did not ride together because I was faster and needed to maintain the pace that was comfortable for me. I liked to start as early as possible and arrive as early as I could so I could avail myself of the facilities before the majority of riders arrived.

Riders who were HIV positive or had AIDS had bikes with flags indicating who they were. I found myself feeling compassion for what these people would face in their lives, also admiration for their part in the ride.

Every evening there was some kind of entertainment, sometimes comedy with riders in drag. Those who were gay or lesbian couples sat together and walked together hand-in-hand. It was the first time I experienced so many gay and lesbian persons and their affection for one another.

I was riding with three persons on my mind, none of whom I had ever met. Two were young boys who had died of AIDS, infected through transfusions of blood. The other was the brother of a member of the church, who was HIV positive.

I became aware of the two boys when I was asked to bring the message at a World AIDS Day service in McHenry County. If I had heard of young people dying of AIDS, it had never registered as it did that night when they and a few others were remembered in the memorial part of the service. I met their parents and their two boys accompanied me in my heart as I rode. Someone had a T-shirt made for me with pictures of these three.

One of the hardest days was also the shortest, about 60 miles. Most of it was on what had been a railroad right-of-way. It was gravel and there was virtually no roll to the trail so pumping the pedals continuously was required and was very tiring. It was wonderful to get on pavement again. When we left the gravel we were in a small town in Wisconsin where people had apples, water and other goodies for us.

All along the way there were those who had water hoses running to cool us as we rode by, or food or bottles of water. The show of such great support by the locals was truly encouraging.

Next we had to face THE HILL. That's what they called it, requiring the most strenuous effort of the entire ride. I was determined to ride the up the hill all the way and not walk my bike as some were doing. I had practiced steep hill climbing especially in the Lake Geneva area in Wisconsin. I made it all the way up THE HILL although I had to stop once or twice to catch my breath, but always I got back on my bike and rode to the top. A personal victory!

On the fifth day we crossed the Wisconsin-Illinois border. There at the border were my wife, Sherry and the parents of the two boys for whom I was riding. They cheered as I rode by.

That night we camped near McHenry, a few miles north of Crystal Lake. I remember sitting with June when a couple from the church came up to us. Of course I was not wearing my hairpiece, something impossible when wearing a helmet. I had not been seen by anyone from the church without it. There was nothing to be done. They said nothing and neither did I.

The sixth and final day! I didn't know it was Gay Pride Day and there would be a parade. I may not have even known about Gay Pride. The destination: Grant Park in Chicago. I would be riding through Chicago. I was excited and nervous. It was a relatively short day and the plan was for small groups to be spaced out so we wouldn't completely shut down traffic.

What a day! At rest stops we were given instruction for the next portion of the ride. We crossed the city limits and rode into downtown Chicago. We had to be careful, to be aware of the possible danger of someone opening a car door as we were passing. People all along the route were cheering us on.

Crossing the Chicago River was the scariest part. The bridge is a metal grid. It felt like riding on ice. I was afraid I would crash. Fortunately there were no accidents.

Arriving in Grant Park was wonderful. Five hundred miles on my bike came to a close. There were shirts given out to commemorate our participation. Food was available. There was a closing ceremony and many of us, yes me included, lifted our bikes over our heads in jubilation!

Finally we were reunited with family and friends who had come to welcome us. Several of us went to a restaurant in Chicago for dinner. During that time the Gay Pride parade took place. I could only catch glimpses from where I was sitting, but wished I could have seen more.

On Sunday I spoke at the last service and made a blubbering fool of myself. I was so emotional and spoke far too long. How do you put into words in a few minutes everything you experience when participating in something like this?

But one of the men in the congregation stood and began applauding and then everyone was joining in. The Ride was over! My life would never be the same again.

HE THINKS YOU ARE GOD!

The church in Crystal Lake had more and more young families with children. I love children and loved having them in worship. I would tell the congregation when little ones made a bit of noise, "Those are sounds pleasing to God."

We had as many as 400 children and youth in Vacation Bible School, many from the community as well as the church.

One Sunday as people were leaving worship, a mother told me what her little boy, perhaps a three-year-old said. "He thinks you are God."

I replied politely, "Please correct that with him. Please!" I guess wearing a robe and being told he was in God's house communicated that message to him.

INVESTMENTS IN MEXICO

In 1994 construction was underway for the expansion of the church facility. In the middle of the year I learned that the associate pastor was to be appointed to a similar position at a nearby church. Apparently he was not happy in his relationship with me. At least that is how I read it. He was very popular with the congregation and had charge of the youth ministry, among other responsibilities.

I have come to the awareness while writing this book that being an associate pastor with me was not a happy situation for the associate. If he/she was popular I saw that as a threat to my role as senior pastor. I did not affirm their gifts and allow them the freedom to exercise those gifts that would have given them a greater sense of their worth as a pastor.

That was mentioned at my retirement celebration when the current associate with whom I had what I think was a good relationship said, "When I told my friends I was going to Crystal Lake as the associate, they said, 'With Ray Miller?' I guess I had a reputation I was not aware of.

With the departure of the associate in the middle of the year that left me as the lone pastor, with more responsibilities, picking up what he had been doing, as well as my own. Some lay people helped with the youth, but I was spending a lot of time with the committee overseeing the construction project and was now preaching every Sunday with no time off. I was becoming exhausted. I needed to get away for a few days. I talked with June and she said that would be a good plan during her Spring break.

It was April. I went to a travel agent and said, "Where can I go for a few days that is warm and cheap?"

She mentioned a couple of ideas, then said: "Here is an Apple vacation in Los Cabos, Baja Sur California."

"Where is that?" She showed me pictures. Desert! That is what I saw, but also some hotels that looked quite decent. "We'll go. Five days, four nights."

Getting there was a trial. We flew to Los Angeles and had a layover of a few hours. But we arrived at last. As we descended for landing at the airport in San Jose del Cabo, we looked down at the terrain and it looked uninhabitable: sand, a few scrubby trees, and mountains rising up sharply. Where are we going? The airport was very basic. There was one runway and few planes and the terminal was lacking in amenities. But we were there.

Before we could get out of the terminal we were bombarded with men shouting about free transportation, free this and free that, and a car for one day. The shouting was to get people to meetings where timeshare sales were presented. I was and still am a sucker for anything 'free.' OK? We signed up. We finally managed to get to our hotel in San Jose on the free bus we were promised.

The next day we were picked up at our hotel and transported to Cabo San Lucas to the Pueblo Bonito resort. June and I had vowed we were not going to buy anything. No way! We had a lovely salesperson. She gave us a great sales pitch. June kept asking questions that sounded like she was starting to become interested.

We were even taken on a tour of the city then to an upscale subdivision called Pedregal where a number of famous and wealthy people had luxury homes. We needed to buy dramamine for our fishing trip the next day, and our salesperson stopped at a pharmacy so we could get it.

Back to the resort and more talk. The end result was that we signed up for two Junior Suites, the smallest units available. That gave us one week each year for each unit. They arranged for a car for us and we returned to San Jose del Cabo. That night I did not sleep. I kept thinking, "How are we going to pay for this?" By morning I had it figured out.

We drove back to Pueblo Bonito the next day, and, as we stood there looking at the beautiful view of "Land's End," the rock that forms an arch with the Pacific Ocean on one side and the Gulf of Cortez on the other side, I thought, *There is no way we would ever be able to come here year after year if we had to pay the full price for a unit.* We had 26 years on the contract.

But that wasn't the end of it. A year or two later they began construction on another Pueblo Bonito resort next door to be called Pueblo Bonito Rosé. A tour of the resort that was under construction took place and we ended up buying a Presidential unit on the fifth floor with a fantastic view. We would have that luxurious unit for the third week of January every year.

Another year and another purchase, this time an Executive Suite at PB Rosé. In all we purchased five weeks of timeshare thinking that when we retired we would spend several weeks a year there, or trade for some other place in the world.

But that's not all. When I married Saundra Craft in 2005 after my wife's death, we went on another timeshare presentation at the newest Pueblo Bonito resort, Sunset Beach, on the Pacific. Saundra loved the location and together we bought a presidential unit there. So I was awash in timeshares.

Over the years, I have traded timeshare weeks for vacations in Puerto Vallarta, Mazatlan, Granby and Steamboat Springs,

Colorado before we moved there, Maine, Vermont, Italy, Huatulco, Mexico, and Switzerland, even for a week in Spain.

I have also donated weeks to charities for their auctions at fund-raising events, helping them raise much-needed funds for their work.

TRAVELS

I don't remember how I met up with a travel agency in the north suburbs of Chicago, but that encounter led to several journeys. It was approaching 1990 and I wanted to go to the renowned *Passion Play* in Oberammergau, Bavaria. I had heard about this event that was held every ten years to commemorate the survival of the people of Oberammergau from the plague that raged through Europe in 1347.

I worked with the travel agency and recruited about 42 persons to go on the trip. That meant June and I got to go free. In addition to the Play, we toured parts of Italy as far south as Rome and some parts of southern Germany as far west as the Black Forest.

One thing I learned about the passion play was that Adolf Hitler attended the play and approved of it because he saw anti-Semitism in the dialogue of the play. There was controversy over this and the second time we went in 2000.we noticed that the script had been changed to make Jesus' crucifixion as having been perpetrated by all humankind.

Oberammergau is located in the beautiful hills of Bavaria. The exterior of many homes are painted with scenes from fairy tales and nursery rhymes, so the town exudes a storybook feeling.

One frightening incident that occurred during that trip took place in Rome. The bus dropped us off at St Peter's. We were given a certain amount of time to explore on our own then we were to meet at the fountain in the center of St Peter's square. After that the group would cross the street to a shop and wait for the bus to return.

All was going smoothly. We boarded the bus and I checked to see that everyone was on board. OOPPSS! One person was missing, our good friend, Fairy Pearson. Fairy was an absolutely delightful woman, but she would become confused at times. We couldn't go without Fairy. I knew that Fairy did not know the name of the hotel where we were to stay so she would be stranded.

The bus driver said we had to go on. I declared, "No! We had to find Fairy." He agreed to circle around St Peter's and allow us a couple minutes to look for her. June and I got off the bus and began to look. What a relief! There she was wandering around the fountain in St Peter's Square, seemingly unconcerned. I rushed over to her and hurried her to the bus and we were off again. *Oh the trials and tribulations of a tour leader.*

Leaving Oberammergau we traveled through Bavaria to Munich. Along the way, as I marveled at the beautiful forests and tranquil countryside, I kept thinking about how these very woods were places where some of the horror of World War II took place. How is it that there can be so much evil in the world when there is so much that is peaceful and wonderful?

In Munich we went to the Hofbrauhaus and were entertained, drank beer and sang, "Ein, zwei, drei, vier, funf, lift your stein and drink your beer...." June and I shared a tankard. It was a good time, a good send off from Germany.

ISRAEL AND EGYPT

Next was a trip to Israel and Egypt. This time there were a few less participants, maybe thirty.

Visiting the traditional religious sites was a wonderful experience. Thinking about how Jesus had walked that ground on which we were now walking was very moving. We crossed the Sea of Galilee and read appropriate scripture, sat and rested where the Sermon on the Mount was possibly delivered, went to the Jordan where John the Baptist carried on his ministry and baptized Jesus.

But one of the experiences that left a mark on me came when several of us walked the route Jesus would have taken from the Mount of Olives to Jerusalem on the day we call Palm Sunday. Along the way we passed a cemetery with above ground tombs (it was too rocky for burial in the ground) on which people who visited those tombs had placed a little stone to mark the visit.

We passed the Garden of Gethsemane. It was fenced off, but we could see the olive trees that dated back, perhaps to the time of Jesus.

That led us to Jerusalem and we walked the Via Dolorosa, the route Jesus would have taken as he was led to the place where he would be nailed to a cross. The narrow passageway was lined on both sides with small shops. People filled the street, many tourists of course. Vendors were shouting out their wares. I thought that this is just the way it must have been when Jesus walked this way. And probably, unlike our usual portrayals, there would not have been many people paying attention. It was just another person being led off to be crucified by the Romans.

Because of tensions between the Arabs and Jews, there were places we could not go. June and I experienced this first hand. The principal of June's school in Chicago, a Jewess and her husband, were in Jerusalem for Passover, staying at the King David Hotel. They invited us to come to the hotel for dinner. We were staying on the Mount of Olives in the Arab section of Jerusalem.

We took a taxi and asked the driver if he would pick us up later that evening. He said that he would not and that we would not be able to find anyone who would drive us back to our hotel. That made me quite nervous. Panicking, of course.

Sure enough, when it was time to go, there was no taxi driver willing to risk driving us to the Mount of Olives. Finally the husband of the principal secured a cab, perhaps with a bribe. The route he took to get us to the hotel was nothing like the route we had taken before. The driver was constantly on the phone, probably getting directions for the safest way to travel.

We traveled south in Israel to the Dead Sea, to Masada where the ancient Israelites made a last stand against the Romans, to Eilat, a resort city at the very southern tip of Israel. There, looking east we saw Saudi Arabia and to the west, Egypt.

The next day we crossed into Egypt. That proved to be a lengthy process. We waited and waited to be allowed to enter Egypt. At last we walked across the border and boarded the Egyptian bus.

I noticed that we had an extra person on board. Our Egyptian guide would not share who this was, but I figured it out. He was a guard, there to ensure our safe passage across the Sinai Desert.

As we crossed the rocky desert we stopped for the night in a village at the foot of what tradition says is Mount Sinai. At 3 o'clock we were awakened to prepare to walk up the mountain where, according to the Bible, Moses met God. The goal was to be at the top for sunrise. We walked by torchlight. I thought these would be torches like I had seen in movies about Jesus' trial and crucifixion. However, the word torches used in the brochure was the British word for flashlights.

It was amazing. Groups from many countries were walking ahead and behind us, often singing hymns in their native languages.

Along the way we found there in the dark Bedouins offering to sell tea and offering camels to ride for the next leg of the ascent.

June had trouble making her way up the mountain. Finally she said, "I'll just sit here and wait until you come back." Reluctantly I left her and continued on. Not long after all of us who were making the hike had arrived at the top we saw June joining us as well. As a result all of us got there just as the sun was coming up in the east.

SCANDINAVIA

There were approximately 25 in the next venture to Denmark, Norway, and Sweden. We convinced the tour leader to deviate from the plan for Denmark and to take us to the Legoland Park. I can picture it still.

There were model trains that ran under the walkways among a variety of village buildings, all made of Legos. There were recreations of the U.S. Capitol, the Statue of Liberty, and Mount Rushmore, with signs indicating how many Legos were used in each structure, some in the millions. Amazing!

More than anything else on this journey I loved Norway. The Viking Museum, the Kon Tiki Museum, the Sculpture Garden with hundreds of sculptures created by the sculptor Vigeland, all portraying some part of the human experience from birth to death. Fantastic!

We then traveled through the mountains we experienced one of the architectural achievements of the Norwegians . It was a tunnel through a mountain. This is not the usual tunnel that runs in a relatively straight line. This tunnel started at the top of the mountain and wound its way inside the mountain to the valley below.

Our journey took us to a site where, during World War II, Germans had constructed what is called The Baby Barn. Hitler was enamored with the blond haired Norwegians. To create his perfect white, blond haired race young blond women were taken to this building where they were impregnated by German soldiers in order to produce the perfect race, yet another of the atrocities perpetuated by this insane man.

SOUTH AFRICA AFTER APARTHEID

I was invited to join a group of Lutheran religious leaders to go on a mission to South Africa to help train Christian leaders there in useful ways to grow the church through education. I was to be in a support role and to preach at a church service on Sunday morning.

I didn't realize that these people were from the Missouri Synod Lutheran Church a very conservative denomination whose clergy do not consider Christians from other denominational churches to believe quite as they do.

This became clear when we had Holy Communion as a group and were to serve the communion elements to those on our right. The man to whom I was to serve communion knew that I was Methodist and was very hesitant to be served by someone who was not Missouri Synod Lutheran. That experience colored my time there. I am sure that he went to confession afterwards to be absolved of the sin of being served by someone like me.

I was not aware that I would be with people who were so rejecting of my way of practicing the faith. Had I realized that I probably would not have gone, but I'm glad I did go.

Most of the participants on this trip knew each other and didn't make any effort to include me, and truthfully I hesitated reaching out to them in friendship.

My assignment was to preach at a large non-denominational church. I had been told that these churches expected sermons of about 45 minutes in length. That was wrong information. A couple other members of the group went with me. My sermon was all right, but I was uncomfortable in that setting.

We visited what was called an *exotic* restaurant. It was a buffet with the meat of many of the wild animals of Africa: elephant, giraffe, impala, crocodile and something they called worms was available. I'm not sure exactly what the worms were, but they did look like little fat worms. I ate some crocodile, which tasted like white chicken, some giraffe and had a couple other dishes all of which were made in heavy sauce, but I could not bring myself to eat worms.

Other highlights included visiting a Zulu village and hearing about life for the black members of that society. We ended our time at Kruger National Park where we toured in open jeeps to view the wildlife. It was wonderful.

While there I read a story in a Johannesburg newspaper that touched me and instilled in me a desire to be in ministry to persons suffering from HIV/AIDS. The story follows:

> *His head is always bowed as he sits on his empty crate at the entrance to the Rosebank Mall holding his cardboard sign reading "Hungry and homeless because I have AIDS." Instead of looking pleadingly at people for help, Tom keeps his eyes at shoe level. Rather than feeling sorry for himself he tries to keep his mind occupied by "counting the shoes passing and trying to calculate how much each pair is worth."*
>
> *Tom is there everyday because begging outside this suburban shopping mall is his only means of temporary survival.*
>
> *He calls himself Tom, although he keeps his true identity concealed to avoid causing his family,*

particularly his mother, grief. She does not know he has AIDS.

Tom keeps himself quite presentable in his attempt to maintain a semblance of dignity despite having to beg. His long brown hair is always neat and clean as are his clothes. He is emaciated, weighing now only about half what he once did. He lost his job after testing HIV positive and can no longer find employment.

Most people walk around the 31-year-old man averting their eyes. Some glare at him and a few make derisive comments, but there are those who give Tom money or food. He is surprised when some people take time to talk to him and wish him well.

Tom believes he was infected because he had too many different girlfriends. But he has no idea who infected him and when.

Tom is not sure how long he has to live. He says, "I chose not to go on some AIDS program because I don't want a countdown on my T4 cells. If I'm going to die I will.

He has met other AIDS sufferers who do not fit the image in his head of skeletons covered in scabs. Seeing them made him realize that people with AIDS were not different from anyone else. He certainly does not picture himself as abnormal. "I am still me, like I was before, with a few minor changes due to circumstances."

—A story from, 1997

I am glad I got to visit South Africa and longed to return when I could see more of this great country. I also had hoped to go on safari, but that is a dream that will remain unfulfilled.

CHINA

Later on I was invited by this same travel agency to be part of a group going to China for twelve days, hosted by Northwest Airlines and the Chinese tourist agency. The idea was that we would see and experience the *new* China and then recruit groups to go there.

I was thrilled to be invited to go: the palaces of the emperors, the magnificent temples of the Buddhists, the Great Wall where we discovered immediately next to the Wall, the largest Kentucky Fried Chicken restaurant in the world at that time.

We went to Xian to see the incredible Terra Cotta Warriors, sculpted individually, no two exactly alike. It is believed these were created to guard the tomb of one of the emperors.

We departed Xian on a train to Shanghai from where we would fly home. While on the train I needed to urinate and went to the toilet. After relieving myself, I needed to flush. There was a hose to be used for that purpose. I was holding the hose trying to figure out how to make it work when I suddenly got the water turned on but the hose by now was directed toward my rear. My jeans were totally soaked. I had to stand the rest of the way to Shanghai to try to dry out.

In Shanghai we were served platters of food with chicken feet on top. I should have tried eating some, but could not bring myself to do so. Chicken feet are considered a delicacy in China.

We returned home and despite an attempt to find people who might be interested in traveling to China, I could not do so. There would be no return trip.

VISIT TO THE DMZ

It was 1988, just six weeks before the Summer Olympics would be hosted in South Korea, when our plane landed in Seoul. June and I were two of thirteen on a mission team to explore the fantastic growth of the Christian church in Korea. We visited many churches from Presbyterian to Methodist to Catholic to an Assembly of God church, the largest church in the world at that time with over 600,000 members.

Often Methodist Churches hosted us for lunch and sometimes for dinner. At one, a poor congregation, we were each served a whole chicken and sat on kindergarten-size chairs at low tables. We were told that some of the people would probably go without dinner because of the sacrifice they were making for us.

At another church the pastor told how in that village all the men were herded into the church by the Japanese occupiers in the 1940s and were cremated when the church was set on fire. The years of Japanese control were severe, and the efforts to put down resistance more often brutal.

Seoul is a beautiful, modern city, rebuilt after its destruction during the Korean War in the 1950s.

One unforgettable experience took place the first morning after our arrival. It was Sunday and we were scheduled to go to one of the Methodist churches in the city for worship. I decided to go for a run. In my skimpy running clothes I set out from the hotel. "I'll just run in one direction for a while and then turn around and run back." Smart idea!

But during the run I thought, "Why not just run around the block. I can always see the name on top of the hotel." Bad idea! What I didn't realize was that the streets to the left and right of the main boulevard were not laid out in rectangles and after you left the main drag they twisted and turned. Soon I realized that I could not see the name of the hotel. I was lost in Seoul!

I had no ID, did not have a card from the hotel, had no cash and didn't speak a word of Korean. I started approaching people on the street and would say, "Hotel Seoul?" People just shrugged me off. Here was this white guy, dripping wet with sweat, dressed in little running clothes, looking like a maniac.

Finally someone must have recognized the word hotel and pointed down the street to a hotel, not my hotel, but maybe, just maybe someone there spoke English. The receptionist gave me directions but I still couldn't find my way back. At last I saw two guys who looked American with motorcycles. They were my salvation.

When I got to the hotel, June was frantic. It was about time to leave for church and I had to shower and dress. Shakespeare penned, "All's well that ends well." So it does.

We were fortunate to be hosted for lunch at the home of Kim Dae Jung and his wife. He was a political leader in opposition to Japanese occupation of Korea who was seized by the Japanese and taken to Japan. Eventually he was to be returned by ship. It was believed that the Japanese intended to throw him overboard on the way back to Korea. Therefore, American planes shadowed that ship until it arrived safely in South Korea.

When we visited in 1986 he was still living in a compound with guard towers at each corner of the walls that surrounded the house.

While he was imprisoned he was given a small scrap of paper on which he could write letters to his family. These letters are contained in his book titled, *Prison Writings*. They read much like the letters of Paul, particularly those in which Kim Dai Jung encouraged faith in his family. Here are a couple paragraphs from one letter to his son Hong-up:

> *Despite my imprisonment and precarious future, I still feel happy that I have few worries about my family. I know that I can entrust you to God's care in everything.*
>
> *Faith in God simply means love. Of the two kinds of love—love of oneself and love of God and one's neighbors—one is selfish, isolated and demeaning, while the other, the love of the Creator above all things in the universe and the genuine love of one's neighbors, leads to happiness and eternal life.*
>
> —Page 5

In a letter to his wife, November 21, 1980, he wrote:

> *Unfailing belief in the resurrection provides me with the great strength to sustain my faith. I struggle with every ounce of my strength not to lose sight of Him and to keep hold of His love. Always my prayer is:*
>
> *I believe the Lord Jesus loves me. Jesus has brought me to my present circumstances, and He would not have done so if it were not best for me. I cannot know what Jesus intends; I can only obey and praise him. I am trusting in his love.*

> *No matter what my feelings, no matter how harsh my circumstances, and no matter what tomorrow may bring, I am determined to keep my hope that Jesus will always be with me, that He will never leave me.*
>
> —"On His Impending Death and
> Faith in Resurrection"
> Prison Writings, p. 3

Kim Dae Jung was elected president from 1998-2003 and won the Nobel Peace Prize in 2000. He died in 2009.

At one point we traveled north from Seoul to the Demilitarized Zone at the 38th parallel that separates the two Koreas. We went to an orientation room where we were given the history of the DMZ and told the proper way to conduct ourselves while there.

Then we waited and waited. Finally the bishop, who was our group's leader, was called out of the room. After a few minutes he came back and said that the problem was that I was wearing Nike shoes and the concern was that I might make a dash for North Korea and give them a great propaganda scoop. Really? I had not heard that we were not to wear anything like running shoes. The bishop assured them that I would not do that and we were allowed to go out.

The room where representatives from the two Koreas would meet had a table that straddled the 38th parallel. On one side of the table there was a small flag of the Democratic Republic of Korea (the north) and on the other, the flag of the south. Apparently they played a game of one-upmanship by continuously raising their flag just a little bit higher than that of the other.

Across the DMZ we could see the North Korean soldiers watching us through their binoculars. We were allowed to walk around the conference table, hence, for a moment I was actually in North

Korea. (I was there before Donald Trump stepped into North Korea, June 19, 2019, but there was no press coverage for me.)

There was one experience that caused my heart to race. We had flown to the city of Pusan in the southeastern part of the country. Pusan was the area that was the last piece of Korea held by the allies when the North Korean forces marched south.

During the time there we were taken to a farming village surrounded by a wall and given a certain amount of time to visit the community on our own. Then we were to meet at the gate. At the appointed time we boarded the bus and headed for the airport to return to Seoul. After a few minutes I noticed that Lib Nightengale, a member of the church I was then serving, was not on the bus.

The bus turned around and headed back. I was so nervous. I knew that Lib was a person accustomed to taking care of herself and I was really worried that she would take a ride from someone. However, when we got back to the village, there was Lib, standing by the gate. She said that she had been offered rides, but declined, thank goodness. So all was well.

HONG KONG

Before returning to the States, we traveled to Hong Kong for a few days. One of the planned excursions was to an amusement park. Our tour leader told us before we departed to be sure to wear our name tags, "Because you all look alike to me." Touché.

At the park we all decided to ride a roller coaster. After boarding I realized that this coaster did a loop and we would be turning upside down. My hairpiece!! I made sure it did not come off, and, at the top of the loop, put my hand on my head to be sure it was secure.

While in Hong Kong I had a suit made in less than 24 hours by one of the many tailors. I loved that suit, but unfortunately I outgrew it in girth and sent it off to Goodwill.

I LOVE ITALY

The first time I went to Italy was in the early 1990's. June's mother, Grace Urzi Rabito, had come to Chicago when she was five years old. Her father, Guy Rabito, was also five when he came with his parents to Chicago. They came from the same town, Santa Croce Camerina in the southeastern part of Sicily, but their families did not know each other in Italy. Guy's family name was actually Arrabito but at immigration on Ellis Island they shortened it to Rabito

Grace always wanted to return to Sicily to see the house where she was born. So we planned the trip, six of us: June's sister and her husband, George, June's mother, June and I and a close family friend. We rented a large van that could accommodate the six of us plus our luggage.

Our journey began with a flight to Catania, Sicily, on Christmas Day. After we arrived, I drove the van, following a cousin at night to Santa Croce Camerina. The widow of another cousin welcomed us into her home for the five days we would be there. She was known as the "rich widow." It was a three-story house that her late husband had built for her, with marble floors and space heaters among other accoutrements. It was late December and while I had expected a place on the Mediterranean to be warm, in fact it was cold, partly because of dampness. It was there that I bought the heaviest wool pants I ever would own.

At night we slept under heavy duvets. When you slid into bed under the duvet you did not move except for getting out of bed. If you got out of bed your feet would freeze on the marble floor. Since we were occupying four bedrooms with space heaters, if all of them were turned on at the same time the fuse would blow because it was overloaded. .

Giovanna was a wonderful hostess. She helped us find the house Grace was born in, a little square house with common walls on each side attached to other little domiciles. In some respects staying for five days in Santa Croce was like going back a hundred years. Water was delivered on a certain day by truck and filled a container on the roof. If you were not home, you did not get water that week.

Trucks came down the narrow streets, not much more than the width of our alleys in America, carrying all kinds of food for sale. From the bakery down the street wafted the wonderful aroma of breads baking.

At night only the men, dressed in black suits, were to walk on the plaza in front of the church, a centuries old tradition. One evening June and I walked across that sacred space, generating many disapproving looks from the men.

Every day widows were expected to walk to the cemetery to visit the graves of their deceased spouses or parents. Widows were to dress in black. Giovanna hated that and wore black dresses with some white included in the design. She was a rebel.

Another cousin who owned a jewelry store took us to visit his villa on the Mediterranean, then to Syracusa and finally to a farm where we had hot ricotta. We did not realize that this was a multi-course dinner: fish, sausage, beef and with each course appropriate bread and wine. We had eaten a couple bowls of ricotta before we realized that that was just the beginning. So we were stuffed. But the evening was wonderful.

The trip north from Santa Cruce Camerina was fairly uneventful. A visit to Mount Etna in the winter was a bit challenging. There were icy patches on the roadway. When someone pointed this out, June's Mother kept saying, "God forbid! Let's go back," but I was not to be deterred. We arrived at the base of the ski area and had a delicious lunch before heading back down the mountain.

We spent Saturday, December 31 in Messina. On Sunday morning we attended worship at a Catholic church before taking the ferry across to the toe of mainland Italy. Next we visited Pompeii with a guide whose main occupation was in the arts. He explained the city in great and informative detail.

A visit to the Isle of Capri in January is not to be recommended. Mom spent the time huddled wherever she could find warmth. And there were few shops open and not much to see.

When we arrived in Rome I found the hotel where we were to stay, dropped off the passengers and the luggage, then with June went to return the van to the rental company. We found that their office was on a pedestrian street. I thought I would park along a nearby street and walk to the office. However, a police officer thought otherwise. We could not park there even for a few minutes.

We tried to explain our dilemma and somehow he understood and hailed a cab to show us to the underground garage where we would leave the van. For some reason June got in the cab and I followed behind. I stayed really close to the cab because it occurred to me that if we were separated we would all be in trouble. I had both passports and the itinerary with the name of the hotel where we were staying. As always, I was panicking. But finally we got to the garage.

The cab driver said I should park the car while he waited above the underground lot with June. I drove down the circular drive and found I was in the motorcycle lane and could not enter the garage. There was nothing else to do but back up the circular ramp and take the other ramp for cars. Backing up has never been one of my skills but carefully and with some new-found skill, I made it. When I managed to get the car in the garage, I realized a lot of time had passed and wondered if June and the cabbie would still be where I left them, but there they were.

We walked to the hotel and enjoyed the streets of Rome and slowly calmed our nerves.

LOST

Getting lost has followed me throughout my life. Running in Seoul, Korea has already been mentioned. Lost in Wisconsin while biking, another time. But there were other times and each time I was filled with tremendous anxiety. Worry has characterized me and often saps my strength.

We were visiting my sister Kathleen and her family in Orlando in the 80's. I was into running at that time and set out at dusk one day when the heat had abated for a run. Gradually the sun went down and I decided it was time to get back to the house. Suddenly I realized that I did not know how to get back. In many suburban developments the streets don't run in parallel lines. I tried several times to find something that looked familiar, to no avail.

Finally I saw a man outside his home, I asked for his help and he gave me correct directions. I was so relieved that as I ran down their cul-de-sac I actually, (the truth) ran into someone else's house. I only realized what I had done when I saw the people in the living room and they were not my sister's family.

Earlier when I was in junior high, I had gone to the theater alone, which I often did.   When I came out of the theater it was dark and I was disoriented. I started walking in the direction I thought was correct. When I saw the river, the Allegheny, I realized that I was going in the wrong a direction.

When I was in Guatemala for Spanish School in Quetzeltenango (Xela) in 2011, I walked everywhere. I had just arrived in Xela and checked in at the school. The woman in whose home I would be staying, Aldina, met me at the school and walked with me to her house, about six blocks away.

After settling into my room, I decided to go out for a walk and see something of the area where I would be staying for six weeks. I had been given a key to the house.

When it was time to return home I found the street with no problem. I knew I would know the right door to enter because there was a red vinyl covered couch sitting outside. But when I arrived on the street there was no couch to be seen.

I tried my key in the door of one of the houses fronting on the sidewalk. It didn't work. I didn't know what to do. I didn't think it wise to walk down the street trying the key in every door.

Then I saw someone on the other side of the block. I knew there was a young man named Roberto staying at Aldina's as well as I. So I approached this man and asked where Roberto lived and he was able to point out the right house.

Getting lost in Xela occurred a number of times. I would walk to the outdoor markets and get my directions confused. But nearly always I could find someone who understood enough of my Spanish to give me good directions.

This also happened, many years before. It was December 1989, our first year in Crystal Lake. It was a Friday evening and we were getting together in the south suburbs with our birthday group for our traditional Christmas gathering. June took the train to Park Ridge every working day where she picked up the car we kept there and drove the rest of the way to her school. The plan was, I would take the train to Park Ridge where she would pick me up and we would travel to the south suburbs together. I was bringing the gifts we had for our friends.

I had never made this trip on the train before. I was a little anxious about getting off at the right place. The conductors voice calling out the stops was virtually impossible to understand. So I kept close watch. As I looked out the window I saw a sign along the road that ran parallel to the tracks that indicated we had entered Park Ridge and at the next stop I got off. All of a sudden I realized that this was the wrong place. I had gotten off one stop too soon.

What to do? There was a public phone, but someone was using it and would not hang up. (Pre cell phone days.) I knew June would be waiting at the train station for me to get off. When I didn't get off, I didn't know what she would do. I feared she might drive off looking for me. I was afraid we might not connect. So I decided to run, carrying two giant shopping bags filled with gifts, and I was in a long, heavy overcoat.

I had no idea how far it would be to the next stop. I looked for a cab. None! Finally, when I realized that it was several miles to the downtown Park Ridge Station and that it would take me a long time to get there on foot, I made another plan.

I saw someone come out of an office building and get in his car. Apparently he was heading home from work. As he pulled out of the parking lot I knocked on the window of the passenger side of his car. Instead of driving away shaking his head at this man with a wild look on his face, he opened the window. I said, "I got off at the wrong station and I am to meet my wife at the Park Ridge Station. Could you drive me there?" And he did. I shared that experience with our friends and we all had a good laugh. (I had recovered from my case of acute anxiety.)

The amazing thing is that June didn't seem it unusual that I arrived by car instead of train. Unusual? You bet. But I wanted to get to the Park Ridge Station to meet June so badly that I forgot about being ashamed, and just did what I needed to do.

I still get panicky if I think I am lost, like leaving a Rockies game in Denver and forgetting how to find the light rail to get home. But I've never had to sleep outside.

In one way I guess I am not like the typical man. I am not afraid to ask for help with directions. Now that I am older, I am grateful for GPS that gets me to my destination without fail.

ROCKY MOUNTAIN HIGH INFECTS US
1999

As retirement approached (I was 64 at retirement) there was one more thing I wanted to do. I wanted to learn how to ride a motorcycle. Members of the church who were cyclists encouraged me. June decided she would take lessons along with me so we enrolled for the week long class.

It was ridiculous. June could not handle the cycle we were given and gave up after a session or two. I was having trouble with it too, but hung in for the week.

The last day was the examination, and if you passed, you got a license. I had a wedding rehearsal that night so got to the testing course late, after dark. My exam with the bike was a disaster. I fell once and that alone disqualified me. Thus ended the motorcycle quest.

Then came retirement. June had already retired in 1998, and that made me feel that if I retired, we would have more time together and, as it turned out, I'm glad I did. But when I told June I was going to retire she was not thrilled. "I wanted to have some time to do the things I wanted to do," she said. However, I was wearing out with the demands of the church and I thought it was a good time to leave. The church was in a strong position. So the die was cast.

I don't remember the reason but I negotiated with the District Superintendent to retire the first day of September instead of the first day of July which was the normal practice for appointments to take place. Now the decision needed to be made. Where?

Over the years we had considered several places. We thought we would go to Hot Springs Village, Arkansas, a golfing mecca, where two couples from the birthday group had already settled. When visiting them on one occasion we went on a tour of available lots that were for sale. We wanted something with a view. We found one that probably would only have had a view of the house across the street. Nevertheless we bought that lot for around $16,000.

Earlier we had gone on one of those *free* four day three night trips to Lehigh Acres, Florida, just east of Fort Myers. No matter where we were, initially I could see all the positives about living in that place. Only later on did I realize I had been looking through rose-colored glasses. We made an investment and bought a corner lot. The investment was around $6,000. It seemed like a great decision and we were told that this property would only increase in value. Right!

My tendency toward impulse buying had been seen earlier when we were living in Glenview. I had always thought it would be great to have some place where we could get away for a day or two, someplace close by, a get-away place.

I became aware of a new development north of us that would be like a campground, with a variety of facilities including cabins, recreation facilities, restaurants and more. It sounded like just what we wanted. Construction had already started on one of the buildings. So we bought a membership for about $4,000.

So what happened? The getaway membership in Illinois went bankrupt and took our $4,000 down with it. We decided Florida would be too hot and humid so we finally sold for a couple thousand. More money lost.

We decided Arkansas would be too gloomy in winter and too hot and humid in the summer. While it was a golfers paradise, neither of us were golfers. So we put it up for sale, but because there were so many lots for sale in HSV, the only ones selling were those on waterfront or fronting a golf course. We finally sold for $2,500.

Add it up. We lost a lot of money. Plus, we had a financial advisor who invested some of our meager funds in limited partnerships, most of which went bankrupt, and though we didn't lose all we invested, this was another loss of an opportunity for our investments to grow for retirement.

Meanwhile, we had traded weeks of timeshare for a couple resorts in Colorado, one near Winter Park and the other in Steamboat Springs. Then our son moved to Colorado.

That seemed a difficult move for Randy because he was moving away from family that always meant a lot to him. At that time he was working for a law firm in Chicago's Loop area and rode the train everyday. He was tired of that and was looking around. Learning that the corporate offices for Boston Chicken (now Boston Market),were located in Naperville where he lived, was looking for an attorney he applied. They called him in and offered him the position. "But," they started with, "We're moving our headquarters to Colorado." He struggled with the decision, but decided it was a good move for him, career wise.

So we visited and each time toured a different part of Colorado. Then I decided to get away from Crystal Lake for a ten-day personal retreat and learned of a place near *Garden of the Gods* called Glen Eyrie. It was February. While there, I called June and said, "You can't believe February in Colorado. Every day is cloudless with temperatures warm enough that I can sit outside with a sweater for an hour or so at noontime."

I wanted June to experience what I had. We arranged to go to Glen Eyrie in April. While there we had a snowstorm that dumped a huge amount of snow. The electricity went out and so did we. I thought we would never get up the incline that led out of the resort, but we did. Our next stop was to be Fort Collins, but we heard that I-25 north over Monument Pass, north of Colorado Springs, was very difficult or impossible. We found a room at a motel for the night.

The next day we headed north and saw that the further we went the less snow we saw, so that by the time we got to Fort Collins, there was virtually no snow on the ground. Well, that is April in Colorado, one of the snowiest months.

Ultimately we made the decision to move to Colorado. Next step, "Where?" We checked out just about every town and city from Colorado Springs to Fort Collins.

Believe it or not, the name of the realtor we had in Colorado Springs was Melchizedek, very biblical and very appropriate because the Springs, while beautiful, also has a very conservative religious bent with organizations like Focus on the Family plus a strong military presence. All of this did not mesh with our Christian theological beliefs.

During the time we were being shown possibilities in Colorado Springs and Fort Collins, we stayed one weekend at the home of a friend, Olive Aithie-Wilkison, in Littleton. Randy was staying there to take care of the house while Olive was on a trip around the world.

Sunday morning Randy and I decided to roller blade on the bike trail along the South Platte River that was nearby before going to church. On our way back to the house, I did something that caused me to take a hard fall that knocked me out temporarily.

Randy came up to me and wanted to know if I wanted him to get the car so he could get me home. "No! Get me on my feet and I'll skate back," and I did.

"Don't tell mom what happened," I stated. I took a painful shower, got dressed, and we went to Trinity United Methodist Church in downtown Denver. I was hurting quite badly and near the end of the service said I needed to leave. We went home and I lay on the couch, but the pain was so severe in my chest I finally decided I needed to go to the emergency room.

Three broken ribs. For the remainder of our time I carried a plastic device with a hose and mouthpiece that I was required to use frequently. Breathe in until the little red ball rises to a designated mark on the device, then again and again.

One day Randy wanted to take us to St. Mary's glacier. When we arrived, Randy and I decided to hike the glacier. On the way I noticed an animal that I thought looked something like a wolf. The animal seemed to follow us up the glacier always lurking in the trees. At that time of year the glacier was mostly boulders, no snow. It made me nervous and finally I told Randy I thought we should head back, which we did. The animal continued to follow us and when we got to the bottom I realized this was not a wolf, but a dog. In fact, there were no wolves in Colorado at that time. Enough excitement for that day.

June and I continued our search for a retirement location. The deciding factor for me was the bike-friendly reputation of Fort Collins. I wanted to bike and Colorado Springs seemed a more difficult place for me. We looked for and found a lot that could provide a walkout lower level and lovely views front and back. So we decided on that location, Globe Court.

I wanted this to be the house June wanted because she had never had the opportunity to have a say in where we lived. We signed the contract for a house to be built that was going to cost far more than I thought we could afford, however I knew we would figure it out and we did. (I thought we could afford $150,000 but the contract was for $275,000.)

FAREWELL TO CRYSTAL LAKE AND TO FULL TIME MINISTRY
September 1, 1999

We were both excited about the new chapter that was about to open for us: new location, new freedom, new friends, a new life.

There were all the goodbyes that would take place: people lamenting our departure, dinners out, some of it emotional. It began to set in that we were leaving a place and people we loved and going on to something new that was dawning.

Now there was packing to be done, decisions made as to what to transport across country and what to sell. Some of it was difficult, letting go of things, some of which had been part of our lives since we were first married.

Then there was the retirement celebration the church planned. It was amazing. A scroll of my life stretched down one of the hallways of the church. There were pictures, some from my life, others cartoonish. The last message was that I had chosen to retire in 1999 because that was the same year Michael Jordan was retiring

August 31 we departed Crystal Lake. Sherry Walker, a good friend, was there with signs and balloons as we drove out of the parking lot of the church after our final farewell to the staff.

June was driving her baby, the Chrysler convertible, I, the Buick Park Avenue we bought used and a car I loved. We had walkie-talkies that were loaned to us so we could keep in touch as we drove. The drive was uneventful until we got close to the Wyoming border. That's when the skies got extremely ominous, the wind started blowing and the weather report on the radio told of possible tornados. At one point the wind and rain were so intense we pulled off I-80 and sat beside a motel until it seemed safe to go on.

There was an urgency to get to Fort Collins because we had tickets to our first Colorado State University football game Labor Day weekend at Mile High Stadium. We had ordered season tickets before we moved so we could go to our first game against rival, University of Colorado. If anything would win our hearts and make us CSU fans for life it was being at that game, won by CSU 41-14.

THE WAITING GAME

It was going to be a couple weeks before we could access our house. Our furniture was in storage. We decided to drive to San Diego to see our granddaughter, Alexandra. We headed south through New Mexico and then west to Tucson, where we visited with friends from Crystal Lake.

The drive west took us close to the Mexican border and through desert land. The temperature soared. The heat gauge in the Buick climbed and I feared that it would overheat, so we turned off the air conditioning and even turned the heater on to try to keep the engine cooler. Once we got into the mountains in Southern California the temperature moderated and I knew everything would be okay. Of course I worried through that part of the trip.

We enjoyed a few days with Alexandra. Alexandra was always a delight to be with. She had a vivid imagination for a little girl. Born in April 1995, Alexandra moved to San Diego with her mother when her parents marriage ended.

We were there when she was four years old. For four days we played make believe, took walks and marveled at the geese along the shore of a little pond. I saw the droppings the geese left behind and tried to be careful not to step in any of it. Alexandra saw the marvelous feathers they left behind and wanted to collect them all.

We watched videos, engaged in little dramas, one in which I became her Dad and June became her Mom; and another in which she was the beautiful queen, June became the princess, her father became the prince and I was turned into a frog because I laughed at the Queen. She never turned me back, so it is a frog that is writing this book!

We also played hide and seek, I with a stuffed monkey, and she with miniature Barbies, and we all laughed and had a great time. We read stories and told stories. Those are memorable days with our oldest granddaughter.

During those magical days with our granddaughter we were given the opportunity to see the world through her eyes and what a wonderful world it is.

It is a world of love in which kisses are given, not as routine but because they are a true expression of affection; a world in which hands are held in crossing the street when walking in unfamiliar places because there is a feeling of safety and confidence when you're holding someone's hand. It is a world in which relationships seem more important than food, a world where imagination is free to roam and explore.

When we looked into the face of Alexandra, we saw the beauty and perfection of someone who made us think of the great gift God gives us in children. Alexandra helped me to know what love is and helped me to grow in love.

We were still staying with Randy in Denver waiting for the go-ahead to move into our house. The scheduled day for the movers to come with our belongings was approaching, but there was still work to be done by the builder.

On the day we were to officially occupy our new house, we got word that the city would not give the go-ahead because of cracked sidewalk in front of our house. The movers were on the way and as always I freaked out. What was going to happen?

The realtor assured me that they would get a waiver that would permit occupancy, and that did happen. So while the furniture was being moved into the house, painters were still applying paint to some of the walls. At last after months of planning and anticipation we slept in the first house we ever owned that very night.

ENTER A BUICK PARK AVENUE

June loved her Chrysler Sebring convertible and the car of my dreams was the Buick Park Avenue. Our friend Dick had a Park Avenue and he let me drive it once and I fell in love. We were living in Crystal Lake, Illinois at that time and were looking for a car to replace the Le Sabre we had driven over 200,000 miles. The Park Avenue was not a new car but a pre-owned car. We found it at an Enterprise car resale lot. *We once called such cars used.* It cost more than we intended to pay, but we bought it anyway.

It was in excellent condition, having been leased for the previous two years and driven only approximately 20,000 miles. I was in heaven driving that car. It felt so luxurious. But things started to happen.

On our return trip from San Diego we stopped for work that was taking place on the highway meaning one-way traffic. I turned off the ignition while we waited and when trying to start again it took several attempts for the motor to kick in. We arrived in Gunnison. I pulled into a gas station and when I tried to start it, it simply would not start.

The car was towed to a mechanic nearby. He told us that he needed a part that was available in Montrose or Grand Junction. They could ship the part that would take a couple of days or we could rent a car and drive to Montrose to get the part. We chose the latter and the next day we continued on to Denver.

The incident with the Buick in Gunnison when the car would not start was not the only problem we had with that car. We were staying in Denver with Randy waiting for our house to be completed. I was driving south on Wadsworth Boulevard in the car, heading to a mall when it stopped right on the road. I had to get out of the car and push it to get it off that busy road. Eventually it started again and I got back to Randy's.

Another time, June and I had gone to Winter Park across Berthoud Pass to make arrangements for our birthday group who were coming to Colorado for our annual get-together. We had just crested Berthoud Pass on our way home when once again the car stopped. I tried to use my cell phone to call AAA, but there was no service.

I put up the hood and hung a rag outside to indicate we needed help. A car with two young men stopped to see if they could help. I asked if they would call AAA for me when they got down the mountain and had cell phone service and gave them my AAA information. They said they would, but AAA never came.

At last a couple returning from some church event stopped. The man took me to the top of the pass where my phone worked and I called AAA. We returned to my car where June and his wife were waiting, and I decided to try once again and the car started.

I made the decision to get off the mountain instead of waiting for the AAA truck. I thought I would keep the car window down and if we saw the truck coming up the mountain I would try to signal them that we were the ones they were coming to help. That was a rather ridiculous idea, but I thought we could try.

Then after we moved into our house we were driving from Fort Collins to Laramie, Wyoming for the Colorado State-Wyoming football game. We had just gotten out of town a short distance when I felt the car hesitate like something wasn't just right. The highway between Fort Collins and Laramie is rather desolate and cell phone service is very sketchy. Not wanting to risk having the car break down along that highway, I turned around and drove back home so we could get June's convertible. We did so and started back to Laramie.

Once again we were on the road to Laramie when I remembered we had left the tickets in the Buick, so back to the house to get the tickets and then off to Laramie again. With tickets in hand and a car we trusted, I drove many miles over the speed limit *(don't ask me how many miles over)* to Laramie and we were there in time for the opening kickoff. It was all worthwhile because Colorado State won the game.

Shortly afterwards we traded it in for an Oldsmobile Silhouette.

NOW WHAT?

It took a couple months to get unpacked and settled. Then I asked myself the question, Now what? I was a workaholic through the years of my ministry, so having no reason to get up in the morning with anything to do left me feeling a little depressed.

Then I remembered that when I was a college student I had obtained a position as substitute mail carrier during the holiday season to assist with the mountain of mail that was delivered during that time of year. Of course that was in the 1950's. So I went to the post office and inquired. No, they did not hire additional help for the Christmas season. As I was walking out of the office, I said, "Well, do you have any other part-time work?"

The immediate response was, "Yes we do. We need substitute mail carriers." I took the information home and consulted with June. She agreed that I should apply. (I think she wanted me out of the house, at least some of the time.)

So after passing the preliminary tests that required a lot of memorization and concentration, and after two weeks of training at the main Post Office in Denver, I was qualified to be a sub and was assigned to a route.

The first day I handled that route alone was December 19, 1999. That was the day with the heaviest mail of the year, Christmas mail. It took me hours just to sort the mail and get it ready for delivery. By the time I left the post office to start my rounds it was already late afternoon. Because I was new, it took me much longer than it should have to deliver the mail. In fact, since it was December, it was becoming dark very early. I was trying to deliver mail to mailboxes when I could not even see the addresses on the boxes. I had no flashlight, no headlight, nothing.

Finally, because it was getting to be so late I received a call from the carrier supervisor at the post office asking how soon I would be back to the post office. I'm sure my voice sounded panicky. I told him where I was on the route and how far I still needed to go. He said he would send someone to help me finish up, which he did. Otherwise I don't know when I could have finished. After that, it was a piece of cake, or almost.

I did have a couple harrowing experiences as a carrier. One day I was delivering mail on a route that was not my own. I pulled up to a cluster box and could not find the key to open the box. We had been warned to never lose that key because if we did we would have to pay to have all the boxes throughout Fort Collins re-keyed, thousands of dollars.

I looked everywhere, practically tore my car apart, but the key was not to be found. I called the PO and talked with the supervisor and told him what had happened. He spoke to the superintendent whose message to me was, "You had better find that key."

I called June and told her and asked her to pray that I find it. Shortly after that phone call I calmed down and thought, *I'll retrace my route and see if I may have left it at one of the boxes.* Sure enough, the key was hanging from a cluster box with two boxes wide open. I was so relieved to have found it and started to breathe again. After calming down. I proceeded to complete the route.

There was another hair-raising experience in my postal years. I was delivering a package to a home when, either someone shouted at me or I happened to catch a glimpse out of the corner of my eye. I saw my car slowly moving up the grade on the street where the house was located. I dropped the package and rushed to my car, managed to get the door open and put on the brakes. I had forgotten to set my car in park. When I think of all of the possible scenarios had I not seen what was happening, I still get shivers up my back!

At first I only worked one day a week, and when the regular carrier for that route was on vacation or sick. However, as time went on I was asked to fill in for other routes and after three years found myself working 40 hours a week.

I met with the supervisor of carriers and expressed my concern. His response was, "The postmaster says that you have to come in whenever you are needed."

I replied, "I really don't want to work that many hours."

He asked, "Then do you want to resign?"

I firmly said, "Yes."

He pulled out retirement papers. I signed and my career with the post office came to an end. I was sad to leave the post office because I had really enjoyed my job, but I didn't want to work full time. So that was that.

It was fortunate that I quit because in a few months my life would be turned upside down when June died.

BACK TO THE PASTORATE

Meanwhile, I had been in conversation with the district superintendent of the Peaks and Plains District of the United Methodist Church about helping in a church and substituting when necessary. He told me of a small church a half hour from Fort Collins that needed a pastor. It was a full-time position. I wasn't interested in an every Sunday commitment, so we left it at that.

Later he approached me again about helping one Sunday a month to celebrate the sacraments. A lay deacon would be in charge the rest of the time.

I met with the committee at the church and we came to an agreement. I was to be paid a relatively small salary but that was fine with me.

Things went along well, I thought. I preached one Sunday a month and celebrated communion. Later I taught an adult Sunday School class and helped in any way I could. I loved the people of that little congregation that usually numbered around 40 each Sunday. They increased my salary for the next year.

However the relationship between the deacon and myself became strained. It's hard to be a retired pastor, at least at first because you can always see things in the church that you attend that you would do differently. After three years I realized that the deacon did not want me at the church. She convinced the church board to reduce my salary to half of what it had been. I felt that I could not go with that and that the relationship with the deacon was such that it was best for me to resign, which I did.

Then in 2007 I was asked if I'd be interested in a part time position at my church, First United Methodist Church of Fort Collins. I said "Yes." My responsibilities included being in charge of the annual stewardship campaign (something I had always avoided as a full-time pastor), teaching, occasional preaching, visiting in nursing homes and hospitals and wherever I was needed.

I found in my teaching discoveries for myself that I could share with participants in classes, including one at a nursing home.

One Sunday I was teaching an adult Sunday School class. In the midst of the teaching one of the members, a truly beloved woman said, "He has two different colored shoes on." Indeed I did, one brown, one black. They were similar in style and because of colorblindness I had made a mistake. I wanted to hide my feet for the rest of the morning. I was so self-conscious.

I loved my work and believe I made a contribution to the life of the congregation.

JUNE'S DEATH

In 2003 June was diagnosed with Hodgkin's disease. This is a form of Hodgkin's that responds well to treatment. She went through 13 chemotherapy injections and seemed to be doing very well.

In the Fall of that year the birthday group was gathering at Gulf Shores, Alabama for our annual reunion. We had a wonderful time sitting on the beach, playing games, and exploring the area. June was feeling great after the 13 chemotherapy treatments.

In November of that year she awakened me during the night and said she was having trouble breathing. I helped her get out of bed but she could not walk on her own. She rested her arms on my arms and while I was walking backward she managed to walk forward and I got her into the car. I took her to the emergency room where they diagnosed double pneumonia. Later they determined it was not pneumonia but something rare that causes fibers to grow in the lungs, hence interfering with the ability to breathe.

The doctor said that this condition occurs on occasion when a particular drug is used in chemotherapy. They also said that when that drug is used there needed to be frequent CAT scans to monitor any negative effect it might be having on the body. To my knowledge there has been no CAT scans done throughout her chemo treatment.

She was put into an ICU room and when her condition didn't improve she was moved to a more specialized ICU where she had her own nurse. For a few days she lingered with no progress being made.

Finally the doctor said that she needed to be put into an induced coma. They told me that there was no cure for this disease but that the body just had to fight it off. The night before they inserted the tachometer, we had our last conversation. She told me that she knew she wouldn't make it and she told me the names of two of my friends that she said I should consider marrying. We talked about what funeral and burial plans we would make when the time came. She said she didn't want to be cremated and I agreed. We expressed our love for one another. We prayed. And that was to be the last conversation we would ever have.

After a week or so sitting in that room all day I decided I needed to do something to give myself a break. I went Christmas shopping for the family. I think that sounds strange but it was therapeutic.

I decided I needed to make arrangements with a funeral director and met with one I knew, selected the casket and made all the other decisions that have to be made. I went to the cemetery and chose the lot where we would be buried, then selected a headstone and the inscription for it. From my experience as a pastor I knew how difficult it is if all of that needed to be done after a death occurred.

At last my kids and I agreed that the life support should be removed. The nursing staff was wonderful with several standing with us as the tubes were withdrawn and she gradually stopped breathing. The date was December 21, 2003.

We went through Christmas as usual. There was a movie on TV starring Jack Nicholson, *About Schmidt*, about a man whose wife had died and who didn't know what to do with his life. It was difficult to watch his struggle. I thought that was a picture of what my life would be like going forward. In seeing the struggle of that character and his eventual recreation of a life that was purposeful gave me hope.

The funeral service was held at First United Methodist Church in Fort Collins, and a memorial service later at the United Methodist Church in Crystal Lake for those who could not come west. Many people came to each service to give tribute to a great lady.

Our granddaughter, Alexandra, felt grandma's loss very deeply. She wrote a note to her beloved Grandma and placed it in the casket. At the service she also stood and spoke about the "best Grandma there ever was."

Three years later, Randy and Melissa welcomed their fourth child whom they named Juniette. Of course her name brought to mind the name of Junetta, her grandmother. I was thrilled that June would be remembered in this way, in the name of her grandchild whom she would never see, at least in this lifetime.

I was in shock as I tried to discern what my life would be without my best friend.

I learned that when a person experiences a sudden change, like death of a loved one, that often there are several accidents of one kind or another yhat follow, caused by the distraction of the death. That was true for me. First I was pumping gas, tried to step over the hose, tripped and twisted so that I strained my hamstring. Second, I decided I wanted a dog to replace Obie, like the last dog that we had. I wanted another yellow lab. Someone at Hospice told me about a person who had one left out of the litter.

I was so anxious to get a dog that when I went to see her I bought her right there on the spot. It was a major mistake. I had trouble getting her in the car because she was so scared. I hired a trainer who came to the house and tried to work with Abby, the name I gave her. Abby would go into the corner and could not be enticed to come out. The training ceased

Abby was difficult to walk because she resisted the collar and leash, so when she needed to eliminate she did it on the carpet in the house .

Then the third thing happened. I was rushed to the hospital with double pneumonia. My neighbor who took me to the hospital was willing to take care of Abby, cleaning the carpet, trying to walk her and feeding her. At last I realized I could not keep Abby so found a good home for her where there was a large fenced in area where she could roam.

THE LEGACY OF MY WIFE JUNE

June was an extraordinary woman, a partner in ministry and a person of strong faith. But she was also one who gave in so many ways besides the church.

She was a teacher in the Chicago Public School System for 38 years. After graduating from the University of Illinois at Champaign-Urbana, she was concerned that she would not be accepted into that school district which operates separate from the rest of the schools in Illinois. As a teenager she had contracted bells palsy that left her with paralysis on the left side of her face. At the time of her meeting with the committee that would decide whether or not she would be hired, the paralysis was hardly noticeable, but she thought this would be disqualifying.

June met with a committee as part of the application process. She was accepted. So she began her career as an educator. Her first assignment was to a school on the near west side of Chicago teaching kindergarten. She had two classes, morning and afternoon with around 45-50 pupils in each class and no assistant.

June continued her education and graduated with a master's degree from Governor's State University in 1978 and then at least 20 hours beyond that.

She involved me in research for one of the projects she chose during her Master's studies. This was to determine how many people entering an elevator would smile at you if you smiled at them. We went to Marshall Fields and rode elevators, up and down, up and down, up and down, she on one elevator, I on another. I thought surely someone would report that a weirdo was acting strangely on the elevator, but that did not happen.

Every time I received an appointment to a new church, she would find herself needing to travel long distances until she could get a transfer, which usually meant to one of the more difficult schools.

In one instance in the early 70's, she took a position at a school in a troubled part of the south side of Chicago. She was one of less than six white teachers in this school that had only black students. It was a time when gangs would occasionally invade schools and cause havoc. The librarian at that school was worried about June's safety and gave her a way to escape if something like that happened. I never knew when I said goodbye to June in the morning if I would see her alive again. As it turned out her tenure there was for only one year.

She was then appointed to a school on the southwest side of Chicago in a racially changing neighborhood. Because she had pursued and obtained the master's degree in counseling, she was given the position of school counselor.

One morning June was leaving for school. As she backed out of the driveway and was starting forward, she was waving at me and drove into a light post, breaking her nose. No school that day. A visit to the hospital instead. She was asked what kind of relationship we had, checking for possible spousal abuse. That's a question that was being asked then.

An incident happened at her new school when a troubled former student entered the building, shot and killed the beloved principal, severely wounded the assistant principal and a custodian. Fortunately June was on an upper floor, so was saved from the carnage.

Then I moved north to Glenview and ultimately June was assigned to the Clara Barton School in northeast Chicago near Evanston. This school had students who came from seventeen different countries, many of whom had limited English. She was beloved by the students in that school and expressed her love for them in ways that were appropriate.

When we moved to Crystal Lake, 50 miles northwest of Chicago, June continued at that school, traveling by train to Park Ridge, where she kept an old car, then driving the rest of the way to school.

I would drive June to the train station in the morning and meet her train in the evening. She was notoriously late getting out of the house and I had to speed to the train, sometimes crossing the tracks just ahead of the train to get her there.

One time we missed the train. So I hurriedly drove to Barrington further east where she could board the train. There is an advantage to being a pastor with a lead foot. I was a nervous wreck, but she got to school.

The car June kept at the train station in Park Ridge was the Buick Le Sabre that had been driven nearly 200,000 miles. She decided to have a contest with members of the birthday group. Each person was to choose the day and time they thought the Le Sabre would pass the 200,000 mile mark. Whoever was closest to the exact time was going to win a prize. June loved playing games.

June and her mother had a game they liked to play. I learned about this game when we were in an exclusive store like Saks Fifth Avenue. She told a clerk that she wanted to see the swimming suits they had. I was aghast. I said, "Do you really want to buy something here?" She replied, "Shh." Later she told me that she and her mother would look at very expensive items, ask questions about them but never buy them. Just a game. Playing rich.

I played that game a couple times. This is the most memorable. June always said she wanted to live in Lake Point Tower when we retired, a very expensive high rise on the shore of Lake Michigan near the Loop. They were having an open house with several renowned designers creating the interiors of five units. We went for the tour. I asked the tour guide how much one of these units would cost. She immediately seized on what she took to be the possibility that we might be a buyer.

When the tour ended she took us to the sales office. I said, "My wife wants to live here when we retire, can you tell us the price?" A sales person was called and we so we could see all of the possibilities of ownership: size, because you could buy two units and move the walls to make a larger space for a larger home, the views north, south, east and west and how the price varied according to the view, the parking garage, the private park on the roof, etc.

When we left I told June, "We could probably rent a space in the garage and not much else. But we saw it.

When June's mother died she received an inheritance of about $30,000. That was *her* money and she was going to invest it the way she wanted without help from a financial advisor. She embarked on a thorough study of mutual funds to determine which one she was going to choose and in which she would invest her inheritance.

She had papers spread all over the dining room table and spent hours researching. Finally she made her decision and most of the mutual funds she chose worked well. She became so possessive of her investments that she was not willing to take money out even when some started to decline in value. But that was June. She would do it her way.

June was my constant supporter in whatever I attempted. When I signed up to do the AIDS ride, she helped me purchase all the things I needed to enter that ride, spending several thousand dollars.

When I started in-line skating she gave me a card picturing an older couple on skates with the caption: "You're never really old as long as you can laugh at yourself." Inside she wrote: "I'm so happy for you and proud of your great achievement. Keep up the good work. You look outstanding on your roller blades." She added, "Please read the message on the back of this card." It read:

> *Life and Other Journeys*
> *Life isn't a destination—it's a journey.*
> *We all come upon unexpected curves*
> *and turning points, mountaintops and valleys.*
> *Everything that happens to us*
> *shapes who we are becoming.*
> *And in the adventure of each day,*
> *we discover the best in ourselves.*

Her love for me was a major contributing factor in the success of my ministry. Her wise counsel helped me avoid pitfalls. Her love for me made me feel special. I felt important. Her love built up my self-worth and self-esteem.

How does one do so much in her life that stretched over only 67 years? I remember how we went on a hot air balloon ride and when we landed, the basket tipped over, but no one was hurt. She loved it. In Mexico we each did parasailing and both of us had a good time.

Once we went to an Indian restaurant in Chicago and she decided she wanted the hottest sauce they had. After eating a few bites her esophagus and stomach were burning so badly she had to go to the restroom. But when she came back she finished her meal.

In retirement, although she had only four years to live, she became very active in the Fort Collins community, qualifying to be a CASA worker, Court Appointed Special Advocate, served as an officer in the Newcomers Club in the city, an organization people could join for four years, became a volunteer with the Fort Collins Symphony Women's Guild, and another group that worked with disabled youth, and was one of the workers who monitored visits by parents who were not permitted to see their children without supervision.

We also had season tickets to the Fort Collins symphony, the Denver Center for the Performing Arts Theatre Company, the Colorado State football games, the CSU men's basketball games and one year to the women's basketball season. In addition we attended many women's CSU volleyball games where we met up with friends from the Newcomers Club.

There was one point of contention, shopping. When we went grocery shopping, June would take the time to study the product cost. Take for example the labels on every brand of green beans to determine which was the best value. If I went alone I chose the one I came to first, which might not be the best value.

Then there was shopping for clothes. One day she wanted to buy a new pair of shoes and insisted I come with her. After trying on what seemed like dozens of shoes, she narrowed it down to three candidates. Once again she tried on each pair, after which she asked me which one I liked best. I gave her my opinion. She bought one of the others.

While her life was cut short, she lived it to the fullest.

A PSYCHIC?

I decided to go to a Hospice program for those who had lost loved ones. Most of the people who were in that group had lost parents or other special people, no one who had lost a spouse. So I felt some of what took place did not really apply to my situation.

When the eight-week class ended, a friend, Don Miller, whose wife had died shortly before June, went with me to a hospice evening group. It was a strange experience to say the least. During the free-flowing meeting people talked about how they had experienced their deceased loved ones. Some spoke of visions, of lights turning on next to the deceased's favorite chair, of a rocking chair moving without any obvious assistance. Don and I looked at each other in astonishment and on the way home we decided we did not need to return to that group.

However, the stories people told at Hospice and what some family members and others had told me about seeing or experiencing the presence of a deceased loved one made me wonder, "Why haven't I received some message from June?"

I mentioned this to the counselor I was seeing at that time. He said, "Would you like to see a psychic? If so, I know someone you could see." So, one day I went to the house of a psychic who was well known, having had a local radio program at one time.

She told me she would record the session and give me the tape afterwards. Much of what she told me seemed like things one could easily report even if not in contact with someone from the world beyond.

However, there were a couple of things she could not have known that she said June told her. One was that I should start writing the three books I said I was going to write when I retired: one was a book of Christmas Eve services I had done (I was so proud of them), one was my life story (I am doing that right now), and I think the other was a book of my sermons (which I thought were so good, but probably weren't as good as I thought) and that was all.

Then the psychic said that June said she had to go because she was teaching a class. Did the psychic know that June had been a teacher in this life? I don't know but that experience has left me wondering if any of what she said was true and if so if it was a peek into the afterlife. Pretty awesome if true.

MISSION ACCOMPLISHED
GUATEMALA

It was 2007 and I heard of a group from First United Methodist Church in Fort Collins that was going on a mission trip to Guatemala. This group was going to help construct a house for a Methodist pastor who lived in the mountains near Santa Cruz Del Quiché. They encouraged me to go with them and I decided to do so. I was starting to fulfill my intention to go on a mission trip every year in retirement.

When I went to Guatemala I discovered what wonderful people the Guatemalans are, and I had the feeling that I wanted to do more. So in 2009 I went once again on another mission trip to the same area of Guatemala, this time as part of a support team for a dental mission.

My experience in Central America among the Quiché people created in me he desire to study Spanish again, something I had started in the 70's. I learned of Spanish language schools in Xela (shay-la), Quetzaltenango, the second largest city in Guatemala. It was one-on-one instruction with no English being spoken at all. It was 2011.

We did many things other than the studies that took place during the day. There were cultural experiences, such as learning how to make tortillas, taking a hike up a volcano, and learning how to do the salsa. That was an experience!

There were more men than women who came to the salsa event. Therefore I was teamed up with another man as my partner. Neither one of us was very light on his feet and we had difficulty dancing together. It was absolutely hilarious and ludicrous. Finally we decided we could not do it.

We also heard from a man who had been one of the guerrillas during the Guatemalan Civil War that lasted from 1960 to 1996. He had lived in a small village in Quiché and had witnessed the Guatemalan army come to his village and shoot his father who refused to join the army. He was 14 at the time and fled to Mexico where he trained for one year to be a guerilla.

He was in his first military confrontation with the Guatemalan Army when, looking up, he saw someone, a white man in the lead, obviously one of the American 'advisors' we had sent there, in the front. He asked the man next to him what he should do. The man said, "Kill him." This former guerilla had nothing good to say about the involvement of the United States in their civil war.

Several of us went to a restaurant for lunch in the center of the city. I noticed a sign advertising *pie queso*. The word *pie* in Spanish is the word for foot and *queso* is cheese. I said to the other students there, "What does 'foot cheese' mean?" Someone has said we learn more from our mistakes than when things are going well.

They laughed and one said *pie* also means pie just like in the United States. Cheese pie. I learned something that day.

After the classes were over I went to Santa Cruz Del Quiche, a two- hour bus ride over the mountains, to help teach in the English classes at the John Wesley school. I thought I was to be the assistant, but when I entered the first class with the English teacher, she gestured in such a way as to indicate that I was to do the teaching. I was not prepared, but what could I do?

So for six weeks I muddled through the teaching. Afterwards I was brazen enough to suggest to one of the directors of the school that if they wanted me to come and teach English the next year, I would consider it. He said they would love to have me come. So in 2012, I would be an English teacher in Guatemala.

PARTNERS

When I moved to Fort Collins there was one thing I knew I would miss, the children in my last church. I had always been supportive of the young people of all ages. In Melrose Park, Harvey, Trinity, Glenview, and Crystal Lake, whether I was in charge of the youth program or not, I made it a priority to do what I could to let them know they were valued.

It must have been evident to the youth. Years after I retired I received an email from a young woman who was in one of the high school groups. She told me how much it meant to her that I was always in the parking lot of the church when the youth were heading out on a mission trip and how I was always there to welcome them home. Funny how things you just do can make an impression that lasts.

I had decided that in retirement I wanted to be a Big Brother to a youth. In Fort Collins, the program is called Partners. There are Senior Partners and Junior Partners. I applied to be a Senior Partner and was accepted.

One day I was called to the office and told there was a youth, nine years old, named Ross. They told me something about him, how in his earlier years he had been subjected to all kinds of abuse. His parents had not provided well for Ross and his younger sister Ashley. There were times when their mother would bring men home and the kids witnessed their mother having sex.

At one point their mother shot and killed a man she had brought home. When the trial took place Ross was told to say that the man had attacked his mother and threatened to kill her so she could plead self-defense, even though that may not have been true. To tell a child to lie makes a lasting impression.

As a result the first years of his life were traumatic and left scars that lingered on and probably will scar him for life. Ross and his sister Ashley were placed in the custody of their grandmother, Saundra Craft and her husband Charlie, who died a few weeks after the kids came to Fort Collins, leaving Saundra as the sole custodian of the children.

I was asked to become the Senior Partner for Ross, although he had asked for someone around 30 (I was told all the kids make the same request. I met Ross and his grandmother in their home and we started a relationship.

Ross was very shy at first, but eventually warmed up. The program asked that a Senior Partner and a Junior Partner meet for about three hours every week. Included in the suggestions were fun times (which we did a lot), help with homework (which we did rarely, (Ross has ADHD and had trouble concentrating), and participation in the activities of the Partners organization.

We joined with the other Partners in building a path at the Visitor Center along I-25, shoveling crushed asphalt into wheelbarrows and dumping it where others would put it on the designated path and tamp it down. Ross became tired of doing that and ended up sitting in a wheelbarrow.

Another time we went to a park, camped overnight in a mosquito infested area along a creek, and set traps to determine the population of Woodland Jumping Mice in the area. This was the least liked activity we did.

The most exciting group activity was going to a ranch where we rode horses along a trail that at times seemed very treacherous. Because of the number of Partners who came, it was necessary to go in two groups. We were in the first group and were supposed to wait at the stables until the second group completed their ride.

However, shortly after we came back and the others had left, the weather began to change very suddenly (that's Colorado). An extremely strong wind started blowing and then it started snowing. The wind blew the snow horizontally. I was so glad that we had been in the first group because we were all dressed in nothing but jeans or shorts and T-shirts.

Finally, I said to Ross, "Let's go!" and we started for home. I watched the temperature gauge in the car go down steadily from a high in the 70's until it was close to 32 degrees.

We skied, sometimes staying overnight at the resort, but only when another father and son went with us to ensure I was never in jeopardy from any possible charge of abuse. Ross loved to ski among the trees and at times would disappear and not come back on the ski run for some time which caused me to be concerned should he hit a tree and be lying there somewhere. But that never happened. *(I always seem to expect the worst possible outcome of whatever I am doing.)*

We went to movies, rode bumper cars, played laser tag which exhausted me and which I always lost, went to Elitch Gardens where he loved a ride that was made to look like a ship and swung back and forth, back and forth. He convinced me to ride with him. I did – ONE TIME! He wanted me to go again. I said, "No Way! Not me." So he rode alone several times.

Another time it was to a water park where there was a wave pool. The waves would come. I would grab him and toss him into the wave. He loved it, but my arms got tired. Well, I was around 65 and had reason to tire.

One October night we went to see a Vampire movie, not really my thing, but he wanted to go. On the way home in the dark with a spooky moon overhead I kept saying, "I'm going to suck your blood," pretending to be a vampire. I used a Dracula type voice. Ross kept saying, "Don't do that." I think it may have scared him."

The trombone was Ross' instrument of choice. He was in the high school band when they were invited to march in the St. Patrick's Day parade in Dublin, Ireland. The hour of the parade in Colorado was something like 3 o'clock in the morning. Some parents said we could see the parade through some hookup I didn't really understand. So there we sat, a few parents trying to discern a band out of the TV picture that was mostly foggy.

I was so excited when he was elected King of Homecoming. What a great experience for him. One of the many issues he has struggled with is self-esteem, so to be elected by his fellow students was really great.

Another issue Ross struggled with was that he is short. He longed to be tall, but that never happened. Like me stressing over my weight, Ross stressed over the fact that he was short, which at times left him feeling like he didn't quite measure up to some of the other guys.

Ross' grandmother provided every possible opportunity for both of her grandchildren: tennis and golf lessons, extra tutoring to help with schooling, summer camps, etc.

Ross' dream for years has been to become a firefighter. He tried college twice and it wasn't for him, but the dream continued. Finally after moving to Arkansas he became part of an Emergency Medical Team (EMT) connected with a fire department in the northern part of that state.

Later he moved to Las Vegas where he tried a different occupation, but that didn't work out. Ross' dream of becoming a paramedic still burns strongly in him, and I believe he will accomplish that goal. Ross was and still is a young man whom I always thought of as a grandson and whom I love.

I believe I was a good Senior Partner for Ross and he brought a lot of joy into my life and hopefully I in his.

A NEW SPOUSE

In April 2004 I called Ross' grandmother and asked if she would like to go for brunch one morning. Because she had lost her husband a few years before I thought it would be helpful for me to talk to someone who had gone through what I was going through after June's death.

She agreed. I picked her up to go to a small restaurant called The Egg and I for brunch one day. She was so funny. She didn't want anyone seeing her getting into a car with a man so she slipped out of the house and slid into the car as quickly as she could.

We had brunch that must have lasted three hours. We talked and laughed. It was so refreshing to have someone to talk to. We dated afterwards on several occasions. She didn't want the children or anyone in the neighborhood to know we were seeing each other. During that time we were having such a good time, going to movies, to dinners, and one time took a picnic to a site along the Poudre River in Poudre Canyon outside Fort Collins.

We had a favorite song by Kenny Rogers we played over and over, "You Decorated My Life." The refrain follows:

> *And you decorated my life*
> *Created a world*
> *Where dreams are a part*
> *And you decorated my life*
> *By paintin' your life*

All over my heart
You decorated my life.

Often when we were in the car going somewhere, we would play the CD and sing along, over and over.

There were times when we saw each other by pretending that we were going to walk her dog in the evening. I could not be seen coming to her house, so parked down the street and waited until she came with her dog Buddy. Then I joined for the walk. We were like teenagers sneaking out of the house.

I was smitten and began talking marriage, the exact opposite of what I had always counseled people who had experienced a loss to do, to make no major decisions for at least a year after experiencing a great loss.

Saundra cautioned me about marriage. More than once she said she thought we should not get married. She said the children would drive me crazy, that I had no idea what it was like to live with them.

I had only known my relationship with Ross and the fun we had been having. Being someone who has sometimes had a messiah complex, I thought I could be a great help for Saundra and give the kids a male figure in their lives. I was going to be the savior on a great white steed riding into their lives, bringing love and stability. We had gotten counseling on the issues involved in creating a blended family, most of which was not helpful.

I persisted and we finally decided on marriage. I proposed to Saundra in the traditional way. Kneeling by our table at a very nice restaurant in Fort Collins, I asked her to marry me. She said "Yes." Then I placed a ring on her finger.

At first we set a date that was much too soon after June's death. My kids resisted an early date therefore we were married on February 19, 2005 with a large reception of about 100 friends and family at our new home a few doors from where Saundra had lived.

When we told Ross and Ashley that we were going to marry, Ashley looked at us and said, "But you're old." Ross just looked at us with an expression of absolute astonishment on his face.

Subsequently the four of us made a trip to Idaho to visit with Saundra's father. He, as well as all of Saundra's family in Idaho, are Mormons. Ross and I were staying at a motel. Saundra and Ashley were at her father's house.

She told me the next day that she was sure he had walked to the motel, thinking that Saundra had gone there and that we were having sex. When he returned she heard him in the bathroom praying loud enough that she could gather the drift of it, praying that Saundra would not marry me because I was not Mormon.

Her father was very deaf, so to communicate it was necessary to shout. We did have a conversation in which I asked him to bless our marriage. He said he did not understand why I could not become a Mormon because it wasn't that different from being a Methodist. Obviously neither of us knew much about the other's faith. The one thing we had in common was that he, like I, was an avowed Democrat.

Her father died when we were at the Vail Ski Resort where Ross and I were having a great time skiing. When Saundra received word that her father had died, she went back to Fort Collins immediately, packed and drove to Idaho. I, with the kids, left the next day and went to be at the funeral. Saundra was so funny. At the visitation, she kept introducing me to friends and family as "my latest husband."

At the funeral the bishop in charge said that Ross Covington had been translated to the second estate. I believe that means, in Mormon theology, that he had been faithful in all things that are expected of a true Mormon and now he is in what we might call heaven.

Over the next couple of years we returned to Rexburg, Idaho where she had grown up, first for a family reunion, then her high school reunion. In keeping with what I had experienced at my high school reunions, I wore a suit. I was definitely overdressed, no suits except mine. The food was like a potluck and the only beverage available was water. Now I knew what reunions among Mormons were like.

OUR NEW HOME, SAUNDRA'S DREAM

Once we had made the decision to marry, we had another decision to make, where to live. There was a house close to where Saundra was currently living in the Ptarmigan subdivision, an upscale golf community with many large houses, some huge. She told me that that was her dream house and it was for sale. We went to see it and because I wanted Saundra to have her dream house, just as I wanted June to have the house of her dreams, I said we'd buy it.

We then completed the lower level of the house and enclosed the lower patio to create a sunroom, as Saundra called it. All told our house had more than 5,000 square feet of living space.

In truth I never felt at home in that house. It seemed far too big. I knew that part of the issue was to have enough space so that Ross and Ashley could have some separation from one another.

As I've said, I have always been intimidated by wealth. Wealth suggested to me people who were more sophisticated, more cultured than this guy who grew up in a factory town in very modest circumstances. I thought some of the people seemed snooty and that just confirmed my feelings.

But it was our home and we had many wonderful times during the few years we lived there. Troubles began to surface, however, and I realized that Saundra was right when she said we should not get married. For one thing, I stopped having the three hours with Ross like I had had before. I did not know how to be a grandparent, never having had any grandparents with whom I could relate (all of mine were gone before I was 11 years old). I vacillated between trying to be a friend and being a disciplinarian. Saundra seemed overwhelmed with the kids and their struggles and she would say, "Ray you need to take over." Then shortly after she would say, "I'll take charge." There was no consistency that made it difficult for all of us.

We had some wonderful travels, however. We went to Cabo San Lucas, to the resort where I had purchased timeshare. Subsequently we purchased another unit, another week in a different Pueblo Bonito resort. We traveled to Huatulco in the southwestern part of Mexico, then to New England, where we visited the birthplace of Joseph Smith, founder of the Mormon church (Ross was still going to the Mormon church), to Ben and Jerry's, to the Calvin Coolidge birthplace, and to the Vermont Country Store and many places in between.

We left Vermont and traveled through Pennsylvania including the Amish country where Ross found and bought a T-shirt that advertised Intercourse, Pennsylvania (it had a different meaning when that town had been named). On the way to Pittsburgh from where we would return home, we stopped and marveled at the Frank Lloyd Wright house called Falling Waters.

On another occasion we went to Chicago on Thanksgiving Day, only to discover no restaurants were open where we could have Thanksgiving dinner, so we had hamburgers at the little café in the hotel We wandered through Millennium Park and were amazed by "The Bean" sculpture. This piece of art is also called "Cloud Gate" created by British artist Sir Anish Kapoor. Eighty percent of its surface reflects the sky. One cannot resist touching it and walking through it. We also enjoyed Christkindle Market, and of course shopped at Water Tower Place that was adorned with beautiful Christmas decorations.

Saundra and I took a cruise from Amsterdam to Vienna and with the kids vacationed in several places in Mexico.

However, things at home got worse and finally Saundra and I agreed that perhaps if I moved out of the house for a time that things might get better. So I took an apartment for a few months and never lived on Kite Court again.

LIVING ON A WORKING FARM

In the summer of 2007 we traveled to Italy. We planned to spend a week at an agriturismo, a farm where there were about four or five accommodations built into the side of one of the farm buildings for tourists. But there was a problem. We could not find the entrance into the farm from the highway because all of the walls along the road were covered with vines. Back and forth I drove, looking, looking, asking for help. Finally we found it.

On Saturday we were invited by the family at the farm to share in the luncheon they had for all their employees each week. There were a few people who spoke some English so we could have conversation.

It was fun to be actually living there for a week, shopping for groceries and preparing our meals. When we left we felt we knew a little about what it was like to actually live in Tuscany. We loved it.

It was time to leave and head to Milan. Again, our hotel was in the historic center of the city. I tried to find my way in this huge city, but the names of streets seemed to change every time the street took a slight turn. I could not find the way.

We asked a police officer on a bike and she told us we could not drive in the part of town where our hotel was located. Great! We asked a biker for directions and he said, "Follow me." So here we are in Milan following a bicyclist, but that didn't work either.

Then I saw it! A secure parking garage. Okay. We'll park there and take a cab to the hotel. Hopefully we'll find the lot when we are to leave.

We loved Milan as every other place we visited. We had made arrangements to see 'The Last Supper' by DaVinci. As it turned out it wasn't one of the most memorable experiences of this journey, but we thoroughly enjoyed our time in Milan. Time to move on to our next stop, at a timeshare in the northern mountains of Italy, not far from the border with Austria.

North of Verona we got into very rural country and noticed that most signs were now in Italian and German. This was an area populated by many Germans and had actually been part of Germany at one time.

It was also an area with apple orchards and we were there at harvest time. Apples right off the tree are so delicious and reminded me of the years my family would travel to Michigan in the fall to pick apples.

A sidebar: One time when we were picking apples in Michigan I was on the top rung of the ladder reaching for the most beautiful apple, lost my balance, and fell to the ground landing on my back. In the process one of my fingers caught my glasses and flipped them off. It was dusk and hard to see, but eventually we found the glasses and, miraculously they were not broken.

(back to Italy) The resort where we stayed had chalet décor. We were so perfectly located. One day we went to the city of Balzano where a museum dedicated to *Otzi The Iceman* is located. This 5,000 year old man was discovered in the Italian Alps and was so perfectly preserved it has been possible to see much of the clothing he wore, the weapons he had, how he was killed (hit in the back with a weapon), and even the contents of the last meal he had, and where that food had come from.

Another day we took the train from Balzano to Innsbruck, Austria, through Brenner Pass. I had been to Austria several times so it wasn't exciting for me, but Saundra had never been there so we enjoyed being there together. What I did enjoy more was the Pass and remembering its importance during WWII.

There were castles near our lodging that were easily accessible, some with magnificent floral gardens.

One evening we had dinner at the resort. There was to be a program of German music, dancing and other entertainment. During dinner a little glass of schnapps was brought for each of us. I decided to sip it and in so doing went into a major coughing fit. That brought a lot of laughter from the other guests. A man at another table indicated that the way to drink schnapps was to down it all with one swallow. That worked better, but I decided I could go through the rest of my life without schnapps.

These three weeks, which gave us an opportunity to immerse ourselves in the Italian lifestyle and culture, have been highlights of my travel life.

LIVING IN AN APARTMENT

I had never lived in an apartment. Well, not completely true. When we were living in Chicago in the parsonage of the first church I was appointed to, we lived in a two-flat with someone living above. We could hear her walking about at times, but it wasn't a bad experience.

Nor was the apartment in 2009 a bad experience. It was a second floor two bedroom apartment near a lovely park. I rode my bike in the park, walked a lot and found myself working at a project I had long said I was going to do: creating scrapbooks for each of my kids with all of the things June and I had saved about their lives over the years.

I had no idea what I was getting into when I started, but like this memoir, I knew that I would not stop until these books were completed.

I knew nothing about scrapbooking and, because of my partial colorblindness, I could never be sure if materials I used in the book complimented each other or not.

Going through all the things I had for each of them, programs from events they were involved in, a clip of hair, the first lost tooth, baptismal clothes we had saved, all went into the books.

Sorting through all the photos, I separated those that related to each and made copies of those that related to both of them. The pages were arranged with those things relating to June's family together, then our family, then each of the kids in their own separate lives. I tried to incorporate a little humor as well.

I was giving these books to the kids on Christmas and was concerned that one book would be larger than the other. So I counted the pages. There were exactly 56 pages in each one using both sides of the pages used to tell each of their stories.

When I gave them to Randy and Jackie on Christmas Day, I was pleased that they stopped the gift giving for a time to leaf through and see what was in the albums I had given them as my gift of Love.

A PARTING OF WAYS

That school year of 2009 ended with Ashley failing to pass a few of her courses and was going to need to repeat them in the next year. Saundra thought that it would be embarrassing for Ashley to return to the same school and repeat classes she had taken the year before, so one day, quite unexpectedly, she said, "I'm going to move either to Houston or Idaho." Her younger son lived in Houston at that time and Idaho was where her roots had been as a youth and where most of her family lived..

I was not about to move to Houston or Idaho, because my roots and my family were now in Colorado and I loved living there. So we had a parting of the ways and were left selling this 'dream house' during the economic recession of 2009, which meant we were able to sell for only what we had originally paid, but not for the tens of thousands of dollars for upgrades we had invested in it.

Our parting was amicable, however. Unfortunately, shortly after moving, Ashley announced that she was going to go to Houston to live with her other grandmother, so going to school in Idaho never happened. Shortly after we had our marriage annulled.

Despite all that had transpired, Saundra and I have continued a wonderful friendship.

TEACHING ENGLISH

In January 2012, I went to Guatemala to teach English, and was there until the end of the school term at the beginning of November.

I was hosted by a Guatemalan family comprised of mama called Lydia *grandde,* papa was Fernando, Brenda the daughter who had two children called little Lydia and Emiliano, and Lesther, the son of Lydia and Fernando. Living with them, eating with them, doing all kinds of activities including going to church with them caused my love for this family to grow.

Teaching was hard work because there were no textbooks to provide guidance. I had to make up all the lesson plans myself.

One day I took a trip to the resort city of Panajachel on the shores of Lake Atitlan. The day I arrived there I walked around the city, down to the waterfront, got something to eat, checked into my hotel, and decided to take a nap. I rarely go to sleep when taking a nap, but on this day I did.

Sometime later I awoke and felt quite rested. I decided to go out and find a restaurant for breakfast. It seemed very dark for being early in the morning, but other than commenting to myself on that, I continued my search for a place to eat.

I found one, went in and was seated. I asked what time it was and was told it was 8:30. I asked if I could get eggs and toast and was told that I would have to go to the rear of the restaurant where I would be able to get that. That seemed strange.

I then asked for a newspaper, if they had one, which they did. The paper looked the same as the one I had read the day before. I said to the waitress, "This isn't today's newspaper it's yesterday's." She looked at me in a strange sort of way and said that's all they had.

I got something to eat and was walking back to the hotel. It still wasn't getting light. When I got to the hotel I asked the clerk at the desk to tell me what day it was. He also looked at me strangely, but told me the day. I was so confused. It wasn't the day I thought it was. At long last I realized I was completely wrong. I had slept and when I woke up I thought it was the next morning when in reality it was night of the same day I took my nap. It took a while for me to adjust to reality.

My Guatemalan family

LITTLETON HERE I COME

I intended to return in 2013, but instead made what was a life-changing decision, something that would prove to be more important than I could have imagined at the time.

I decided to move closer to my children and grandchildren who were living in Denver and Highlands Ranch. I thought that if I didn't have to travel on Interstate 25 to get to see them that we would have more time together. The move was good in many ways.

The first floor condo I bought faces the public golf course, so I have a wonderful grassy front lawn that I don't have to care for. I am not a golfer so do not use the golf course except for walks. I don't golf because one time when I was living in Glenview three men talked me into golfing with them. I could not drive nor putt the ball well. We never completed the 18 holes because I took so much time.

Another time June and I went to a driving range. I swung the golf club, it slipped out of my hands and sailed past others who were there. Then I swung again and the club flew out into the parking but didn't hit any cars. That was the end of golf for me and fortunately no one was killed.

Living close by, within walking distance, was my friend, Olive Aithie-Wilkison, one of the Birthday Group from Harvey.

The people living in the condos were not particularly friendly at first, other than saying, "Hello" when passing on the sidewalk with their dogs but the longer I lived there, the more people I got to know. It became home.

I joined the 24-hour Fitness Gym within walking distance, explored the area around and found everything I needed in close proximity. Jackie was particularly helpful getting me settled, deciding where wall décor should go, and how to arrange the furniture.

As 2014 drew near I decided that I would like to teach English in Guatemala once again and the school welcomed me back. So in January I made my way to Santa Cruz on my own.

Everything was going as before except that I had a couple of additional classes to teach. Then something happened in March of that year that totally changed the life I was living.

PHILOMENA AND THE AFTERMATH

> *Only you can prevent you from being who you are...It is never easy. The hard part though is figuring out who you are, defining what you want. Once that is accomplished, then being brave enough to be that person and getting what that person wants is probably really quite easy.*
>
> *Thursdays Child*
> Victoria Poole

It was March 2014. I was ensconced in Santa Cruz del Quiché in Guatemala. I had heard about a movie that had been nominated for several Academy Awards called *Philomena*. I could not see the movie in Guatemala so chose instead to read the book. I was gripped by the story of a woman whose son, Anthony, was taken from her at the age of three by nuns in a convent in Ireland and adopted out to a family living in Atlanta. His name was changed to Michael Hess.

As I read on, I learned about the son, Anthony (Michael), whose mother was trying to find him in the U.S. He had graduated from Notre Dame and Georgetown University and was a lawyer in the first Bush administration, a position that, at times, necessitated working for anti-gay legislation. Because he was gay and still in the closet, had he been 'outed' as a gay person, he would have lost his job in an administration that was strongly anti-gay.

Secretly he had a partner and they had a home in eastern Virginia. Ultimately, Anthony (Michael) died of AIDS.

Years before I had read a book, the title of which I do not remember, by an author whose name I also do not remember. In that book the author talked about how all of us have a little box inside ourselves in which we put those things we do not want to deal with, the things we want to hide. She said every once in awhile we might take a look inside and then close it up again.

I remember talking about that at times with persons individually and with classes I taught. I had never forgotten what she said. Now, suddenly, after reading about Anthony and what he had kept hidden, how, if he had revealed his true self, he would have lost his job and his public life, I saw a reflection of myself.

At that moment the little box inside in which I had hidden my true sexual identity exploded and I was faced with and finally accepted fully that I am a gay man and that I have always been gay. Immediately I had two reactions: one, a huge sense of release (euphoria), but also a need to talk with someone about it.

Soon we were scheduled to have a break from school for a week. I returned home, but first made appointments to see my psychiatrist and also the counselor I had been seeing for thirteen years. The first was very supportive and I felt a great sense of relief. Here was someone who had known me for years and who accepted what I told him without judgment.

The second, my counselor, was shocked and maybe disgusted. His demeanor showed it. We had scheduled a two-hour meeting during which I told him about what had happened and the great sense of freedom I now felt. I was about to read a document I had prepared about my life when he said something like, "Give me those papers and I'll shred them right now." I decided this meeting was over, excused myself and left feeling angry. I knew I would never see him again.

I returned to Guatemala, but there was no way I could teach the remainder of the school year so I gave notice that I would be leaving when the current session ended in July.

While continuing to teach I was very distracted by what was happening inside me. I knew I needed to find a counselor close to where I now lived in Littleton, so I went online, searching for someone skilled in working with gay men. There were two responses. Why I chose the one I did I do not know. At any rate he was perfect for me.

When I got home I contacted him and set up an appointment. When I went into his office he asked if I was the person from Guatemala who had contacted him, to which I responded, "Yes." He said he was glad that I had come to see him.

I could not have found a better person to help me maneuver my way into the gay community. We talked a lot about why I had waited so long to come out. I was open with him about my life and he assured me that he could help me, which he did.

REVEALING MYSELF

> *Even when I found myself most attracted to girls, I knew that the male figures were still there, lurking somewhere behind consciousness, and would soon return.*
>
> —*Fire Shut Up in My Bones*
> Charles M. Blow, Chapter 6

The only way I can describe my feelings after allowing the secret in the box out is euphoria. I was free after living for nearly 80 years in hiding. I wanted everyone to know and to rejoice with me. Yes, I was *Free at last. Free at last. Thank God Almighty I'm free at last.*

Justin and I talked about how to reveal myself to those who were important to me. I said I should probably start with my children. He said, "When do you think you will tell them?"

I responded, "In a couple months."

When we met next I told him I had met with Randy and Jackie and told them. He smiled gently and replied, "I knew you would. Two months went by quickly, didn't they?"

I had invited Randy and Jackie to have lunch one day. There was something I wanted to tell them and I wanted to tell them both at the same time.

We had barely sat down and even before ordering lunch Jackie turned to me and questioned, "Well, Dad, what is it you want to tell us?" That's Jackie. Get to the point. And she was right.

I started by stating how much I had loved June, their mother, and how wonderful our years of marriage had been and how much I loved them, the fruit of our marriage. "But," I continued, "there was something that I had known for as long as I could remember, at least since I was in high school, and that was that I had always been attracted to men. I am gay." I said that being gay is not a choice, it's who God made me Why would anyone choose to be gay given the persecution that gay people have had to endure and still do.

I tried to explain what had happened that enabled me to step out of the closet now. I tried as best I could to help them understand that I am the same person I was before, but that I had at last come to terms with my true sexuality.

Jackie's response was: "Dad, we love you and we want you to be happy." She has always been in my corner it seems.

Randy said, "Dad, I'm not surprised because one time when I was looking in your chest of drawers I found a magazine featuring hunky men." Randy has also been supportive of my new life.

While I am sure this was difficult for both of them to think that I was one person and all along I was someone else, at least in this part of my life, nevertheless I felt their acceptance and support. This was something I needed to know, that I would still be loved by the people closest to me. I am so grateful to have children who have been so accepting and. supportive.

My experience with the Walk to Emmaus, when I thought everyone would be so happy for my discovery of a personal, loving relationship with God and would rejoice with me. But it didn't work out that way. People who thought they knew me found they were dealing with someone they didn't seem to know.

The same thing happened now when I shared my freedom with persons who had known me. Having had such a great experience with my kids, I wanted others to know, others who had been important in my life. I scheduled a luncheon with the man who had been senior pastor at the church in Fort Collins when I was on staff. At the restaurant I shared my story. It seemed he was receptive, however, I have never heard anything from him since that day, therefore deciding that my revelation to him was not well received.

I told a couple I had considered good friends from Fort Collins, and they seemed supportive as well, however there has been minimal and finally no contact between them and me.

I realize now, too late, that not everyone needed to know the discovery I had made and accepted. When appropriate it could be shared, but initiating the sharing was not proper.

Eventually my euphoric state waned and I began living as a gay man. But how does one find one's way into the gay community at age 79? My counselor was the key to discovering the way.

An aside: One day when I was meeting with Justin, he asked if I had any questions for him. I did: how old are you and do you have a partner, for he had shared that he too was gay. He replied "26 and yes." He could have been my grandson.

The people I have never told and never will are my two sisters and their families. They all live in the eastern and southern part of the United States. I rarely see them although we frequently have phone conversations.. They are fundamentalist Christians and knowing I am gay would lead them to believe I am going to Hell. No need to burden them with that. I long for them to know and to accept me, but I've decided telling them would be for me and not them.

One of the persons I shared my newfound identity with was then the pastor of the First United Methodist Church in Fort

Collins. I did so because I knew that congregation was considering becoming a reconciling congregation, meaning they officially would go on record as welcoming and incorporating all persons into their midst regardless of marital status, ethnicity, sexual orientation, race or land of origin. I offered to help with that in any way I could.

In the course of that conversation the pastor told me about the Denver Gay Men's Chorus as a possible way to meet people. The chorus is made up of more than 100 gay men. I knew they were having a Christmas concert that was to be performed at a United Methodist Church near Littleton. I decided to go and see for myself this gay chorus. Jackie went with me and I found it to be an amazingly professional group.

One of the numbers they did that night was "Silent Night," sung first with vocal only, then vocal with sign language and finally with only sign language. It was beautiful and very moving.

There is a lot of choreography in the performance and all music is memorized. I told Jackie I thought I wanted to audition for the chorus. She said, "Dad, do you think you can do it?"

I easily responded, "I'd like to try."

So I arranged to audition and was accepted as a bass. Rehearsals for the next concert, all Beatles music, began immediately after the New Year with performances in March.

Rehearsals are held in the fellowship hall at Christ United Methodist Church in Denver, and that is how I found my church. Rehearsing every Sunday night for three hours was tiring and challenging. Shortly before the concert, a retreat was held at a casino in Blackhawk, Colorado. We worked hard on this production.

There was need for a number of narrators at various points in the concert. I tried out for these and the director asked if I would be willing to do a short monologue prior to "When I'm 64," telling my story of coming out. Here is what I said:

When I'm 64. I wish! For me that was 16 years ago. You see I just turned 80 this month, and it has been quite a ride. Aging! .

I have always thought of life as a book, each chapter building on what had happened before. A new chapter opened for me last March. You see that is when I stepped out of the closet. Inside myself there was a little box in which I kept locked away what I didn't want to deal with and who I really am. I cannot explain how it happened but one day an explosion erupted inside me. The door on that little box blew off and it could not be locked again. On that day I finally acknowledged who I really am, a gay man.

The years up to now have left many wonderful memories of 43 years of marriage, two wonderful children and four grandchildren whom I deeply love. But now I am reveling in the beauty of my newly resurrected life and embracing the challenge of being a new person. And, I am trying to live to the best I can, a life of honesty, authenticity, and integrity.

Several times during my narration people cheered and applauded. Several of the chorus members, mostly young ones, told me how moved they were, even to tears, when they heard my words. Following this narration I exited the stage and at a later point in the song came out using a walker and did a little dance with a walker. I loved doing this and the reception it was given.

Randy, Jackie and Warren *(I'll tell about Warren later.)* attended.

I started rehearsing for the next concert about Harvey Milk, the gay city council member in San Francisco who was assassinated. I got as far as the retreat when I had to bow out. I was not able to perform the wonderful moving music because I had to have shoulder surgery. During the Beatles concert when we sang "Imagine," a number of us were to hold poster boards with words on it like Free, No Judgment, Love, and others printed on them. I held that sign up high as instructed, but had difficulty doing so, therefore singers on both sides of me held my arms at the elbows. However, the strain on my right shoulder was so intense that I had to have shoulder replacement surgery. I was sad to leave the chorus, and although I started in on the next concert finally I made the decision to retire. I was no longer ready to commit the time and energy needed. While my involvement with the chorus was a wonderful experience, it was time to move on.

There was another factor that entered into that decision. Someone had come into my life with who I preferred to spend Sunday evenings.

A NEW LOVE, A NEW LIFE

I wanted so much to find someone compatible with whom I could share my life, and he with me. I learned of a group of older gay men called Primetimers that met every Wednesday at a bar/restaurant in Denver. One day I got up enough nerve to go to their luncheon. People were fairly friendly although I noticed that there were men who always sat together at the same table every week. I found a seat at a different table during each of the next few weeks, trying to make friends.

One day I asked how a person went about meeting others beyond this group. One of the men named John, told me about a website called Match.com for gay men. I was hesitant to take that step, but finally had the courage to do so. I posted my name, age, and interests plus my photo. I confess I shaved a few years off my actual age. I thought, "Who would want to hook up with an octogenarian?"

One day there was a message from a man who saw my posting. We arranged to meet at a restaurant. He was in his mid-forties. As we ate, he kept looking around the restaurant to see if there was anyone there he knew. He was very nervous.

He told me he liked older men and had had an older man in his life for a number of years. That man had died. Then I became aware that if I said the word gay, or if I talked about being in the Gay Men's Chorus he asked me not to talk about that in the restaurant, or at least to keep my voice low.

He said he and the older man with whom he had had a relationship went to the same church, but they never traveled together nor sat together. Right away we both knew this was not going to be a match.

There was another man who contacted me and we agreed to meet for coffee at a Barnes & Noble. When he came in it was apparent I would not be interested and that was confirmed as we talked. He showed up looking a mess, old ball cap and a T-shirt stretched over his ample stomach. He, like the previous guy, was not really out as a gay man and I could not have a relationship with someone who was still in hiding.

Primetimers chose one night every month as the 'bar night.' The idea was that men would go to the designated bar on that night. I decided to go. I had never gone to a bar before. This time it was to be at the Broadway in Denver. When I entered there were few men there. I ordered a drink and sat at one of the tables. No one approached me nor I them. So when I finished my drink I left. That was it for bars.

Then one day at Primetimers a man sat across the table from me.

We talked. He told me he had seen my picture and profile on Match.com. Like me, he is a father with a son and two granddaughters. Like me, he had been married for more than 40 years. He had been involved in music at the University of Denver from which he graduated. He majored in graphic arts, taught at DU for a few years, afterwards becoming a high school teacher of graphic arts.

He and his wife were both interested in art and both had done some painting. One of Warren's paintings is in the Kirkland Museum in Denver.

In his younger years before marriage he said that he had had several relationships, most of which were very short term. There was only one man whom he had truly loved, but when Warren moved away from San Francisco where he had been going to college for a short time, that relationship ended.

Warren's wife had died a few years before we met and my wife had died about 11 years before. We found so much common ground. We agreed to meet at his house either that day or soon after. When I arrived at his house Warren asked if I would like to go in the hot tub in his backyard and I said I would like that. He loves to remind me what it was like. I had trouble getting into the tub and made a rather whale-like splash. Then getting out was equally difficult. We laughed about that, and laugh about it still. *He has never suggested the hot tub again.*

Our relationship blossomed. Warren was going to the Colorado Symphony with his friend Richard, a long-time friendship. I got tickets to half of the season and the three of us traveled together. Later, I too got full season tickets. He went to the Broadway show series with another friend and soon I was going as well. My life was expanding and I loved it.

Now we attend plays, ballet, concerts, and opera. We've also gone to Santa Fe for their operas during the summer and thoroughly enjoy those experiences.

I became a fan of ballet decades before. June and I discovered the Joffrey ballet Company that performed in Chicago every year. The name of one of their male dancers is Christian Holder, black, with a magnificent body. One year he performed a solo wearing only tight white shorts. I watched all of this unfolding on the stage, I was not only impressed by his dancing but jealous of his statuesque body. I've never forgotten that performance.

There are days when we go to the Denver Art Museum, the Museum of Contemporary Art, the Museum of Nature and Science, or the Botanic Gardens. Through this I have become more aware of and now participate in so many of the events that Denver has to offer and loving it.

Many of these are new to me but not so for Warren because Warren has lived in Denver for more than 50 years, in the same house, and has gone just about everywhere and done nearly everything there is to do.

We both love to travel. Warren has been in more than 40 countries and 49 states missing only Alaska. I've traveled to at least 24 countries, so travel was to be part of our life together.

Because of my participation in the Gay Men's Chorus I came to the realization that Christ United Methodist Church must be very welcoming of LGBTQ by allowing Chorus practices to take place there. One Sunday I went to worship and found a small but welcoming congregation. I became a regular at worship. One Sunday Warren (my partner by then) surprised me by coming to worship, walked down the aisle and sat next to me. It was very emotional for me. I now had someone with whom to worship.

Once Warren and I became partners I decided I wanted to learn how to cook. I subscribed to a magazine, *Cooking Light*, where I found many wonderful recipes. I also went online looking for recipes for specific ingredients I wanted to use. At times I would experiment by adding something that was not in the recipe or not adding something that was recommended. Some of the dishes I cooked were excellent, according to Warren.

I created my own cookbook with recipes I had made rating them excellent, very good, and good. Anything that was rated less than very good was discarded.

This was not my first attempt at cooking, however. When we were living in Crystal Lake I found a recipe for spaghetti sauce in the newspaper. I decided to make it and surprise June. We would have spaghetti for dinner that night. As the sauce cooked it filled the house with a wonderful aroma.

When June arrived home I asked her, "What is a clove of garlic?" She told me a clove is one section of a garlic head. Whoops! I had put two whole heads of garlic in the sauce I was making. We had it for dinner and I thought it was delicious, as did June. But she said we could not keep the remaining sauce in the house because it would make our house smell so garlicky. I overruled.

Another cooking experience took place after June died. I thought I should learn how to cook and told my children that cooking lessons were something they could give me for a Christmas gift, which they did. The cooking lessons were fun. But then life changed again when Saundra Craft entered my life. For Saundra the kitchen was her domain and I was to stay out of it.

Then came cooking for Warren. I have enjoyed doing that immensely. Warren has been a great help with the cooking. I choose the recipe, prepare the ingredients, and Warren does much of the actual cooking with me telling him how to do it. I love being the 'boss.'

Warren and I have created a life that is comfortable, and yet is always exciting.

We have traveled to Norway, New England, Peru, New York, plus Puerto Vallarta, and Cabo San Lucas, Mexico.

Warren told me that he and his wife had a cabin in the mountains near Blackhawk at approximately 9000 feet. I loved the cabin immediately. It is not at all like the cabin we had when I was growing up. It is surrounded by wonderful trees and in the spring, wild flowers grow along the dirt road in front of the cabin.

When we go there, with no television and internet, we play cards, do crossword puzzles, play dominoes and a new game of cards we've learned "Head and Foot." We read and enjoy the relative quiet and beauty and we listen to music. When it is cool we light a fire in the fireplace, making the cabin very cozy.

There is electric heat, an electric stove, refrigerator, running water and now hot water. What more could you want?

A few miles down the road on the outskirts of the casino town Blackhawk, there is a small restaurant where you can get sandwiches and lattes. A mile or so up the mountain from there is the historic town of Central City, a gold rush town that had more

than 20,000 residents during the gold rush, now with less that ten percent of that. During the summer, operas are performed in the old Opera House, a few of which we have attended.

One problem in our relationship is that Warren does not like sports. Most of my gay friends are like him. I enjoy watching pro sports on TV, especially the Steelers, and I check in on the Pirates. He has gone to a couple of college football games with me and says he will go again, but I think he will be bored. *I think it's a small sacrifice for love.*

One of the interesting things about our lives is that we both had dogs, or stated accurately, I had a full-time dog, a Cavalier King Charles Spaniel named Calvin (after the Calvin and Hobbes cartoon), and he has a 'timeshare dog,' part Yorkie and part

Bishon, named Roxie. He and his wife along with another couple purchased this dog together. So Warren had Roxie one week and the other couple the next week and if either goes away the other takes care of the dog. What a great arrangement! For me, when I go away I need to hire a dog and house sitter.

I loved my dog but at the age of 13+, Calvin had to be put to sleep. Three weeks later Roxie was also put to sleep. I decided not to get another dog. Then, somewhere I heard about a ferret rescue in Denver. I went to see the ferrets *(at that time I didn't know what a ferret is)*. They were so cute and didn't require much care so I adopted two we call Bonnie and Clyde. Bonnie is a cute girl, with grey and white markings. Clyde is albino. They sleep most of day waking occasionally to eat, do their elimination needs and get treats. Then in the early hours of morning, they waken and begin to play in their tunnels or move things around, like slippers, waste baskets or anything else they can find on the floor. They bring joy into our lives.

We did not live together, each of us having a condo or house, however we spent every evening together. That changed in 2019 when, faced with health issues, we began staying at the house of the one needing care. So now when one of us is ill or has surgery, the other stays to give T.L.C. As time has gone on, we are now living together most of the time.

Every evening we watch the local and national news. Afterwards it is *Jeopardy*, and on Fridays, PBS, to hear the commentary of David Brooks and Mark Shields *(I call them Briggs and Stratton)* on the events of the previous week. Occasionally, we watch something we have recorded or something on Netflix.

There were two guys in the gay coffee group we attended each week who always dressed exactly alike, same shirts, same sweaters, same scarves, same everything. They were married in the church where I attend.

They were often made fun of because of their common dress, so Warren is very sensitive about us wearing anything that looks alike. We both have shirts and jackets that are similar and if one of us is going to wear that shirt or jacket, it's important to tell the other so we won't show up looking alike.

There are people all the time who are asking if we are brothers. Some people think we look alike. Maybe they are just trying to figure out the kind of relationship we have.

SO I LIKE TO BE NEAT

I have been accused, mostly by Warren, of being obsessive. Maybe I am a *little*, but not like this:

> *A young man told his mother that he had a date with a certain young woman. She was delighted he had invited this person to come to his apartment for dinner. When he saw his mother the next time she asked how it had gone. He said, "It was fine but she insisted on washing the dishes." His mother said, "What is the matter with that? I think that was very nice of her." He said, "but we hadn't even eaten yet."*

Now that's obsessive!

All right, so neatness is something I value. I could never go home from my office unless my desk was cleared. I hated showing up the next day and finding a messy desk. I hated starting my day in the morning trying to figure out what was on my desk, what I needed to do, what I could discard, what I should file. I liked a clean slate and a clean desk to start the day.

All right, so I like to keep a neat and orderly house, maybe like Felix in *The Odd Couple* movie. The dinner dishes must be in the dishwasher before going to bed. When I'm at Warren's house he'll say, "I'll take care of the dishes in the morning." Too bad! I have to see to it that the dishes are either washed or in the dishwasher, not tomorrow, *Now!*

So I'm obsessive about my appearance and that is a challenge because I am partially colorblind. If I show up wearing colors, let's say a shirt and slacks that clash, I'm terribly self-conscious even though I doubt anyone notices or cares. I care!

After June died, I would usually take at least two ties to church on Sunday morning and ask someone which tie went best. If I'm shopping, I often grab someone, perhaps another shopper, and ask for help with colors and most are ready to help.

I guess I am also obsessive with the mail. Every day when I pick up the mail I am compelled to open all of it. Warren, well, he has piles of unopened mail, some even first class, that just sit on tables or chairs for days and maybe weeks. I can't do that.

When I come back from a week or longer time away and the mail has accumulated, I have to go through it almost immediately to see what is there. *I keep hoping for a large check, but that hasn't happened.*

I count steps. I don't know when this started, perhaps when I was in physical therapy following my surgery for epidural hematoma and was told to see if I could walk up 80 steps. I did, and that hastened my release. Ever since, I count steps. I believe that staircases with landings should have the same number of steps leading to each landing. It distresses me when they don't.

I guess I am an obsessive person!

A GARDEN IN POTS

One of the joys in my life since meeting Warren is appreciation for living things. When we go to the Botanic Gardens I am so blessed to see so many flowers in bloom, gorgeous specialty gardens, plants and flowers, many foreign to me. Warren knows so much about plants, fostered by his years cultivating and nurturing his own beautiful flowers, primarily in his backyard.

In his garden there are beds of perennials, phlox, blue salvia, Denver daisies, peonies, tickseed, and columbine, which bring an abundance of color to his yard. In addition every spring he plants at least 20 geraniums and hundreds of other annuals, including white impatiens.

I have about 25 pots of flowers arranged neatly on my patio. I move them around from time to time, yes, obsession again, trying to make them the most beautiful *garden* in the neighborhood. I love it when someone walks by and comments on how happy the flowers make them feel. I may have mandevilla, bougainvillea, hibiscus, petunias, dahlias, or geraniums, and an oleander tree I bought as a memorial to my dog, Calvin. I bring several of them indoors during the winter so they will be in my garden again the next summer. I am excited when one of my plants buds, then bursts into bloom.

DREAMS AND NIGHTMARES SOMETIMES COME TRUE

There are two recurring dreams that I have had over the years. First, I would often dream that Sunday morning had come and I had forgotten to prepare a sermon or that there were no bulletins or something else was wrong. That never happened. However there was a time when I was using a wedding liturgy that was included in a booklet along with the marriage certificate. I would use that liturgy, then would give it to the couple after the wedding as a remembrance.

One time I was already in the sanctuary, the processional had concluded, and when I opened the booklet expecting the liturgy for a wedding to be there, it was a surprise! There was something different there than what I expected. It wasn't a liturgy for a wedding. What to do? I could excuse myself and go to my office to get the Book of Worship, or I could wing it. I chose the latter and because I had conducted many weddings, the liturgy was ingrained in my memory. No one knew the difference. Saved from a possible embarrassing situation.

Number two. I've had this dream, or nightmare you might call it, many times. It goes like this. I've been in a shopping mall or in some other facility and when I come out I can't find my car. I think someone has stolen it.

Actually there have been times when I have come out to a parking lot and have not been able to find my car. The reason is

I have come out a door on a different side of the building than where I entered. Eventually I found the car.

But one time Warren and I went to an event in downtown Denver. We both drove to the light rail parking lot and took the train together. When I came back from that event and walked to the place where I had parked my car, my dream, *Nightmare*, had come true, my car was gone.

I called the emergency police line. When I gave my license plate number I was told I had parked in a handicapped space and my car had been towed to a lot many miles north in the city. Thankfully, Warren was there to drive me to that lot where I picked up my car after paying $321 towing charges plus the police ticket that cost me another $150. Now I check carefully to be sure I am not in a handicapped space. Tough and expensive way to learn. *Enough of dreams!*

MY LIFE IN THE 'SPIRITS'

The first time I ever had a hard liquor drink was when I was at my son's home for some family celebration. Randy and others nearly always had a martini. So I said, "I want a martini too."

Apparently it put me in some kind of 'otherworld' because later Jackie said, "You were talking with your Pittsburgh accent." I only remembered that I was laughing quite a bit.

I grew to love martinis. We always go to Sam's #3 restaurant in Denver prior to shows and concerts. Sam's is a very popular place with an extensive menu of nearly every kind of food, food for breakfast, for lunch and for dinner available all the time. The food is good, the portions are huge, and the prices are rather inexpensive. We love to sit in the bar area and have gotten to know some of the regulars.

Our favorite waitress knows what we drink: a sweet Manhattan up (Warren), and a slightly dirty martini for me. For some reason, one night before the symphony, I had two martinis. Warren nearly always had two Manhattans so I wanted two martinis. During the first half of the symphony concert I could not stay awake and kept falling to the side in my seat. Fortunately I was on the aisle and there was no one in the seat to my left. *Never again when attending an event.*

AN EMERGENCY

In 2017 we had great plans for travel. First we were planning to take a cruise up the Norwegian coast on a small working ship. It had been a dream of mine to return to Norway and to do a cruise, but not on a giant cruise ship. However, sometime in mid-2017 Warren was diagnosed with bladder cancer. The cancer had not embedded itself in the wall of the bladder so it was considered treatable. A few weeks later the cancer reappeared and the doctor said it was probably unwise for us to make that trip now.

We also had a trip planned to Vietnam and the Angor Wat temple in Cambodia in 2018 leaving shortly before Thanksgiving and returning just before Christmas. We were both excited about this trip. But because the cancer had returned, we had to cancel once again.

Another trip to Viet Nam was scheduled but on advice from Warren's doctor that journey was also cancelled. even though we had our suitcases packed.

Then I had a situation of my own. Around mid-November, 2017 I fell backwards onto the bathroom tile floor hitting the back of my head. My head didn't hurt so I didn't think anything of it.

A couple weeks later I tripped on the ledge getting into my walk-in shower and couldn't get myself up for quite some time and when I did I knocked the sliding doors off the shower. The falls started coming, twice in the bedroom, where again I had trouble getting myself turned over so I could get up.

I started falling outside. Often it was when I was walking Calvin and would bend over to pick up his feces. I always knew when I was going to fall, but never was hurt. One time I fell into some shrubs while walking Calvin. I saw a neighbor nearby and asked if he could help me get up and walk me home.

There were at least two occasions when driving the car that the wheels of the car brushed the cement divider on the left side of the road. But nothing was registering with me that said I should get help. Slowly but surely, something was happening in my brain that prevented me from thinking clearly.

Then on December 17 Randy stopped at my condo. Warren was there. I had slid off the couch and was sitting on the floor. Randy took one look at me and said, "Dad, I've got to get you to the hospital."

I was admitted and x-rays were taken and sent to Dr. Ben Ruben, a brain and spine specialist. At seven o'clock the next morning Dr. Ruben performed emergency surgery for a subdural hematoma. He told my family that when he saw the x-rays and the amount of blood that had pressed on the right side of the brain he thought I would be in a coma, but I wasn't.

I recovered after ten days in the hospital and having therapy. I was a prize patient, of course. This time was unlike one other time when I balked at the protocol requiring me to have the assistance of a nurse when I needed to go to the bathroom.

Christmas was spent in the hospital. By then I was permitted to walk the halls and even go to the cafeteria. All of my family came to the hospital. We sat in a circle in a room large enough to accommodate all of us. In some ways that was the most wonderful Christmas. No one was going to the kitchen to prepare or check on Christmas dinner. There was no pile of gifts to be opened.

Instead we talked, told stories, shared memories, and laughed. It was wonderful and a Christmas I will always remember fondly.

NORWAY AT LAST

Finally in June 2019 we managed to go to Norway and take the trip up the coast making 34 stops, many very short, taking on and disembarking supplies, people, vehicles, etc. At some of the longer stops we were able to get off the ship and visit the towns and villages. Our journey took us to the very top of the world where Norway borders Russia.

Because we were on a small ship we were able to go deep into the fjords. Tucked in the fjords we found beautiful waterfalls, mountains and cliffs, so magnificent as to make describing the scenery hard to put into words.

Before and after the cruise we spent a few days in Bergen, Trondheim, and Oslo. We marveled at the hundreds of sculptures created by one sculptor in the Vigeland sculpture park in Oslo depicting the many aspects of human life, from birth to death. We visited the Viking museum in Oslo, the old town in Bergen with wooden buildings and stave churches, the great cathedral in Trondheim and a museum dedicated to royalty. We managed all of this despite the fact that I was suffering from plantar fasciitis.

In September we traveled to Vermont, spending a week in the northern part of the state at Smuggler's Notch Resort. While there we took a tram up a mountain and enjoyed the wonderful view. When we were ready to return to the base we realized the tram had stopped working. We were told we could walk down, an option not even considered because Warren was suffering from sciatica. We are definitely showing signs of aging.

After several hours we were taken down by means of an all-terrain vehicle on the rough ski runs that, without snow, are simply rocky, rutty trails.

LOST IN PITTSBURGH

It was in the summer of 2018 that I decided to make a quick trip to Pennsylvania to visit my older sister and brother-in-law. My sister, Mary Jane, is four years older than I and has had multiple physical problems. It was time to spend these days with them while they were both doing relatively well.

Landing at Pittsburgh International Airport, I rented a small Hyundai and drove the 60 miles to their apartment in Lower Burrell, a town near where we grew up. Each of the few days I was there we talked about many things, often recalling experiences from our childhood. We laughed a lot at some of the things remembered, some of which were not funny at the time.

While there I made my favorite macaroni and cheese for my sister and brother-in-law and they shared it with some of their children. I got rave reviews for the Mac & Cheese (of course I loved their responses).

Because my flight home was early the next morning, I decided to get a motel room near the airport. I did not want to drive through Pittsburgh to the airport in the morning during rush hour. I set out from my sister's apartment in late evening, around nine o'clock. It was raining hard.

The first mistake I made had to do with getting on the limited access highway toward the city. Unfortunately I took the ramp that took me on the lanes that went away from instead of toward the city. So I turned around and headed in the right direction.

When I got to the city the rain was coming down in buckets, making it hard to see. With poor visibility and because I was not paying attention, when I crossed the Fort Pitt Bridge that leads into the Fort Pitt Tunnel, I found myself instead getting off on a street that ran parallel to the Monongahela River. I tried to find a way to get back up to the bridge so I could get through the tunnel, but to no avail.

By now I was truly panicked. There were no people on the streets that I could ask for directions, no stores or bars open where I could get help. Finally *(why wasn't I doing this all along?)* I took out my phone and used GPS.

The directions took me on a zigzag route, but at last I was on the road to the airport. First problem resolved.

I knew there was a gas station somewhere near the airport but I failed to see it because I was completely disoriented. Then I made a left turn into an area that turned out to be a huge parking lot. I had not gone through an entrance to the parking lot and now I could not find a way out. At last I saw a moving car. Help at last. I drove to that car and asked where the exit was and got directions.

When I got there it was a tollbooth and of course I was going out without a ticket indicating when I had come in. The operator looked at me askance, but finally let me out without paying anything. I had decided to go to the car rental return and pay them to fill the gas tank. However when I exited the parking lot, the gas station was right there.

I found the car rental return. Relief! But when the attendant checked out the car he called my attention to something broken on the fender on the right side. Another problem. It must have happened when I went into the car lot the wrong way! But! Another miracle. He said, "That is such a cheaply made car I'm not going to charge you for the damage."

When I finally got to the motel I was so relieved to be there I gave the driver a very generous tip. With a look of surprise, he said, "Are you sure?" I replied, "I'm so glad to get here. Yes, I want you to have it." I collapsed on the bed completely exhausted emotionally and after calming down, got some needed rest. Shakespeare wrote, "All's well that ends well." I believe! All that aside, it was a great visit and I'm truly glad I went.

VOLUNTEERING

My life as a pastor had been one of service to others. Now I needed to find a volunteer position that would fill that need in me. Warren told me about something he was doing at a food bank, Metro Caring, in Denver. I visited that facility, applied, and was accepted for a position as a Community Navigator.

At Metro Caring people needed to make an appointment to come for food and could come only once per month. My job was to meet with the client in a cubicle that was my 'office' to determine how they were doing, if they needed any of our other services, and then print out their shopping list that indicated what was felt would be needed by that client or family for one week.

I loved meeting with the people and found myself giving counsel and a listening ear to what many were going through. It seemed a perfect fit for me. Those who received food stamps often told me they got $16 or less per month. I thought it would be good if the officials in Washington spent a few days meeting these people face-to-face then they would have a much better knowledge of what they were doing when they allocated money to help the least among us.

When I heard an accent that didn't sound like a person born in the United States I would ask what country they were from. I kept a list of all the countries, a list that grew to approximately 30 different nations, truly a melting pot. People were from every continent except Antarctica. Of course the majority were from right here in the United States. I believe that's what our country is, a melting pot of peoples from throughout the world. And I believe that is what makes our country great.

I resigned from that work after 3 ½ years. However it was a wonderful experience.

I also became a "Friendly Visitor" in a program operated by the GLBTQ Center in Denver. When the Center learned of a gay person in a nursing home they would ask that person if they would like to have someone visit them or call them on a regular basis. I thought I would like to do that.

Bill Mackey was given to me as someone the organization thought I would relate to well. He is a very simple man, I was told apologetically. That proved true. While at first Bill said very little and could not even remember my name, eventually he began to open up. I learned that he was born in Grand Junction, Colorado and came to Denver when he was a teenager. He had little education and worked at menial jobs such as dishwashing at a nursing home. When he lost that job he became homeless.

Bill's feet were wrapped in large soft booties, due to an infection in his left foot. Meanwhile he began losing his sight and developed what the doctor called thick cataracts. Eventually he could see nothing at all. But no cataract surgery was possible until the infection in his foot had healed.

I learned from Bill that when he was homeless and lived outdoors in winter, he slept under a bridge. The shelters, he told me were too crowded. When sleeping outside he would receive a blanket from the Salvation Army and some food. It must have been during that time that his feet became severely frostbitten, and that was the source of the foot problem.

I accompanied Bill to multiple visits to both the foot doctor and the eye doctor. I watched as the doctor peeled away dead skin from the two toes that were infected. Again and again the doctor tried to find a way to heal the toes, but to no avail. It was so painful to witness.

By now I had become Bill's POA (Power of Attorney) in order for me to receive medical information. Bill had no one else. No family (he had not been in touch with his mother since he left Grand Junction 50 years ago) and there was no one else.

Finally the doctor asked Bill if he would be willing to have two of his toes amputated on his left foot, the ones that would not heal. Bill consented and after the surgery the foot healed. It was now possible to have cataract surgery. This was performed and Bill could see again. Now he could maneuver his wheelchair himself and move about without help. The quality of his life improved. He gained freedom.

In the six years now that I have been visiting Bill and his roommate Aldo, I look forward to the twice-weekly visits. They are always concerned about me if for some reason I do not get there on the designated day.

I once asked Bill if he was gay because I had no indication that he was. He said "Yes," but we never talked further. Having his roommate present does not make conversation about that comfortable for Bill.

ANTHONY ONCE AGAIN

To be nobody but yourself in a world which is doing its best, night and day, to make you everybody else—means to fight the hardest battle which any human being can fight, and never stop fighting.

—e.e.cummings

Then came Anthony the son of Philomena, and the life-changing acceptance of myself as a gay man. I discovered in Anthony one who made me aware that I was not the only person who had ever been trapped into living a life that was not who he or she is. I was free of what had bound me.

Jane Fonda once said, *"There are days when I feel I should pack it all in, that I'm a complete fraud, and I am afraid that the world will discover that."*

The conditions were right. I was no longer a pastor, I was single, I had moved to Littleton, Colorado and I was in Guatemala, isolated from everyone back home who knew me and it happened. I believe God had prepared the way for me to accept myself at last as the person I had always been.

STRAIGHT MASQUERADE

There was a preacher who got tired of everything. He was a worn out preacher. He had had enough of schedules, meetings, sermons... everything. So he quit. He started looking for a job.

The only thing he could find was at the zoo. They needed someone to dress up in a gorilla costume and be in the gorilla cage because they did not have a gorilla at that time.

He took the job. He was having a pretty good time too, entertaining people who came. One day a large busload of kids came and he was having a ball entertaining them. He started swinging on the big rubber tire they sometimes have in the gorilla cage. He swung higher and higher and suddenly lost his grip.

He flew over the fence into the next cage, the lion cage. The lion started towards him. He started screaming, "I'm not a gorilla, I'm a preacher!" The lion walked over, looked down at him and said "Get up! I'm a preacher too."

Coming to the point of finally being able to say, "This is who I am, a gay man," was a journey of 79 years. The first realization of my attraction to men far more than women began at least in high school. I don't know where I learned what it meant to be gay, certainly not in high school. I do know that I felt a lot of shame, as do many in the LGBTQ community, because of the way some particularly handsome and well-built men aroused me.

Why was I more interested in seeing pictures of men like Robert Redford (June loved him too), Brad Pitt, Keanu Reeves, and Heath Ledger, plus my trainer at the health club, than with those of Elizabeth Taylor, Veronica Lake, Marilyn Monroe, and other screen beauties. I can appreciate their beauty, but I was not sexually attracted, as many of my classmates were, to girls with big boobs and rear ends. Why not me, I wondered.? There must be something wrong with me.

I don't remember being attracted to any particular guy in school. Being in the locker room with guys and listening to their talk about the size of someone's sex organ, embarrassed me, because I was afraid if I actually saw such, I would be aroused and that would betray me.

In college other than my crush on my blonde roommate, I did not find myself attracted sexually to any guy.

Then came seminary and the walk along Lake Michigan at Northwestern University. I discovered that at night there was activity of all kinds taking place. It was there I had my first gay experience. Afterwards there was not only shame at what I had done but also the desire for more. However I also had fear because had I been discovered by someone from the Seminary I would have been expelled. Outing me would have destroyed my life. I knew that if that happened, I would have to find a way to end my life, rather than go on in such disgrace. But I continued on this potentially destructive path.

It was these conflicting emotions and actions that resulted

in my decision to leave seminary when I was only a few months from graduation and being ordained as clergy. How can I go on in this secret life that the church said was going against God's plan for humans?

Being in the National Guard gave me time to reflect. Once again, discovery of being gay would have resulted in a dishonorable discharge. Why could straight guys go on weekend pass and satisfy their sexual needs without fear, while for me, there was to be no such release?

I would like to say I was celibate as a gay man, but that wasn't the case. How can I explain the shame, the confusion, even the disgust with myself that I was going to need to live with, with part of myself in hiding? I had a wonderful wife, someone I deeply loved, two growing kids of whom I was so proud and a blossoming career as a pastor. Yet there was this part of me hidden inside, causing me to feel schizophrenic. Why was I willing to risk it all? Not much wonder I suffered from depression. There was no one I could confide in.

During the 1980s, like many closeted gays, especially among clergy, I became anti-homosexual, even believing what Pat Robertson said in 2005 that Hurricane Katrina destroyed so much of New Orleans and killed so many people because it was God's judgment on that city due to all the homosexuals living there. To think that I had felt that way simply to cover up my own sexuality is absolutely repulsive to me today.

Life went on until the AIDS crisis broke. I was beside myself worrying over whether I might have contracted HIV. I went to the county health facility where tests were being conducted and was tested. It came back negative. I was so relieved. Had I been positive I could have infected June and even the kids. Now I was determined to leave the dual lifestyle I had practiced and never went back again.

So for about 35 years I lived as a celibate gay man with the stress of being two people, one of which was hidden.

I believe a reason I always felt more comfortable around women than men, was that they posed no threat to my hidden self. When I crocheted, hooked rugs, and did activities usually associated with women, I could say that it was all right for a man to do these things and I referenced Rosie Grier, ex-NFL football player and a real *man* who, it was revealed, did crossstitch.

Often I would say that I did these activities as a means of helping me to lose weight, which was true, because my hands were busy with hooks and needles and not bringing food to my mouth. But I truly loved being creative in these ways.

So for nearly eight decades I held inside part of me that could not be expressed nor revealed. Is it any wonder then that in March 2014, when I read of Anthony, finding in him one whose life read so much like my own, that the acceptance of myself as a gay man came as an emotional explosion?

So now, for however many years I have left, I can be a truly authentic man. I thank God that I have come to this new life before my life on earth came to an end.

Then came Warren. It seems that when straights hear homosexual they think sex, immoral sex. To be in a relationship, as I am, with someone of one's own gender, is far more than simply that. Like heterosexual people, a relationship that leads to a deep commitment to each other is a sharing of life, experiences, stories, companionship, and a commitment to each other:

> *for better, for worse,*
> *in sickness and in health,*
> *for richer, for poorer,*
> *to love and to cherish as long as we both shall live.'*

I still experience depression, but not as severe as once and no debilitating headaches coming from the conflict within. I enjoy the world of art that Warren has opened to me. I enjoy going to sleep with someone I love.

I now believe for myself what I once said to a woman who came to ask me if it was all right for her to attend the wedding of her friend's son who was marrying a man. I said, "Why should we not desire that everyone might have someone to love and with whom to share life?" And that is what I believe to be true and to be God's will for us all.

I have been asked how it was possible for me to live a heterosexual life as a gay man for so many years. In many ways it was difficult living life as two different men. It wasn't until the 1990's I ever knew someone who lived openly, without shame, a gay life with a partner he had had for eleven years. I realize now that my obsession with my work, the long hours I spent at work, were a means of coping with and suppressing part of my true self.

LIVING IN THE '80s

Staying young is the last thing a person ought to do. Life is so much more interesting, so much more exciting when you get to knowing better. I can hardly wait for the morning to begin to spend these last precious years.
—Alice Duer Miller
Poet, novelist, playwright

Fire is seen in the eyes of the young, but it is light that we see in the old man's eyes.
—Victor Hugo

Do any human beings realize life while they live it, every, every miunte?
—*Our Town*
Thornton Wilder

The title, Living in the '80s, is not referring to the 1980s, but to my life as a octogenarian. There is a picture of an older couple eating ice cream cones. The caption says, "The older we get, the more we can't believe how old we are."

That encapsulates my way of thinking in my mid-80s. I never expected to live this long, with a Father who died at 60 and a Mother at 75. But here I am and it's possible there could be more years to come even perhaps reaching 100.

At the LGBTQ Center in Denver, the director of the SAGE groups (Services and Advocacy for GLBT *Elders*) refers to us as Elders. That's a term I resist using to refer to us seniors. Perhaps it is because in 1961 I was ordained an Elder in The United Methodist Church, the term used for ordained clergy in the United Methodist Church.

Or maybe because it sounds so old, like those persons sitting in rocking chairs doling out wisdom, or talking about ancient memories. I resisted being called old until now when I am old. I always said, *I'm not old I'm older.* Well, I've arrived at old. I *AM* old.

With older age come so many positive as well as troubling issues. I love it when I tell someone my age and they say, "But you don't look 85." I want to say, but don't, "Well, what does 85 look like?" I know, my grandmother was around 86 when she died. She was wrinkled and simply sat in a rocking chair in the living room. That's not me.

One thing that happens as we become old is the inability to remember so many things. I find that it is not uncommon to say, "I remember…well I can't remember his name but it begins with 'D,' or whatever the appropriate letter might be" and someone else helps out. That's what we seniors do, help each other maneuver the obstacles of faulty memory.

One of my favorite stories that I used in a sermon goes like this:

> *There were three elderly sisters, Wanda, Martha and Wilma, who lived together. Wanda had gone upstairs to run some bath water. She stuck her foot in the water, then stopped and looked around and said to herself, "Was I getting in the bath or out of the bath? I can't remember." So she called Martha: "Martha, would you come up to the bathroom? I can't seem to remember if I was getting in the bath or out of the bath."*

Martha muttered to herself, "You old woman, what do you mean you can't remember whether you were getting in or out of the bath?" But she made her way to the stairs. She got about half way up, stopped, looked around and said, "Was I going up the stairs or down the stairs? I can't remember." She called for Wilma who was in the kitchen. "Wilma would you come in here? I can't remember if I was going up the stairs or down the stairs."

Wilma sarcastically said under her breath, "Martha, you senile woman, I can't believe you can't remember if you were going up or down the stairs. Thank goodness I'm not as forgetful as you." She knocked on wood for good luck, stopped and looked around then asked, "Was that someone knocking at our front door or at the back door?"

In the end, we all make the life we live, for good or for ill. I think this illustrates it well:
Charlie was sitting on a bench next to one of his fellow workers during his lunch break. He began rummaging in a paper sack. He pulled out a sandwich, unwrapped it and muttered "Ugh! Peanut butter." He opened the next sandwich examined it and again said in disgust, "Ugh! Peanut butter!"

Charlie left both sandwiches on the bench. His friend was thoroughly enjoying a ham and cheese on rye and asked, sympathetically, "If you don't like peanut butter sandwiches, why don't you ask your wife to fix some other kind?"

Charlie frowned and said, "Wife? I pack my lunches myself."

I find that laughter is essential throughout life, but especially as we age. There are many things that could cause a person to become very unhappy. As we age we give up things that have been important in our lives. I have given up skiing, biking, in-line skating, jogging and a number of other physical activities. But I still have a brain and go to bridge and Spanish classes and I can still read.

One of the most frustrating experiences as we age is forgetfulness. The lyrics to this song titled "Looking for My Wallet and Car Keys," written by Steven Walters, makes me laugh because it is just the way it is with me.

Looking for my wallet and my car keys,
Well they can't have gone too far;
And just as soon as I find my glasses
I'm sure I'll see just where they are.

Supposed to meet someone for lunch today,
But I can't remember where
or who it is that I am meeting;
It's in my organizer – somewhere.

I might have left it on the counter;
Maybe outside in the car.
Last time I remember driving
Was to that Memory Enhancement Seminar.

What's that far-off distant ringing
And that strangely familiar tone?
Must be the person I am meeting
Calling me on my brand-new cordless iPhone.

I might have left it under the covers,
or maybe outside on the lawn;
And I got just one more ring to go
before my answering machine kicks on.

Click

"Hi, this is Tom, and your call means a lot to me,
So leave a message at the tone
And I'll do my best to try to remember
To call you back when I get home."

Beep

"Tom, this is Gwendoline, and I'm trying not to cry
But I've been waiting here for over an hour –
I thought you loved me. This is goodbye!"

Hell, the voice sounds familiar
And the name rings a bell.
Let's see now, where was I?
Oh well…

There have been times when I might have wished my life had been different. But now I'm grateful for everything that has happened in my life, each happening a step on the journey that has brought me to the life I have today. I would not change anything, because in times when I screwed up royally, I learned something that was beneficial later on.

The names like sissy and tubby made me more sensitive to those who do not fit the accepted mold; the music of the high school band; the recognition I received in high school and college; the experimentation in matters sexual; the internal stresses; the churches I served, even when there was a conflict that became personal; the wives with whom I found life, hope, support and who enabled me to respond by giving my own gifts to them are inscribed in my memory.

And of course, my children who fulfilled dreams and are living lives greater than anything I have done and believing I had some role in that, plus four beautiful and highly intelligent granddaughters whose interests range from volleyball and school plays to the study of medicine, law and other professions that provide help to many, and Warren, the love of my life.

It's been a journey wild and wonderful and it's not over yet.

I have often quoted Browning:

> *The best is yet to be,*
> *The last of life for which the first was made.*

I LOVE GUATEMALA

I began by talking about my love affair with Guatemala. Perhaps you already know what I am talking about. It was to Guatemala I went on a mission trip in 2007. I had said at the time of my retirement that I wanted to do a mission trip every year during my retired years, as long as I could.

The first trip was under the auspices of an organization called Pura Vida Ministries whose main purpose is to help students stay in school with scholarships provided by volunteers in the United States. That took me into a rural area in the mountains of the Quiché where I assisted in building a home for a Methodist pastor, his wife, and three children who were living in two mud buildings, one for sleeping, one for cooking.

Despite having shoulder pain that led to rotator cuff surgery later, I did all I could to assist in this effort. I separated the little stones from the sand used in making the cement by shaking a rectangular device similar to a sieve. I even tried laying a couple of the cinder blocks on one of the walls.

While there, we visited a Maryknoll Sister, Sister Helen, already nearing 90 years old, who had lived for about 35 years in the small village of Lemoa. She had lived through the horrors of the Civil War 1960-1996, along with the people of Guatemala.

She had the most loving spirit and beautiful smile. When we visited her in her home, we had the traditional homemade chocolate chip cookies and lemonade made from the juice of lemons from her lemon tree.

We visited a family whose daughter, a girl sponsored for education by a Pura Vida volunteer, had died when there was a mudslide that buried her home with her inside. We felt their grief.

Later we visited her grave at the Santa Cruz Cemetery, her body buried in the poor section of the cemetery where there were no headstones, just little homemade wooden crosses with the name of the deceased written on it. Apparently if the grave is not tended in that section, after a few years it is plowed under and a new burial would take place there.

It was 2011 when I decided to go to Xela for Spanish language school. There I lived with Aldina for the six weeks I would be in school. I met members of her extended family and some of her friends during that time. I loved living there, eating what Aldina prepared and walking around the city. Xela is not the most beautiful city in the world, but as I walked to the outdoor markets, the cemetery where I witnessed a funeral taking place, attended a wedding though uninvited, and the parks, I felt I was beginning to know what it was like to live there for both the city dwellers and those in the countryside.

Aldina had a shower that was supposed to emit warm water if you turned it on just right, a French invention that saved heating in a hot water tank. I couldn't figure it out. But I learned how to take a cold shower by first, putting one arm in the cold water, then the other arm, then one leg, and then the other leg. Then I could step in completely for an invigorating shower.

It was while I was living at Aldina's that I learned how Guatemalans love to laugh. One day I was inspired to write a story that later I shared with some of Aldina's friends and family. I wrote in Spanish, but here it is in English.

One morning, when I awoke, I heard a rooster crowing. I thought possibly a neighbor had a rooster. When I was in the bathroom, which was across the patio from the house, the noise of the rooster was louder. When I came out of the bathroom, Aldina was there. She indicated with her head that I should look in the corner of the patio. In that corner was something for me to see, a rooster, one end of a cord tied around one of his legs, with the other end wrapped around a table leg.

Immediately, I knew the future of that rooster. He was going to provide lunch for us one day. I said to him, "Señor Gallo, why are you here?" He said, "I know what my future is. One day I am going to be food for you and the family." "O, Senor Gallo, may I pray with you?"

"Thank you," said the rooster. I prayed, "God of all chickens, when the time comes for Senor Gallo, to lose his head, please give him peace. He is my friend. I talk with him and he is a marvelous rooster."

One day when I got up I did not hear the Rooster crowing. I knew what had occurred. And for lunch we had chicken.

I was so in love with Guatemala that I made a proposition and was accepted at the John Wesley School in Santa Cruz Del Quiché to teach students with names like Esperanza (hope),

Hector (when have you known someone named Hector?), Victor, Cheimy, Jesús, Marcos, Tomás Yohandro, Zulmy and my favorite student of all Jonathan.

Their greetings, their hugs, their joy in playing tricks on me are indelibly marked on my life, and something for which I am eternally grateful. I cannot hear the words Maestro, profe (professor), pastor or just Ray, which they spelled Rey (king in Spanish), without thinking of these young people whom I loved and still do.

Another experience of my love for Guatemala came while living with the family of Fernando in Santa Cruz. They accepted me as family. There are so many memories. I loved living in the city and with the family. I was, and still am *Abuelo* (grandfather) to them.

When I took my dog Calvin with me in both 2012 and 2014, they accepted him as their own and surrounded him with love. When I wasn't there, they would walk him, give him treats, and cuddle with him so that he felt at home.

It was there I ate beef tongue for the first and hopefully last time. I would eat anything that I was served because I did not want to embarrass them. For the most part the food was fine, simple and I was always sustained.

For special occasions I would buy fried chicken, their favorite meal, at Pollo Campero, the most popular restaurant in Santa Cruz serving food like KFC. That was one of the few establishments that served brewed coffee. In most places it was Nescafe.

I became acquainted with some of the storeowners where I would buy school supplies, get gifts, have clothes mended, and whatever else I needed. Nearly every day I walked to Central Park, the park in the center of the city, just a few blocks from my home. There I would buy coffee, a newspaper and walk through the market. Mostly the stalls were all the same, but I loved mingling with the people and buying a few items I might need or want.

It was amazing to see how hard the people worked. In the morning the men and many women would come with their huge packs on their backs of whatever products they were hoping to sell, then in the afternoon pack it all up and carry it out just to return the next day and do the same thing all over again.

It was in Guatemala that I read about Anthony and his life lived in the shadows as a gay man, who could not live life openly as a gay man and felt his effect on my life, freeing me to accept myself as the gay man I had always been. I can remember vividly lying on my bed at their home and having the sudden powerful realization that I could no longer live the masquerade I had been living all my life. Could this have happened in Colorado? I don't know. But far from everyone I knew and the activities I had when at home in Fort Collins and Littleton, I found myself. I love Guatemala for that.

The time came for me to leave Guatemala. The leave-taking with my family was a very sorrowful time. I left behind my 'grandson' Lesther to battle some health problems that I don't understand; Mama Lydia who is seeking medical diagnoses for a condition relating to lymph nodes that I prayed could be treated, Emiliano and his daily tantrums and screams, but at other times is a delightful three year old who brought smiles to many of us, and whose prayers at meal time were long, Lidia *pequeño*, who wanted to be a chef; Brenda whose creativity is outstanding and whose life was filled with teaching, caring for Emiliano, and helping with household chores; and Francisco, who I had gotten to know least, and with whom the conversation was limited to "Ray" and "Como está?"

How can one not love the magnificent scenery that is seen while traveling through the countryside? Great mountains, volcanoes, pristine lakes, all mark the landscape. Of course, there is the garbage thrown along the roadways, the black smoke from exhausts, and roads that are rough to traverse, but this does not diminish the beauty of this land.

However, my greatest love for Guatemala comes from the fact that it was there while reading in bed in my room at the home of the Quiñones' that I released my hidden self and became the person I had always been, but was never allowed myself to be.

It was because I accepted personally and publicly my sexual orientation that I found my partner Warren whom I love with all my heart. I do not think that without Guatemala I would be where I am today. So I am filled with gratitude and will always embrace Guatemala as my love.

ACKNOWLEDGEMENTS

There have been many who have enabled me to write this book. I want to thank my friend and editor, Roberta Binder, whose encouragement kept me going; Deanna Estes for formatting, design, and for her seemingly inexhaustible patience; for my daughter, Jackie Miller, who first planted the idea of publishing, and who, along with my daughter-in-law, Melissa Miller, solved the multitude of computer issues I experienced; to Ray Sylvester and Jerry Gold who made suggestions after reading the text; and to my partner, Warren Morrow, who endured the roller coaster of emotions that often made me want to give up.

I never thought I would actually write a book, especially one that dealt with a gay man who lived for nearly eight decades undercover. No one knew, or perhaps even suspected my true sexual orientation. But one's life is about more than that. There are fun times with family and friends, unexpected surprises, stories to tell, friends with whom to share life, and two wives, one for forty-three years and the other five years. Then there are two children, six granddaughters, and one grandson. There can be regrets to wallow in, wondering how life might have been different had one or two decisions been made differently, but as I reflect on my eighty plus years of life, I am so glad that finally, even at this late date, I can embrace myself as the gay man I am and always have been. As you journey with me in this book, perhaps you will find something about yourself that you may have forgotten. You need not be a gay person to remember: It's all about the great journey of life.

Made in the USA
Las Vegas, NV
21 April 2023

70921675R00203